The
SKEPTICAL
Business Searcher

The
SKEPTICAL
Business Searcher

The Information Advisor's Guide
to Evaluating Web Data, Sites, and Sources

By Robert Berkman
Foreword by Reva Basch

 Information Today, Inc.

Medford, New Jersey

First printing, November 2004

The Skeptical Business Searcher: *The Information Advisor's* **Guide to Evaluating Web Data, Sites, and Sources**

Copyright © 2004 by Robert Berkman.

Publisher's Note: The author and publisher have taken care in preparation of this book but make no expressed or implied warranty of any kind and assume no responsibility for errors or omissions. No liability is assumed for incidental or consequential damages in connection with or arising out of the use of the information or programs contained herein.

Many of the designations used by manufacturers and sellers to distinguish their products are claimed as trademarks. Where those designations appear in this book and Information Today, Inc. was aware of a trademark claim, the designations have been printed with initial capital letters.

Library of Congress Cataloging-in-Publication Data

Berkman, Robert I.
   The skeptical business searcher : the information advisor's guide to evaluating Web data, sites, and sources / by Robert Berkman ; foreword by Reva Basch.
       p. cm.
Includes index.
   ISBN 0-910965-66-8 (pbk.)
   1. Business--Computer network resources. 2. Electronic information resource searching. 3. Business--Research--Methodology. I. Title.
   HF54.56.B4685 2004
     025.06'338--dc22

                                                                            2003020692

Printed and bound in the United States of America.

Publisher: Thomas H. Hogan, Sr.
Editor-in-Chief: John B. Bryans
Managing Editors: Amy M. Holmes, Deborah R. Poulson
Copy Editor: John Eichorn
Graphics Department Director: M. Heide Dengler
Cover Design: Ashlee Caruolo
Interior Design: Erica Pannella
Proofreader: Dorothy Pike
Indexer: Sharon Hughes

Dedication

This book is dedicated to librarians, my favorite trusted source.

Contents

Figures and Sidebars xi

Acknowledgments xvii

Foreword, by Reva Basch xix

About the Web Page xxiii

Chapter 1: The Business Researcher's Challenge 1

    Some Things Haven't Changed 2

    Enter the Quality Checklists 4

    The New Internet 5

    Why This Book? 8

    Seeing the Big Picture 9

    The Internet Emerges.. 12

    Scope of This Book 17

    How to Use This Book 18

**Chapter 2: What to Do Before Using
             a Search Engine** 21

    Basic Library Business Sources 22

    Prescreened Web Sites.. 23

    Invisible Web Sources 27

    Databases on the Invisible Web 30

    Web Indexes and Directories.. 33

    Discussion Groups 39

    Weblogs 39

RSS Feeds 41

Summary 44

Chapter 3: Precision Business Searching 45

Why Only One Search Engine?.. 46

Why Google? 47

How Search Engines Work.. 48

Best Diner in Town?... 49

Precision Searching Techniques 52

Alternatives to Google 65

Chapter 4: What to Do With Questionable Sites 69

How Journalists Use the Web 70

Reassuring Signs 74

Ferreting Out the Facts... 75

Chapter 5: Company and Industry Sources................. 111

Sources for Locating Company-Provided Data 112

How Credible Is Company-Supplied Information?............... 114

Market Research Reports and Data..................................... 123

Investment Research Reports.. 132

Finding and Evaluating Discrete Market Data on the Web ... 134

Company Directories 136

Other Sources 139

Chapter 6: Statistics, Polls, and Surveys....................... 141

Statistical Data 141

U.S. Government Statistics 142

One Strategy: Use Preferred Statistical Sources................... 154

A Primer on Understanding Statistics 155

Polls and Surveys 157

Chapter 7: News, Talk, and Blogs on the Net.............. 163

Online News and Media Services.. 163

Web Discussion Groups, Blogs, and More: Opinions
    and Anecdotal Information.. 170

Mailing Lists 174

Chapter 8: Knowledge, Intuition, and Trust 185
Building Your Own Knowledge 185
Developing Critical Thinking Skills 189
The Art of Asking the Right Questions 194
The Use of Intuition 196
Whom to Trust 198
Determining Truth 200
Business-Related Urban Legends and Myths 202
Seeking Larger Truths on the Internet 203

Chapter 9: Prescreened Business Sites 207
Best of the Business Sites 207
A Sampling of FIND/SVP's Trusted Sites
    (By Industry/Practice Area) 230

Appendix A: Web Site Evaluation Checklists 243

Appendix B: Referenced Sites and Sources 247

About the Author 263

Index 265

Figures

Figure 2.1   Hoover's 25
Figure 2.2   ResourceShelf 25
Figure 2.3   EDGAR 26
Figure 2.4   Embassy.org 26
Figure 2.5   NY Times Tracker 27
Figure 2.6   ProQuest Database 31
Figure 2.7   INFOMINE 34
Figure 2.8   INFOMINE Search Results 34
Figure 2.9   Librarians' Index to the Internet/Browse 35
Figure 2.10   Librarians' Index to the Internet/Sample Search 35
Figure 2.11   Profusion 36
Figure 2.12   BUBL LINK 38
Figure 2.13   Business.com 38
Figure 2.14   Jim Romenesko writes a popular blog covering
              media news 40
Figure 2.15   About.com 42
Figure 2.16   An example of an RSS Reader, NewzCrawler,
              displaying headlines collected from news sources
              like BBC News, Sloan Management Journal,
              Forbes, and Business Week. 43

Figure 3.1   Google remains the leading search engine.............. 46
Figure 3.2   An advanced Google search for PDF pages with
              the exact phrase "corporate scandals" in the title,
              but not the word Enron, and which have been
              updated during the past year 52

Figure 3.3   An advanced search from Google's main search
page. Here I searched for pages limited to
governmental Web sites (site:.gov) in the
PowerPoint format (filetype:ppt) with the word
Worldcom in the title (allintitle:Worldcom) that
that had been updated in the past year. 53

Figure 3.4   Adding the names of your most trusted experts
along with your search query can help filter a
search and retrieve superior results 57

Figure 3.5   The fourth and fifth pages on this listing retrieved
from this Google search (the EV World and
infoshop pages) include a date next to the URL,
indicating that the page is likely to be freshly
indexed and up-to-date. 61

Figure 3.6   Clicking on Google's cache makes it easy to find
your keywords on the page, as Google highlights
each on the Web page in a different color (here
the keywords were: forecast, "hybrid vehicles,"
and China) 63

Figure 3.7   AllTheWeb news search 66

Figure 3.8   IxQuick 68

Figure 4.1   The Center for Consumer Freedom is produced
by an anti-regulatory organization called the
Center for Regulatory Effectiveness 86

Figure 4.2   The Center for Consumer Freedom 87

Figure 4.3   GreenWatch is produced by a conservative
organization that identifies sources of funding
of left-of-center entities and activities 91

Figure 4.4   Grants given by Gap Inc. as identified by Capital
Research Center's "GrantMaker." 91

Figure 4.5   A search on the left-leaning Center for Science
in the Public Interest's "Integrity in Science"
database retrieves a biography of the climate
change skeptic S. Fred Singer. 92

Figure 4.6   Guidestar displays the financial information it
              has collected on the Harvard Business School
              Publishing Corporation, including a link to its
              IRS Form 990 93

Figure 4.7   The full image of Harvard Business School
              Publishing Corporation's Form 990 filing with
              the IRS. 93

Figure 4.8   Common Cause's "Soft Money Laundromat"
              database identifies an individual's business, union,
              and industry contributions to both the Democrats
              and Republicans 95

Figure 4.9   The Soft Money Laundromat also identifies
              contributions to the political parties by a specific
              company. 95

Figure 4.10   The U.S. Occupational Safety and Health
              Administration's (OSHA) "Statistics and Data"
              provides details on companies where accident
              investigations have occurred. 96

Figure 4.11   A listing of investigations conducted by OSHA
              on Eastman Kodak's facilities 96

Figure 4.12   Detailed results of an investigation of a
              specific Eastman Kodak case 97

Figure 4.13   A search on the Federal Election Commission's
              Transaction Query System for political
              contributions by Steven Spielberg 97

Figure 4.14   The Search Systems site identifies what public
              records are available from each state 98

Figure 4.15   A search on the Search Systems site "Public
              Records Locator" identifies sources of public
              records matching the keyword: "contributions." 99

Figure 4.16   A listing of states' public records Web sites can
              be found by browsing BRB publications................... 99

Figure 5.1   As with many company home pages,
              background information on the knowledge

services firm FIND/SVP can be found under
its "Investor Relations" link 113

Figure 5.2 Facts and background data on FIND/SVP are
displayed after clicking on "Investor Relations." 113

Figure 5.3 Emulex's rebuttal of the fictitious press release 117

Figure 5.4 MarketResearch.com's "Search Inside This
Report" helps users indentify which pages of a
report are likely to be most relevant. 131

Figure 5.5 Inputting keywords and phrases commonly
associated with market research like "units
shipped" and "forecast" helps create a more
focused market search. 135

Figure 5.6 A search on Hoover's will retrieve a good
amount of detail on a company at no charge. 137

Figure 6.1 Bureau of Census American Fact Finder 144

Figure 6.2 FEDSTATS Home Page 145

Figure 6.3 Statistics Canada 146

Figure 6.4 Google's top-ranked page is an outdated version
of a federal government booklet—the newer
version is ranked third. 147

Figure 6.5 OMB Watch 150

Figure 7.1 NPR's news archive permits users to search and
listen to individual segments of its broadcasts 168

Figure 7.2 McGee's Musings is an example of a quality
blog. This one covers the field of knowledge
management 172

Figure 7.3 Example of a blogroll 175

Figure 7.4 Cricket Web Forum 176

Figure 7.5 Example of an investor message board 177

Figure 8.1 The Internet is only a source of data, facts,
opinions, and information—not true knowledge
and wisdom—though this site promises
enlightenment 206

Sidebars

Catching Business Information on the Internet 13

Public Information Sources Available to Online Researchers 88

Can't Get a Date? 109

Sample Press Release 115

Acknowledgments

First my thanks to Information Today, Inc. Editor-in-Chief John Bryans and Managing Editors Amy Holmes and Deborah Poulson for their scrutiny of my manuscript and for their suggestions, edits, and probing questions. All of this attention was of immense help in making this a much better book.

Much of what I've written in this book is drawn from my 15+ years as editor of *The Information Advisor*, so I'd like to take this opportunity to thank those people who were so critical in nurturing and helping the publication along since its inception in 1988.

My initial thank you goes to business entrepreneur Mary-Frances Winters for her willingness to take a risk when I approached her with the idea of starting up this publication while working for her market research firm, The Winters Group, in Rochester, New York, back in 1988. During my time at the Winters Group, I also worked closely with Marie Kotas, a librarian and information professional by training, who has worked closely with me on the publication since its inception. In addition to becoming a good friend, Marie has been a much trusted copy editor, proofreader, and overall editorial consultant who ensured that the newsletter was clear, well-written, and as free of mistakes as possible. Thank you Marie for all your years of invaluable assistance!

When I felt it was time to sell the publication in 1993, I was thrilled to discover that Andy Garvin, founder and president of the knowledge services company FIND/SVP was enthused about taking over the publication. I've always been grateful that Andy focused his great store of energy and shared his fertile ideas towards making *The Information Advisor* a success over the years. Several other colleagues at FIND/SVP have been critical in guiding this publication too. Josh Blackman, Sonia Bedikian, and Pat Clifford were all part of a tiny but dedicated team devoted to making sure the publication was of high quality, designed cleanly, and was satisfying to our readers. I would also like to thank previous FIND employee Michael Shor, who also shepherded *The Information Advisor* in its early years at FIND and taught me some good marketing tricks.

I've been blessed to have not one, but two outstanding contributing editors. The first is my friend and colleague, Reva Basch. Reva sent me an unsolicited letter back in 1988 when the publication first launched, and her note was filled with such great insights and ideas that when I responded, my thought was how could I get this talented woman to join the publication. I'm so glad she agreed and helped shape the publication in its early years. Reva was also kind enough to write the foreword to this book.

When in 1995 Reva told me she could no longer continue as contributing editor, I felt that was going to be an unrecoverable blow, but I should have known that Reva had something—or should I say someone—up her sleeve. Reva had already consulted with her good friend and colleague Mary Ellen Bates, as a possible replacement, and I've been privileged to have Mary Ellen as an outstanding contributing editor on this publication since 1995. Thank you Reva and Mary Ellen!

And now, as *The Information Advisor* has become part of Information Today, Inc., I'd like to take the opportunity to extend my thanks to Tom Hogan, Sr. and Dick Kaser for their desire to bring the publication forward to the next stage in its lifecycle. I'm looking forward to lots of new and exciting energy and ideas.

Finally, I'd like to thank my most trusted advisor, my wife Mary. Whenever I'm facing a quandary in my work, she can always be counted on to tell me what she thinks is the wisest and—while not always the easiest—the right thing to do.

Foreword

Information quality is hardly a new issue. Librarians and other research professionals have been uneasy about the reliability, completeness, and currency of electronic documents and data since the advent of online searching more than two decades ago. In 1990, the members of SCOUG (the Southern California Online Users Group), a particularly outspoken group of expert searchers, took as their task the development of a rating scale for online information. My report, "Measuring the Quality of the Data," which appeared in *Database Searcher* (now *Searcher*) magazine that October, chronicled SCOUG's effort and its outcome. Other professional entities took up the cause. Information quality became the theme of dozens of articles, studies, and professional meetings and conferences—in Canada, Great Britain, Scandinavia, Australia, and elsewhere—in the early to mid-'90s.

In 1994–1995, I edited a book called *Electronic Information Delivery: Ensuring Quality and Value* for the U.K.-based Gower Publications. Contributors included such respected information professional writers and thinkers as Stephen Arnold, Anne Mintz, Barbara Quint, Carol Tenopir, Péter Jacsó, and T.R. Halvorson, who examined from their individual perspectives every step of the information chain, from database construction to the role of the intermediary searcher to quality testing, liability issues, economic implications, and recommendations for the future. Clearly the issue of quality information is complex and multifaceted. Visible glitches like typos, transpositions, and garbled text are just the tip of a massive iceberg.

Concern about the quality of digital information in our commercial database services had just about peaked when the Web reared its unruly head. Suddenly, the professional online services looked impeccable by comparison. They offered peer-reviewed (or at least edited) content, structured into more or less standard formats, often with value-added indexing. They were subject to quality control at all stages of the production and distribution process. Quality-wise, the Web was like the Wild West, an unruly, undocumented frontier where the old rules simply did not apply. Effectively, anyone could publish. That was one of the joys, as well as a major drawback, of the World Wide Web. In this new information democracy, biases, misstatements, omissions, and outdated information carried the same weight as impartial, accurate, complete, and current documentation. Suspect sources masqueraded as legitimate-looking sites, while reputable publishers, handicapped by their print legacy and their inability to truly "get" the Web, were sometimes overlooked.

In fact, many knowledge workers and information specialists were reluctant at first to accept this strange and uncontrolled digital environment as a legitimate research resource. Their solution to dealing with dubious information on the Net was to not use it at all. Eventually, of course, that stance became untenable; denial can only go so far. Now, the Web is more ubiquitous than television, a platform and distribution medium for many of our personal as well as professional needs. The established database services have all migrated to the Web, joining a vast collection of primary and secondary research materials offered directly by publishers, trade associations, corporations, government agencies, advocacy groups, and experts in various fields—regionally, nationally, and, increasingly, globally.

The challenge of separating the gold from the garbage has not gone away with the increasing legitimacy of the Web. If anything, it's grown. Unmediated access to information—much of it ostensibly free—does carry a price. That price is vigilance, an ongoing skepticism, a questioning attitude toward new and untested data and unknown information providers. Contemporary information seekers must go into the field with rigorously calibrated b.s.-detectors firmly in place.

Fortunately, such quality assurance tools do exist, and Bob Berkman is an expert at deploying them. He has written several books as well as countless articles on finding and evaluating information for company and industry intelligence, management, and marketing. *The Information Advisor*, a newsletter he founded in 1988, is dedicated to assessing and comparing the quality and value of specific research resources, particularly in the business arena. For a number of years, I was lucky enough to work with Bob as contributing editor. I know that he brings the questioning attitude of an investigative journalist to every source, site, search engine, new technology, or management trend he explores. He covers the pros and cons thoroughly, thoughtfully, and without bias. At the same time, he never loses sight of the big picture, of what additional resources and alternative approaches the information-seeker might pursue. In each issue, he not only evaluates the new, he reminds us of the tried-and-true—and even points out when picking up the phone or consulting a print resource rather than an electronic database might yield a faster, cheaper, better answer.

Bob takes a similar approach in this book, entertaining us with anecdotes and vivid examples, but never losing sight of the fundamentals. He explains the "why" along with the "how," but his overall focus is practical, not theoretical. Bob always has the needs of the working searcher in mind. He illustrates, in detail, how to evaluate the sources you locate online. He identifies particular sites and starting points that are guaranteed to yield reliable, high-quality results. He shares the techniques and tools you can use, the filters you can put in place, the options you might select that will enhance the quality of your results every time you search. He also emphasizes a subject near and dear to my own heart, the importance of critical thinking—that is, taking an active, questioning stance when confronted with new information—and demonstrates exactly how you can develop and hone your own critical-thinking skills.

The Skeptical Business Searcher is not only a guide to evaluating information on the Web. It's an essential supplement to any general text or course on online research, a valuable refresher for experienced information professionals, and—for anyone with an interest in the Web and the extraordinary variety of information and misinformation to be found there—a lively, informative, and entertaining read.

Reva Basch
Executive Editor, Super Searchers book series
Past President, Association of Independent Information Professionals

About the Web Page

This book is supported by a companion Web page at http://books. infotoday.com/skepticalbiz.

There are two major purposes for this Web page. One is to provide you with a listing of hotlinks to the sites listed in this book. Those URLs are being updated on a regular basis, and if one is changed or updated in any way, I signify this right on this page by placing an "UPDATED" indicator next to that URL along with the date of the change. (If sites are removed, I note this alongside the URL along with a date of removal).

The other major purpose of *The Skeptical Business Searcher*'s Web page is to add new and significant sites. I will continue to share resources that I feel are important and relevant to the scope of this book.

I suggest you bookmark and check this page occasionally for updates.

You will also find a link to my own e-mail on the site—if you have an experience or opinion on a source listed, or want to suggest a new site or strategy for evaluating the quality and credibility of business information on the Web, please let me know!

CHAPTER 1

The Business
Researcher's Challenge

Where do you turn when you need to find company, industry, new-product, market, or business-trend information? These days business researchers begin on the Internet. There are few traditional business resources that have not migrated in one way or another to the Net, and there have been countless sources born on the Web as well.

But as the savvy researcher knows all too well, in addition to the trusted names and sources that are now Internet-accessible, an enormous number of sources of unknown origin and veracity exist there as well. They're all mixed together in the same vat, so to speak, from which the researcher must filter and scoop. This has given business researchers a new challenge: how to ensure that those sources taken from the open Web are reliable and credible.

On the one hand, the Web has provided the serious searcher with a wealth of worldwide information never before available, speeded up access, and often lowered the cost of—or even made free—some previously expensive sources. For instance, before the Internet, researchers did not have easy—let alone *free*—access to company press releases, daily newspapers from around the globe, and mountains of government reports and statistics.

Today, all of this and more is available by pushing a few keys while sitting at your desk. Moreover, it's typically formatted with all of the original graphics. The Internet has also aided the business researcher by creating remarkably helpful communities of like-minded professionals, on newsgroups and mailing lists, that share resources, answer questions, identify new sources, and perform other collegial activities. And the Net has made it possible to locate the most obscure data, specialized experts, and those with views and activities far out of the mainstream who previously were difficult to find.

But we've also experienced the flip side of the Web. Free information isn't always quality information, and an abundance of it can cause information overload. Further, the same open characteristics of the Web that provide us with the ability to participate in a worldwide conversation and let us connect with so many interesting people has also made it possible for anyone to be a self-appointed journalist, publisher, expert, or even broadcaster. All of this without necessarily taking any training programs, displaying any qualifications, or having anyone else check their information for accuracy.

None of this is news to today's experienced searcher, though you deal with this reality on a daily basis. You do a Google search for company information and you're directed not to, say, D&B or Standard & Poor's, but to an online directory you've never heard of before. Who is this publisher and where did it get its information? Or you find a local business journal with a Web version of an article that ran in its print version, but is what you found *really* the same as what was in the print publication? And where is the date of this article? Another search, say on trends in a new and growing market that you're researching, sends you to the pages of a popular "Blogger," someone who has created his or her own personal news and opinion page. What are this person's qualifications? Should you believe what he or she is telling you?

These are the problems confronting today's business researcher who ventures onto the Web.

Some Things Haven't Changed

Naturally, the need to evaluate the reliability of an information source goes beyond the Web. Good researchers have always confirmed the origin and veracity of all types of business and nonbusiness information. During the 1980s and early 1990s, most business research was conducted via fee-based online services such as Dialog or LexisNexis (which of course are still heavily used by information professionals, though today they are typically accessed through a Web browser), as well as print sources. When consulting these online sources, there were (and still are) important questions to be asked. Is the online version the equivalent of the original print version? If not, what was omitted? What sorts of quality-control techniques were utilized when entering the data to avoid keying errors?

During this era there was necessary attention paid to data integrity, which in retrospect seems simpler and less burdensome than in today's Internet age. Now there are virtually no quality controls or filters for information to pass through before it is disseminated to millions of people around the globe.

Even before the online information age, there were basic questions that good researchers knew to ask. What is the reputation and mission of this publisher or source? Does the author have an ax to grind? Is there a bias or some ideology that can call his or her credibility into question? How was the data gathered? If the information was derived from a survey or poll, what were the methodologies used?

In the classic text *The Modern Researcher* (Wadsworth, sixth edition, 2003), which was first published in 1992, authors Jacques Barzun and Henry J. Graff lay out what they view as the most fundamental "virtues" that the serious researcher should learn to cultivate: accuracy, love of order, logic, honesty, and self-awareness (pp. 43–48).

The authors explain that the task of ascertaining truthfulness is a daily occurrence for us: "Everybody daily faces the question: Is this true or false? ... The conclusions rest on a combination of knowledge, skepticism, faith, common sense, and intelligent guessing" (p. 96).

We must remain vigilant when encountering even the traditional information sources, which can lead us astray just as easily as a Web site (perhaps *more* easily since our guard may be lowered). In October 2002, for instance, a news story made the rounds on several major news outlets, including the *Washington Post*, the BBC, and several other supposedly trusted sources, that a new World Health Organization (WHO) study was predicting that blonds would soon be a thing of the past, due to the recessive gene associated with that hair color. One minor flaw: WHO never issued the story. In fact, with a little bit of reflection the blunder should have been obvious, since it doesn't make much sense that an organization concerned with health matters would issue a report about the future of blond-haired people. Media organizations that ran this story could have avoided embarrassment by placing a simple phone call to the organization to confirm it. But apparently none did, resulting in a slew of retractions. (The origin of this error, though not totally clear, was allegedly a 2000 article in a German magazine that erroneously cited WHO.)

Today, though, when using unknown Web sources, determining source reliability becomes even more important. There are special issues that need to be examined and new questions that need to be asked, all of which will be discussed in this book.

The bottom line is that the Web has made the job of the business researcher both easier *and* more difficult. It is easier in that the Web has delivered a great diversity of sources and made them quickly available, at no or low cost. The job is more difficult because of both the sheer amount of data we now have to wade through and the difficulty in determining which sources are trustworthy.

Enter the Quality Checklists

So how have business researchers approached the issue of information quality on the Web, and what steps have they taken to deal with it? Librarians and information professionals have weighed in with their own approaches and views. Some just bemoan the problem. Having been burned once or twice, they eschew searching the open Web and advise sticking with tried and true fee-based databases, supplemented with some favorite bookmarks of trusted sites. Others deal with the issue by sticking with government (*.gov*) or education (*.edu*) sites, and remaining skeptical of the dot-coms.

Some have gone a couple of steps beyond by trying to come up with specific guidelines that can be used by all searchers to assess the quality and reliability of what was uncovered on the open Web. These guidelines typically take the form of a criteria checklist that can be used to evaluate a particular Web site.

Personally, I find these checklists quite useful, though only to a point. On the positive side, they help surface the most likely problem areas and remind researchers of areas where attention needs to be paid when looking at sources. They can also be a nice crutch to lean on when venturing out into unknown Web territories, particularly for beginners or students. On the downside, checklists vary in what they ask you to consider. Some leave out areas that others include. Their emphasis on pinpointing a site's potential flaws can narrow your focus and keep you from seeing the bigger issues surrounding how information is created and disseminated.

The other drawback is that checklists do not really offer practical or long-lasting solutions to truly learn what to trust on the Web. It's hard to imagine actually reading down these lists and measuring and rating individual Web sources as you're surfing the Net. It's just too time-consuming and cumbersome. Furthermore, the longer-term solution (thinking critically and analytically about information) is built up over time, sometimes over years, and cannot be substituted with a check-list. So ultimately, while checklists contain useful reminders of what to look for when examining Web sites, I don't see them as an elegant, workable method of evaluating information on the Web.

That said, I'm not in any way against these checklists, as they can be used as a tool to increase awareness and improve one's search-ing. (In fact, in Appendix A you'll find a checklist I wrote myself, plus some others I recommend.) Because they help make sense of the Web's information glut, they are also excellent teaching aids for students or novices in Web-based research.

Furthermore, I'm not certain that many checklist creators ever intended them to be used in a literal manner. Just keep in mind that the checklist alone is not going to "solve" the problem of evaluating information on the Web.

The New Internet

The Internet has changed so much for researchers, mostly for the better. It's also had some fascinating effects. One that's particularly noteworthy is how it has changed what we think of when discussing an information item's "relevancy." Before Web search engines, when you searched a traditional fee-based database, any returned results could and would be deemed as "relevant" to your inquiry, since the search engine made a match between your keywords and the words in the article or other information item. Technically, those items were the relevant ones, even though they weren't always exactly what you wanted.

On the Web today, it seems that you can enter almost any series of random words (as an "AND" search) and nearly always retrieve results. The fact is, when searching such a huge set of information—literally billions of Web pages—probability theory compels that your chances of turning up results—results being defined as pages that include your keywords—are pretty high. But whether those results are truly *meaningful* is another matter altogether.

What I mean by this is as follows. Say you had a hunch that companies that outsource have lower morale among their employees and you wanted to go to the Net to see if there was any confirming data to support this. You go to a search engine, enter, "low morale" and "outsourcing" and lo and behold, you turn up scores of Web pages and discussion forums, which to your surprise—seem to confirm your theory! You find, that, yes there are people discussing and exploring how outsourcing is lowering morale. Similarly, say you are wondering if there is currently a housing bubble in the real estate market, and you enter "housing bubble" into a search engine and, yes, find *lots* of discussion on the subject of an upcoming housing bubble.

But you need to keep in mind that because you are searching such a vast amount of information, the odds become pretty good that you're going to find someone, somewhere, who also happens to believe or is exploring what you are looking into. And finding these kinds of "supporting" views can easily feed into something that all psychologists know about—a phenomenon called "self-confirmation bias"! Simply put, this means we tend to give credence to information and views that support our own pre-existing beliefs and opinions.

Furthermore, the fact that you are searching a set of billions of Web pages means that the odds increase that you'll turn up pages just because they happen to include the keywords you've entered. But many pages will just include your keywords somewhere on the page, unrelated to each other. In this case, you'll get back lots of results, but they won't necessarily be relevant to your query.

So if it's on the Web you seek, you'll more than likely find—just be careful that what you find is relevant, meaningful, and, if you're looking to verify or confirm a theory or point of view, something more than just a case of self-confirmation bias!

Another way in which the Internet has completely changed the scene has been in empowering the researcher to go beyond merely scooping up facts and secondary information and to become a more proactive, directed editor or fact-checker. Indeed, smart researchers today understand that the information-quality problem on the Web isn't necessarily in the believability or credibility of the individual who is posting it. Rather, it's the lack of standard editorial processes that traditional publications go through, such as topic screening, peer review, copyediting, fact-checking, and proofreading. For this reason, it behooves you, the researcher, to assume those roles yourself—that is, to examine what you find with skepticism.

Interestingly, while the Internet has eliminated much of this function, it has also given birth to some tools and sites that make it possible to reintroduce these critical functions, at least partially. In some cases, with additional verifications you're able to go well beyond what the typical researcher has been able to do. For example, in 2002 President George W. Bush said something controversial, and the media took him to task for it. One particular blogger took umbrage at this, but rather than simply note his disagreement, he offered visitors to his site the ability to link to an archived video clip of the event. This way they could judge for themselves whether the President's comments were inappropriate. Now that's the kind of media check that, until not so long ago, hadn't been readily available to information users!

Another way in which the Web has changed information flow is in how quickly both good and bad data is spread. When a dramatic news story breaks or a rumor begins to emerge, the Web, primarily in the form of e-mail forwarding, rapidly and seemingly uncontrollably accelerates the data. In the case of bad information, the result can be that, in a very short time, it's possible for a great many people to believe something that isn't true.

In an informative and amusing April 2000 interview on National Public Radio's *All Things Considered* ("A Cautionary Tale About Facts on the Internet"), author and expert searcher Reva Basch was interviewed about the problem of commonly believed, but untrue information that's passed on via the Web. In response to NPR host David Kestenbaum's query about this phenomenon, Basch replied jokingly that this situation "does call the definition of reality into question. If enough people arrive at a consensus on a fact, does the nature of reality change?" (See Appendix B for the link to the audio of this broadcast.)

Defining reality is a bit beyond the scope of this book, but I will observe that, fortunately, business research does not normally rely on instant access to breaking news or rumors. Typically, it involves more in-depth, deliberative research over a longer period of time. This allows ample opportunity to question the source, analyze it, and get additional confirmations, and then apply the various safeguards we'll discuss throughout this book.

Why This Book?

Why do we need a book to help us evaluate business information on the Web? The problems in establishing the veracity of Web information in general are clear, but what's special about business information and why does it need its own treatment?

For one thing, there's usually much at stake in locating accurate data on the Web and in making sure you're not deceived by erroneous or even deliberate misinformation. Business research is normally performed prior to making some significant business decision. It could be research on whether to introduce a new product, partner with another company, plan to enter a new market, create a competitive strategy, understand changing buyer habits, or keep track of emerging opportunities and threats within your own market. And while a good business decision requires more than accurate and reliable information, it's impossible to make a good decision that's based on bad information. Plus, your own personal credibility is on the line whenever you provide information to another party, as you are implicitly vouching for its accuracy simply by choosing to pass it along.

But it isn't easy finding reliable, trustworthy business information on the Web. Although we've come to appreciate Google's uncanny ability to retrieve relevant results, it's easy to be swamped with too many pages of dubious quality if you don't know how to create a focused, precise search and take advantage of all its powerful features.

As impressive as Google is, it still cannot screen out pages where data is too old, biased, or created from an untrustworthy source. Google cannot tell you which directory has the latest sales figures of the companies you want to track. It can't tell whether a poll was conducted scientifically or not. It cannot tell you if a company is fudging its profits, or if an analyst is giving you biased recommendations, or if an organization's agenda is different than what it appears to be. These are still matters best left to human analysis.

In order to really end up with the best business information on the Web, you need to know when and how to go beyond search engines, when to use other information-gathering tools, and how to pull together collections of pre-screened sites.

This book is designed to tell you what you need to know about all these matters—how to create the best business-information search, use the right research tools, and scrutinize Web sites for credibility—so that you can rely on the business information you find on the Web.

Seeing the Big Picture

For better or worse, doing any type of research has become synonymous with going to the Web. How did we get to this point, and what are some of the larger implications for the serious researcher?

Remember Marshall McLuhan's admonishment: First we shape our tools, and then they shape us. The Internet is an incredibly powerful tool, and it has an equally powerful influence on us. One effect is in how we view the research process, and what it means to be a good researcher. As outlined in *The Modern Researcher*, these virtues include accuracy, love of order, logic, honesty, self-awareness, and imagination.

The Web certainly challenges researchers to maintain these virtues. According to Barzun and Graff, a key characteristic in maintaining accuracy is "the habit of unremitting attention" to what you find. Can you maintain that level of scrutiny when surfing through Web pages and scanning for data while under time pressure? As for imagination, the ability to "imagine the kind of source [you] would like to have before [you] can have it" is imperative. But if research now means simply going to Google and typing in keywords, how good are you in imagining your ideal source?

Similarly, any good investigative researcher will tell you that a thorough investigation means lots of nitty-gritty, detailed work, and often takes many months. It means you'll have to comb through primary documents, find people who know what you need, and interview them. In the old-fashioned journalist vernacular, you need to use up a lot of shoe leather. On the Web, as professors today lament, it's almost too easy to "perform research" simply by scanning the first few pages returned by a search engine.

In *The Road Less Traveled*, M. Scott Peck suggests that if there's anything in our nature that can be termed "original sin," it would be laziness. This is the inertia we all feel that prevents us from doing the necessary work and making the effort that's required to do what we know needs to be done. And unfortunately, doing research on the Web makes it easy for us to indulge our propensity for laziness, to the detriment of our finished product.

Like any media or communication tool, the Web embodies inherent characteristics that determine and influence the way we obtain and use information. But this is a subtle process. Like the old saying about a fish's inability to discover water, we too are becoming immersed in the medium, which may make it impossible to distinguish the new information environment clearly. But because the Web is a new medium, we still have the opportunity to observe its impact. The following are some of the special hazards we'll encounter as we move to a mostly Web-based research world:

1. **Missing Context**—A search engine does not care about context, it merely retrieves for you the page that contains

your keywords. But understanding the context of what you're reading is critical to understanding it. You'll need to do the work necessary to find this larger context.

2. **Emphasis on speed**—If there is a single primary "message" to the Web, it may be speed. Everything is instantly available. Researching can get news that's only a few minutes old. But while speed is important, it's not necessarily a friend of good research. In fact, emphasizing speed increases the chance of making mistakes and merely allows for data access, rather than knowledge building—a process that takes time.

3. **Emphasis on style and graphics**—Web designers and online journalists alike know that it's difficult to read long blocks of text on the Web, and that a page must look appealing to draw people to it. But an emphasis on design can come at the expense of text length, and the written word is still the best way to convey complex ideas. Relying only on shorter "chunking" of text and eschewing longer analyses means there's a greater potential of getting a superficial read of the subject.

4. **Lack of historical perspective**—The Web is a new medium and, other than some specialized archival collections that have been digitized, most pages are no older than the early 1990s. That's fine for most business research purposes, as you rarely need old business information. But on those occasions where you do require historical, archival-type information, it's important to go off the Web and check specialized hard-copy or microfilmed collections.

5. **Search Engine/Keyword Mindset**—Being a good researcher goes beyond creating keywords or even searching online databases. *The Modern Researcher*'s Barzun expressed concern that online searching "presupposes the searcher's knowing ahead of time what he should find out."

Further, he notes that "a database is good for the person who wants to know the length of the Brooklyn Bridge; it is not for the one who wants to understand the respective effects of Norman, Arab, and Spanish influence in Southern Italy" (personal correspondence, October 1, 1995). Or, to put Barzun's point in a business-related context, an online search won't help you understand how the economic forces of the 1990s are going to influence the success of your new product introduction in 2005. In other words, building an in-depth knowledge and understanding of any complex matter takes more than a search.

6. **Bots vs. People**—Scientists and researchers continue to create smarter, more capable automated tools to collect and display information. Some of these are impressive indeed and have the capability to search through millions of articles. These tools cull those articles that meet the profile of what you want to track, summarize them, and then display them in an intuitive, graphical manner. U.S. intelligence agencies even use these programs to identify linkages among people and organizations that are suspected of terrorism. These tools and bots are generally touted for their ability to turn information into knowledge. But only humans have the ability to provide true analysis and insight, and it will remain this way for the foreseeable future. Only people can answer your specific questions by calling on their wealth of experience and knowledge.

The Internet Emerges

It's interesting to go back 10 years and read what was written in the monthly newsletter I founded and edit, *The Information Advisor*. The article that appears in the following sidebar was published in December 1992. George H.W. Bush had just lost the presidential election to Bill Clinton, and the European Union was created earlier that year in Maastricht, Netherlands. An excerpt of the article, "Catching Business

Information on the Internet," provides an interesting glimpse into the technology as we knew it then.

Catching Business Information on the Internet

What do you need to know about "the Internet"? During the last 6 months or so, interest and discussion about this international electronic network has exploded. But much of the writing has been overly technical and dense. Furthermore, few—if any—of these analyses have been relevant for the business researcher. This article will explain, in jargon-free language, what the Internet is, how it can be of use to business researchers, how to sign on, and where to find the latest and most useful sources of information.

What Is the Internet?

The Internet is an enormous conglomeration of electronic computer networks. Currently, it links about 4 million people on 1 million computers in over 100 countries.

Here's a capsule history: The Internet was begun in 1969 by the Department of Defense. It grew in size and scope over the years, and eventually became a publicly run network for fostering study and communication in education, research, and academia. Up until the last year or so, [its] use was restricted to those persons associated with an academic or research institution already on the network. Today, while commercial use of the Internet is still restricted, anyone can sign on and join the network simply by hooking up with one of a number of telecommunication vendors (listed later in this article). The Internet is funded today by the National Science Foundation, and has been supported and nurtured by Vice President-elect Albert Gore.

What do people do on the Internet? Well, as with the well-known and popular bulletin board services like CompuServe, Prodigy, The Well, and others, a primary use is electronic mail and user-to-user communications. Internet users also can subscribe to electronic journals, join special interest groups, and access various information databases.

Business Information Uses

But what can the Internet offer specifically to the business researcher? There are probably four major applications: locating experts and answers, sharing information and problems, accessing documents and books, and searching online databases.

Let's look at each of these areas separately, beginning with the locating of experts.

We spoke with Sharyn Ladner, business librarian at the University of Miami. Ladner is the author of How Special Librarians Really Use the Internet and was speaker at the December 7–8 Meckler Conference on Document Delivery and Libraries/Internet and Libraries. Ladner told us that "the best information tool is a Rolodex. And the Internet is an electronic Rolodex." She enthusiastically describes how researchers have "thrown out hard-to-answer questions" onto the Internet, and in a matter of hours, have received a handful ... of replies. "How many phone calls would you have had to make to get an answer?" Ladner asks.

Related to the opportunity to locate experts is the ability to share information and problems with peers. The Internet currently has a forum for business librarians, called "BUSLIB-L." Its mission is to deal with "all issues related to the collection, storage, and dissemination of business information within a library setting." While still populated mainly by academic rather than purely commercial researchers, Ladner expects that this group will grow quickly. (Other special-interest lists on the Internet cover government documents, chemicals, law, library reference, medicine and health, science, and many other topics.)

Another use for the Internet is directly accessing documents and books from other network participants. Users can search hundreds of libraries' catalogs online, and information specialists can use this function to facilitate traditional interlibrary loans.

Online Searching

Finally, Internet users can conduct database searches of certain popular online hosts, as well as smaller, more specialized databases. Among the big names currently accessible are Dialog and Mead Data Central (Nexis/Lexis). Why would you choose to search these hosts on the Internet? There are pros and cons to searching these files here. Let's look at searching Dialog first.

A major reason why you might want to search Dialog through the Internet is cost. Currently, accessing Dialog through one of the major telecommunication vendors like Tymnet or Sprintnet costs an average of $12 per hour in telecommunication fees. However, it costs only $3 per hour on the Internet (plus regular Internet access fees). The other advantage to searching Dialog on the Internet is more abstract; it relates to the synergy you could achieve by having an electronic communications experience that consisted of a mixture of posting queries, downloading other users' data resources, and searching databases all during a single session. Dialog's Internet connection is managed by ANSI, [which is] located in Michigan.

On the negative side, searching Dialog on the Internet is rather user-unfriendly. You cannot perform certain functions such as capturing log files or utilizing accounting functions [that are] otherwise available.

Searching Mead's files on its own Meadnet system costs $13 per hour in telecommunications costs. Mead has created a version of its communication software to search the Internet. However, the firm tells us that the product is made available to law school and business school users only.

Dialog and Mead are not the only online systems accessible through the Internet. There are also individually accessible database files, which include economic and census reports, and science and technology files. However, no complete list of databases exists.

Access Options

Once you've determined that you want to give the Internet a try, how do you sign on? There are many different ways to connect. ... As mentioned earlier, if you belong to an organization that already is connected to the system, all you need is a password. Otherwise, you'll need to contact a commercial or specialized provider.

Probably the best-known names are CompuServe and Delphi. Once you decide to sign up, be prepared to deal with a sometimes difficult interface and confusing procedures. ...

So, other than evidence that Al Gore was at least a nurturing father figure to the Internet, what can we glean from this 1992 article?

As expected, much has changed since then. Certain Internet service providers mentioned are either no longer in existence or have been absorbed by other companies. And the technical aspects of connecting and navigating the Internet have clearly improved.

But the Internet is still doing what it was doing best even at those nascent, pre-World Wide Web days: It allows us to find other *people*, who remain the best, most reliable sources of expertise. They might be trained information experts like journalists or librarians, or just have knowledge, interest, and a willingness to share what they know. The scholar, teacher, businessperson, author, and passionate amateur expert can all be located in a matter of seconds through the power of the Internet.

You, then, as an intelligent business researcher, will use the Internet as an extraordinarily powerful data-gathering tool and an excellent method for locating knowledgeable people. You must employ your skepticism and skills to ferret out the good and bad data. You can then take the next step and ask your insightful questions, critically assess the information you receive, and work to build your own knowledge and further your own understanding.

Scope of This Book

It's important to make clear what this book covers and what it does not. The most important point to keep in mind is that I am limiting the discussion of business information to what can be found on the *free* Web. Specifically, I am referring to the portion that is accessible by anyone, at no charge. (This includes sites where you may need to register, but not pay a fee.) Also included here are those sites and pages that constitute the "Invisible Web"—these contain information that resides on the Web, but for a variety of reasons are hidden from search engines. These "invisible" pages are covered here, as long as they are free.

What I don't cover are those fee-based traditional databases that have migrated to the Web: large online vendors like Dialog, LexisNexis, and Factiva; the individual databases such as ProQuest, Gale, Moody's, and D&B; and smaller, more specialized data providers such as the Economist Intelligence Unit. Also not covered are fee-based business databases that were born on the Web: SkyMinder and OneSource, for instance.

The reason I've chosen not to include those sites is that they represent known quantities to researchers. And the fact that they can now be accessed on the Web (rather than on proprietary dial-up services or through larger database vendors) does not raise too many new, significant quality issues. So if you've searched, say, D&B's Million Dollar Directory by dialing up to Dialog's service in the past, but you now search it either on DialogWeb or even on D&B's own services, there aren't too many critical quality issues to consider. (Not that there aren't *any* new issues that have arisen from having Web access to some of these sources. For example, you'll want to confirm that the same quality and currency is available via the Web interface as before, in respect to matters like length of archive, update frequency, coverage, advanced search capabilities, and so on.)

There are some sites that fall into a gray area when it comes to categorizing them as free or fee-based. For instance, market-research-report aggregators on the Web allow anyone to search their databases, view initial results, and sometimes view even more (such as a summary or table of contents) for no charge—and some don't even require registration. But if you decide to purchase a report, then you'll need to pony up some money. These kinds of sites—free searching/fee-based viewing—*are* included in the scope of this book.

It might be helpful for me to describe the scope of what I am covering under the broad umbrella of what is called "business research." Obviously, "business research" is a very broad term and can be defined as anything that answers any business-related query, so theoretically any kind of data or source could support a business related question.

In practice, though, there are certain types of information sources that are relied on and utilized most often for business research purposes. These include company information sources, market research reports, statistical data, news and media sources, and online discussion groups and Weblogs. I'll discuss each of these sources in detail in Chapters 5 and 6.

One type of source not covered in this book is information geared toward investors, which generally consists of advice and news on choosing and trading stocks, bonds, commodities, or other investment instruments. These really don't fall under the category of professional business research. Rather, they're mainly geared to consumer or institutional investing.

How to Use This Book

Following this introductory chapter, Chapter 2 will examine some strategies to use before using a Web search engine. I'll review the important non-Internet-based business sources as well as Web sites that have already proven themselves as reliable sources of business-related facts. We'll also examine how information-finding tools (other than search engines) can be more effective for locating reliable business data than standard search engines.

Chapter 3 will in fact focus on search engines—specifically, on using them effectively to pinpoint just the business information you need. I'll tell you how to get the most out of Google: how to make its advanced search features work, filtering out questionable sites from the get-go, analyzing its initial results page to spot the most promising pages, and more. Also included is a summary of what I think are the best of the other search engines and advice on when to use them.

In Chapter 4, I'll tell you what to do when you arrive at a site or source of questionable origin or veracity. Here you'll get some tips from some of the best investigative reporters around on analyzing the truthfulness of a source. You'll also discover the top signs that you may be dealing with a source of dubious quality. You'll learn how to go beyond just reacting to what you see on your screen by using some proactive evaluation strategies to determine whether a source is credible.

The two chapters that follow will help you evaluate specific types of commonly used business information sources. Chapter 5 looks at company information from corporate home pages, market research reports, company directories, and a few other sources. Chapter 6 focuses on statistical data, polls, and surveys. Chapter 7 examines online news and Web discussion groups. For each source I'll discuss the most common quality problems, examine specific Web-related concerns, offer tips on finding out if your source suffers from those problems, and offer advice on how to ensure that you locate quality information.

In Chapter 8, we'll look at some of the overriding, big-picture issues that we need to know about to feel confident that we're gathering quality information on the Web. Here I'll discuss the importance of building your own knowledge on a topic so as to more easily spot bad data, along with the roles of critical thinking, intuition, and trust.

Finally, Chapter 9 is a compilation of filtered and screened business sites, organized by category, that have proven themselves to be reliable and useful sources for business research purposes. An important part of the process of doing research on the Web is to have a set of trusted, stable Web sites at your disposal. The sources listed in this chapter will help you develop such a collection.

Appendix A offers my Web site evaluation checklist along with recommendations of other checklists you'll find freely available on the Web. Appendix B is a chapter-by-chapter listing of resources recommended in the book.

To make *The Skeptical Business Searcher* easier to read, I have placed the URLs for all recommended Web sites in Appendix B. The companion Web page to this book features hot links to these Web pages; this page will be updated on a semiannual basis.

I'd love to hear from you and hope you'll share some of your own tips with me. I'll include them at the Web page and perhaps in a future edition of *The Skeptical Business Searcher*.

Now, let's get out onto the Web and start finding those reliable business sources you need.

CHAPTER 2

What to Do Before Using a Search Engine

What's the best way to ensure you don't get tripped up by bad data on the Web? Don't search the Web.

I say this tongue-in-cheek, of course. While some might advise you to avoid Web search engines completely, to me that's going overboard. As you'll learn in these pages, it is certainly not necessary to go that far—so long as you use the right strategies and tools while on the Web and know how to perform precision searches.

That said, it's perhaps too easy these days to overlook a wide range of options for locating quality, timely business information that doesn't involve using a search engine. These options can help you bypass some of the hazards involved in conducting credible business research.

This chapter will review and identify the following seven major types of business-information resources that can be accessed without a Web search engine:

- Basic Library Business Sources
- Prescreened Web Sites
- Invisible Web Sources
- Web Indexes and Directories
- Discussion Groups
- Blogs
- RSS Feeds

21

Basic Library Business Sources

There's no question that more and more of what used to be available only in libraries has migrated to the Web. Newspapers, journals, government documents, annual reports, and more are available—often for no charge—right on the open Web.

But this doesn't mean that *everything* has migrated to the Net. There are many business sources that are still available only in print, which are better accessed at a library. For some of you, this is familiar territory, so you may want to skip ahead. But for those who are newer to business research, or if you're experienced and just want a refresher, read on.

Examples of information sources that are better accessed in print, and in the library, include:

1. **Business Books**—Obviously, if you're looking for the latest tomes on management, marketing, the knowledge economy, leadership, or other in-depth topics, you're not going to read the full text of those books online. Your best bet is your library, or a large bookstore with a business section. Not only are physical collections like these the best place for finding books, but most of us enjoy scanning titles and covers to decide on the right one. You can't easily browse book titles on the Web—certainly not as efficiently (or enjoyably) as you can at a library or bookstore.

2. **Specialized Directories**—The major publishers of company directories (including D&B, Standard & Poor's, Moody's, Thomas Register, and Hoover's) have made their collections of company data available on the Web. But you'll have to pay a fee to search these, and you may not obtain as much information as the original print directories. You may also lose some of the look-up tools and indexes that let you comfortably browse their print directories. In addition to the major company directories available on the Web, there are hundreds, if not thousands, of smaller directory publishers that cover niche areas. Most of these have not made it to the Web and can only be found in print.

3. **Media Archives**—Nearly all newspaper and journal publishers have Web sites that allow both subscribers and non-subscribers to read their latest issues, and sometimes to search for back issues as well. But access to archives is spotty on the Web; the available resources often do not go back very far and are typically fee-based. In some cases, when you do an archive search you're not finding the exact full text from the print newspaper, but a separate, Web-only edition that the publisher has created. If you want older articles—and a complete archive—your best bet remains either a library that subscribes to the publication or access via a traditional fee-based database.

4. **Primary Documents**—The need to locate original primary documents is unusual in a business search, but if you do have to uncover memos, in-house newsletters, legal documents, maps, historical photographs, and so on, you're not likely to find them on the Web. Although there are some notable digital library collections with scanned-in primary materials (such as the Library of Congress' American Memory Collection and contents from the Vatican's library), the percentage of original physical documents online is still minuscule.

5. **Access to Librarians**—Don't forget that the best search engine remains a trained human, especially a skilled librarian. Spending a few minutes chatting with an information professional at a nearby library can save you hours of unproductive Web searching.

Prescreened Web Sites

Today there are scores of Web sites that have earned reputations for consistently offering reliable, credible business information. Others are known for the quality of experts and specialists that stand behind the sites. If you're aware of or have these Web pages bookmarked, you may not need to run a general search to find an answer or author-itative site. You just link to one of these instead.

Chapter 9 includes an extensive list of the best business sites. Following are examples of the best-known and most often used free sites utilized by business information professionals. (Figures 2.1-2.4 show some of these sites.) They cover the broadest general use for most business research purposes. (Remember, the following are free/registration-only sites—they're not fee-based databases or those that require paid subscriptions.)

Web Site	Type of Data Provided
Hoover's	Primarily company information
ResourceShelf	Resources and news for information professionals
EDGAR	SEC filings of public companies
U.S. Census Bureau	Demographic and statistical data on the U.S.
Newslink	Directory that provides access to international newspapers
Public Records Online	Public records offices for state and local government
MarketResearch.com	Indexing, tables of contents, and excerpts from market research reports
MindBranch.com	Same as above
Embassy.org	Links to embassies around the globe
FirstGov	One-stop shopping site to U.S. federal government data
FedStats	Links to federally generated statistics sources
ITA Trade Development: Industries and Analysts	Access to federal government industry analysts
Thomas	Key source for locating information on legislature, laws
Yahoo! Finance	Descriptive and financial data on public companies

Figure 2.1 *Hoover's*

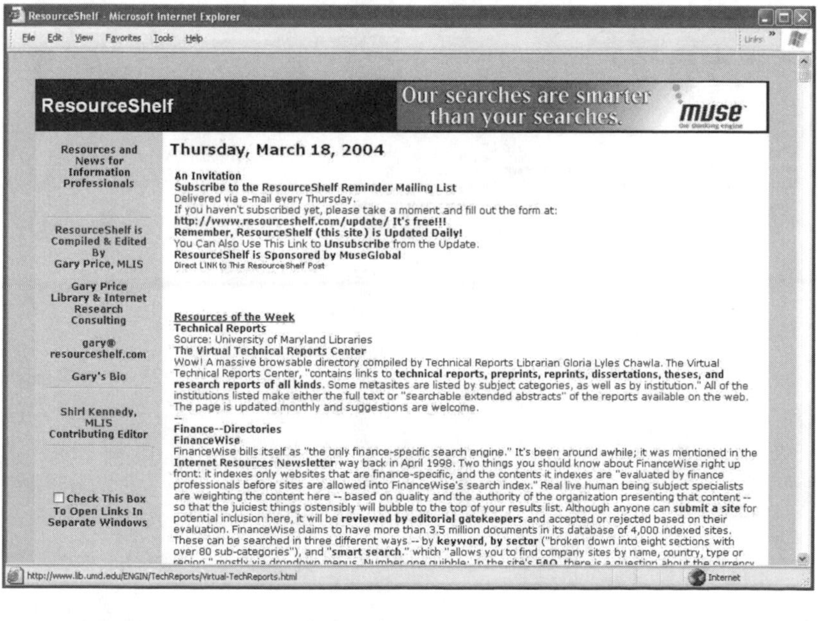

Figure 2.2 *ResourceShelf*

Figure 2.3 EDGAR

Figure 2.4 Embassy.org

When you find a trusted, favorite site, you should take another step and consider using special Web tools to get the most out of it. Two worth considering are e-mail alerts and Web-watching software.

Some sites allow you to register for free e-mail alerts, which are sent to you whenever new information is added that matches a profile you've created. For example, at the *New York Times* Web site, I have an alert set up to let me know whenever the day's paper contains one of several terms that I track. See Figure 2.5 for a sample message that I receive when there's a relevant story in the day's paper.

You may also want to be sent an e-mail alert when a favorite page changes. There are several software programs that allow you to monitor certain URLs, and then let you know when there are changes. A couple of the better-known ones are TrackEngine and WatchThatPage.

Invisible Web Sources

It may come as a surprise to some, but there's a whole world of information on the Web that's not retrievable by all or most search

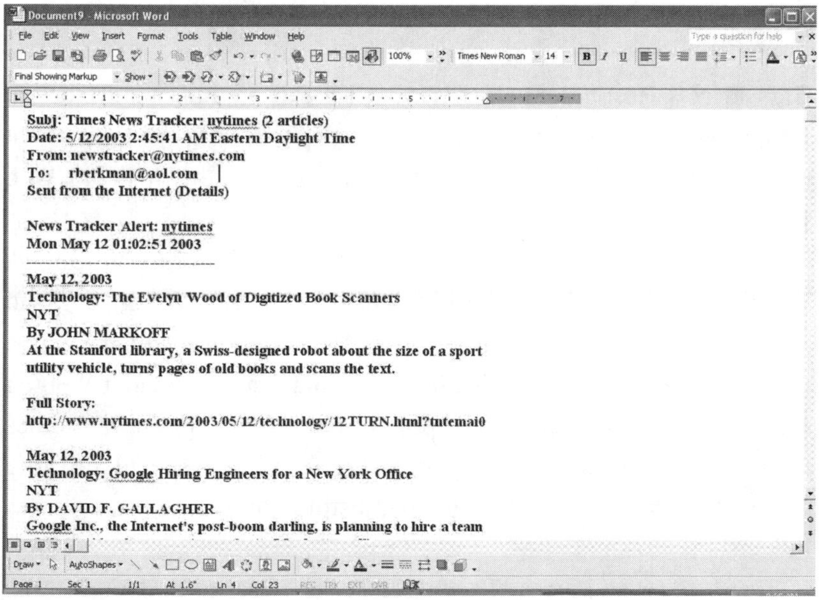

Figure 2.5 *NY Times Tracker*

engines. This is most commonly called the "Invisible Web," and it consists of sites that cannot be indexed by search engines. There are several reasons why a Web site may not be retrievable by search engines: It may require registration or a password; it may consist of unindexed multimedia or non-HTML files; it may be a database, which is generated by a cgi-script and is only retrievable from the site itself; or the owner of the site may have created a "no robots" command in the code, which prohibits the search engine spiders from indexing the site.

While the actual substance of the Invisible Web runs the gamut, some Invisible Web sources that are of interest to the business researcher include:

- Media archives, including both print and audio archives
- U.S. government reports and statistics series
- Searchable databases on various topics
- Library catalogs

There are sites, however, that find their way through the Invisible Web and link to quality resources. These sites can be invaluable tools for business researchers. Some focus specifically on identifying and providing access to online databases, while others locate all types of sources.

My number-one source—head and shoulders above the rest—is Gary Price's ResourceShelf. It's what I'd call a "must read" for the serious business researcher who wants to both keep up with the latest trends and news in research and be alerted to key Invisible Web sources.

Price served for many years as a reference librarian at George Washington University in Washington, D.C., and is well-known and respected in the information industry. He is co-author of the book, *The Invisible Web* (with Chris Sherman), and writes a regular Weblog (blog) in which he identifies important news items and new sources for the information-searching community. Along with identifying these sites, Price often adds his own astute commentary as well as links to the original sites.

There are several types of sources that Price uses to find noteworthy items to post on his Weblog. These include audio programs, newspapers, news wires, company press releases, government documents, conference reports and papers, association studies, and UN Reports.

To get an idea of the topics covered by Price in a typical week, here are the categories of the resources he covered during the week of March 15th, 2004:

- Children—Statistical Data
- Climate
- Courts Statistical Data
- Digital Information
- Digital Libraries
- Elections
- Engineering
- Environment
- Finance Directories
- Geographic Searching
- Government Procurement
- Government Records
- Health Information
- Health Policy Statistical Data
- Industry Briefs
- Information Technology
- Information Industry
- Internet Security
- Journalism
- Library of Congress
- Library Professional Reading
- Online Databases
- Online Research
- Population
- Scholarly Publishing
- Small Business Statistical Data
- Special Libraries
- Technical reports
- Television
- Transportation Statistics
- U.K. Budget

- U.S. State libraries
- Water
- Web Searching

Although ResourceShelf is my favorite source for finding material on the Invisible Web, it is not the only one. A few other favorites are INFOMINE and the Social Science Information Gateway, both of which focus on revealing academic-oriented Invisible Web documents. Another excellent one is Search Systems, which identifies public records available on the Web.

Databases on the Invisible Web

In Chapter 3, I discuss how to perform precision business research on a search engine. I want to help ensure that the sources you retrieve are relevant—certainly one of the most important factors in a quality Web site. But search engines can only take you so far in performing a precision search. If you really want to be precise in pinpointing the information that meets your criteria, your best bet is not to use a search engine, but a database. Furthermore, virtually all database creators assemble their sources from known providers, such as newspapers, trade magazines, government documents, academic journals, and other branded data sources. This gives you some level of assurance before you even begin your search.

There are many thousands of databases available online, covering everything from accounting news to zoological research. The actual sources in these databases vary. Some consist of newspaper and/or trade journal articles, patents, market research reports, chemical formulas, company directories, census series, and so on.

Databases, as you probably know, preceded the existence of the Internet. Back then they were typically available either online from a large fee-based database vendor like Dialog or LexisNexis, via a remote library database provider like ProQuest (see Figure 2.6), or on CD-ROM.

Because pre-Internet databases contained a controlled set of information from a finite number of providers and was organized by a vendor who sold the database, it was easy for that vendor to break down

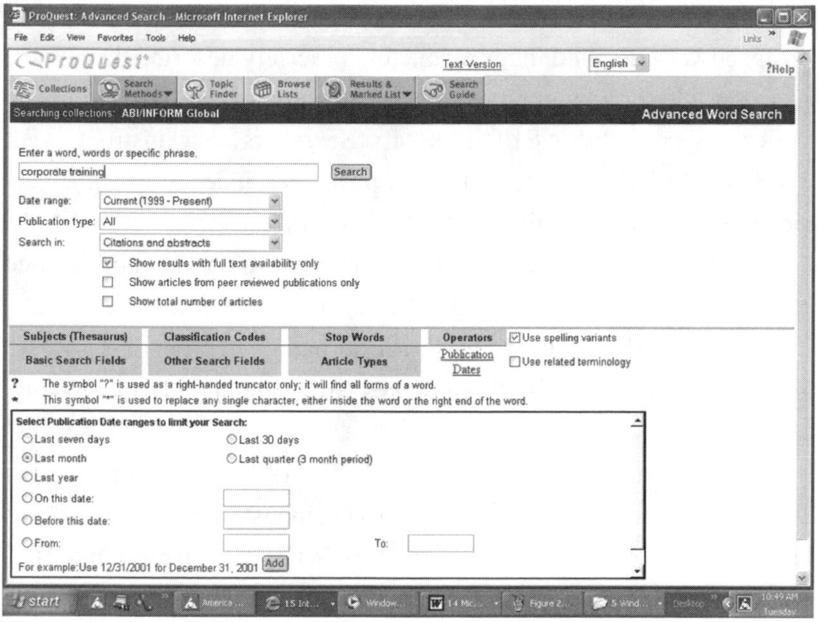

Figure 2.6 *ProQuest Database*

the information inside the database into sections (or "fields") that helped the user search with a great deal of precision. For example, a journal article might be segmented into such fields as author name, journal name, geographic code, abstract of article, date of article, and subject of article. Users could then input a search word and run it not just against entire articles, but against one of those narrow fields. This made searching more precise and resulted in more relevant results.

Arguably the most valuable field created by a database vendor is "subject of article." The best vendors went a step further and created what is called a "controlled vocabulary," a special index designed for use with a specific database. This way users could browse the index and find the preferred term created by the database producers to index related data. The searcher could then use that term to pull up all that indexed information. As an example, ABI/INFORM is a major database of business journals that you can search at many libraries via the ProQuest system, as well as in certain fee-based online subscription services.

Each of the business articles in ABI/INFORM's database is assigned very detailed index terms that precisely describe the subject of the article. Following are examples of some of the "CN" indexing codes assigned by ABI/INFORM. (Searchers can instruct ABI/INFORM to only return articles that have been indexed with the particular code corresponding to the subject of the article.)

Every article in ABI/INFORM's database is assigned very detailed subject index terms that precisely describe the subject of the article. To do this, ABI/INFORM classification names that begin with "M" include managerial skills, market research, metalworking industry, and middle east.

The advantage of this method is as follows. Say that a researcher wants to locate articles on the metalworking industry. He or she can then just enter a CN code to retrieve all articles that have been given that classification. This process takes the guesswork out of how to come up with the right search words to retrieve the most relevant articles.

For the record, a few other outstanding business databases are PROMT, Business & Industry, and TableBase, but, like ABI/INFORM, these are also not available on the free Web.

The Web is not, by any means, a controlled database. Nobody is in charge of splitting all the pages into fields and writing index terms. However, there are some controlled databases that *are* available to access via the free and open Web. You should be aware of these, as they do provide you with the opportunity to perform more precise searches over a controlled set of known information. Some examples of the types of searchable, substantive databases that reside on the free Web include:

- A public records database
- A U.K. company-name database
- A searchable database of tax forms filed by nonprofit organizations
- A database of companies in European white pages and yellow pages directories

The following are my favorite sources that specialize in helping search for and browse databases that reside on the Invisible Web.

INFOMINE

INFOMINE covers not only databases but also directories, larger resource collections, online library card catalogs, e-journals, and books. It is superbly organized with keywords, subject headings, and tables of contents. You can conduct your keyword search on one of many fields as well as restrict it by broad category, one of which is "Business and Economics" (see Figures 2.7 and 2.8).

Librarians' Index to the Internet

The Librarians' Index to the Internet (LII) serves as both a directory to substantive Web sites (see p. 36) and a source that identifies and describes searchable databases. There are a couple of features that make this site such a useful tool. One is that you can browse the category called "Business, Finance, & Jobs" to zero in on the subtopic area where you want to find databases. Another is that its advanced search screen allows you to specify, in the "Category" field, that you want to limit your search only to databases, and not any other kind of LII-indexed resource (see Figures 2.9 and 2.10).

Profusion

I've had some hits and misses when testing the Profusion site, and it can be slow to update, but you can also locate some useful databases here. One nice feature is its ability to browse by category to find a listing of relevant databases (see Figure 2.11).

Web Indexes and Directories

Another way to rely on prescreened business information sites is by searching finder tools like Yahoo!, which are directories or hierarchical indexes. Unlike search engines, these finder tools do not blindly crawl the Web to bring back just any page that happens to include words that match your keywords. Rather, they are built by human beings—often librarians—who ensure that each site included is substantive and categorized correctly under the proper subject headings.

The idea is that when you search (or browse by category) a directory/index, you are limiting your search to a *much* smaller set

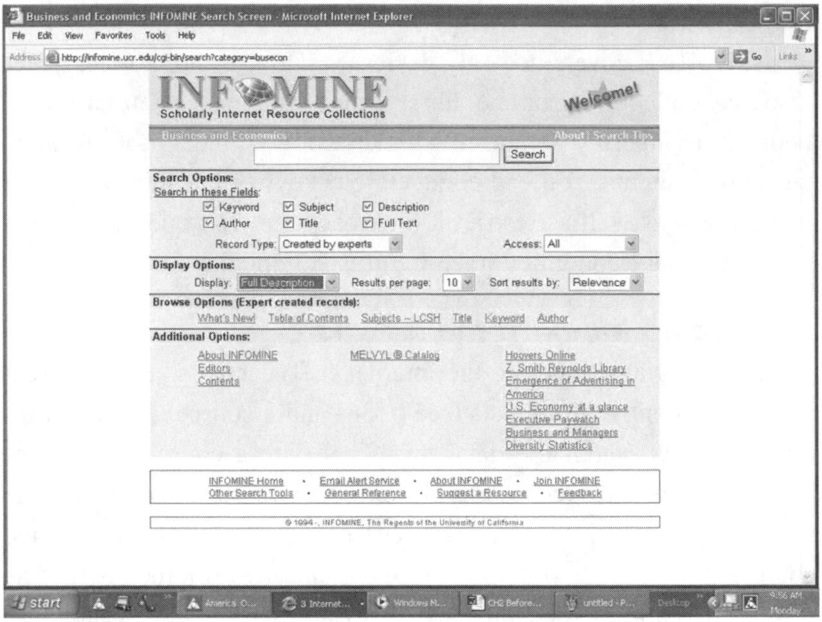

Figure 2.7 *INFOMINE*

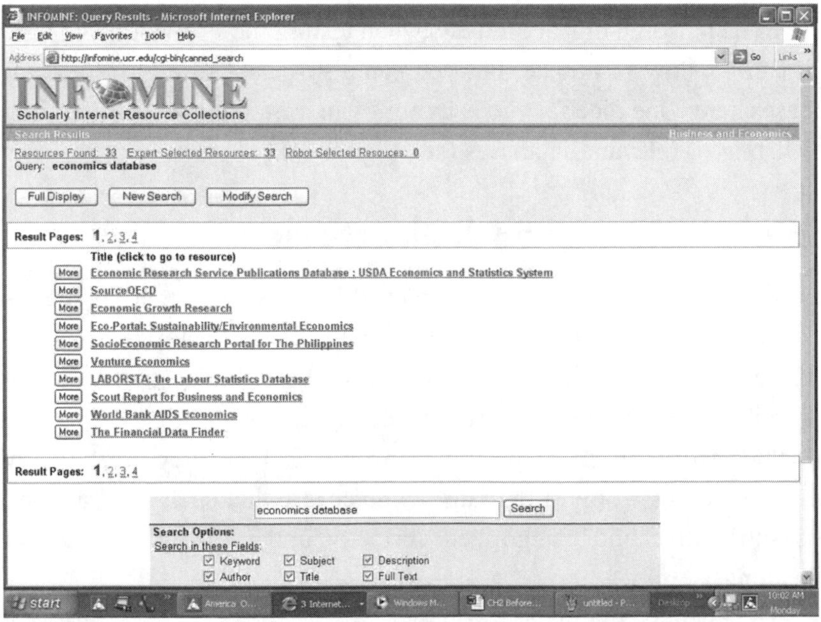

Figure 2.8 *INFOMINE Search Results*

Figure 2.9 *Librarians' Index to the Internet/Browse*

Figure 2.10 *Librarians' Index to the Internet/Sample Search*

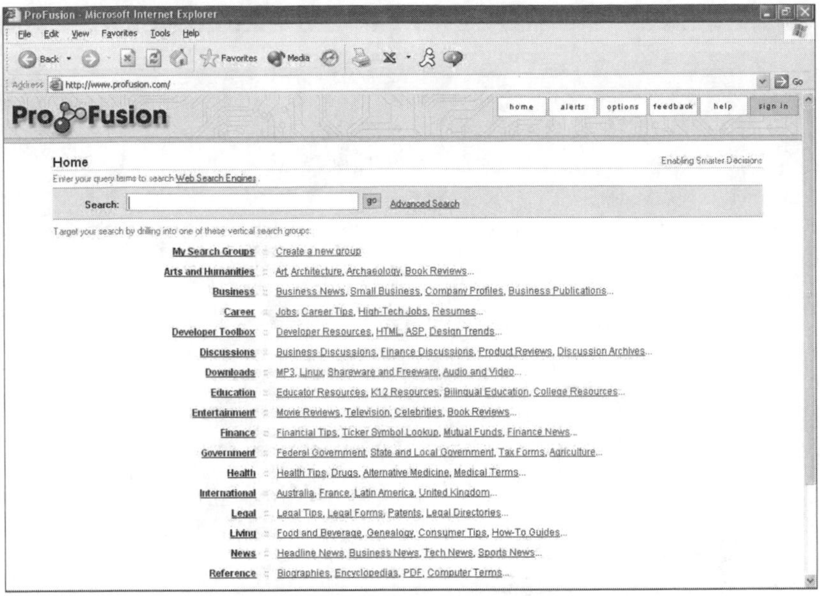

Figure 2.11 Profusion

of Web pages. But your odds are much better that you'll get back relevant, useful sites.

Besides Yahoo!, there are a number of other human-created directories. Following are some of my favorites.

Librarians' Index to the Internet

As previously mentioned, the Librarians' Index to the Internet (LII) is both as a directory and a database search tool. It is created by librarians, is precision-indexed, and includes only useful and substantive sites. Not only can it be browsed or searched, but LII even offers a free alerting-type service where you can be automatically notified by e-mail when new sites are added to the index. What makes this site stand out is its superb organization. I also like its noncommercial approach and the precise search capabilities available in its "advanced search" feature.

BUBL LINK

BUBL LINK is a catalog of about 12,000 selected Internet resources that are maintained by the Centre for Digital Library

Research at the University of Strathclyde in Glasgow. Each resource selected is given a specific subject term cataloging record that corresponds to the traditional Dewey Decimal Classification system. BUBL LINK is an organized collection of well-screened, filtered sites, and you can browse the hierarchical listings and perform advanced searches (see Figure 2.12).

Business.com

Though more commercially oriented than the previously mentioned sources and including a greater number of sales links, Business.com is used to locate prescreened sites. It contains a large collection of business-related sites, so it can be helpful for narrowing your Web search. Just be careful to distinguish Business.com's paid listings from the others (see Figure 2.13).

(One other excellent business Web directory site that should be mentioned is Alacra. However, this is a fee-based, not free site on the Web.)

Yahoo!

Yahoo! is perhaps the biggest and best-known Web directory of them all. Although it's best known as a consumer research tool, it also does a surprisingly nice job of categorizing business sites, primarily under its Yahoo! Finance section. Yahoo! also has a few specific sections that are valuable for locating business sites, and these are listed in Appendix B.

Google

Finally, I very much like Google's general Web directory, which is available under its "Directory" tab. The general directory is actually derived from one of Google's partners, the Open Directory Project (ODP). The ODP, which is one of the best known and oldest of the Internet subject directories, is available not only through Google but can be linked to directly, or accessed via many other popular online services that license ODP's listings. The directory is compiled by a volunteer staff of about 50,000 editors, each of whom specializes in a particular area of expertise. Each editor's job is to scour the Web to locate the best and most relevant sites for their assigned area.

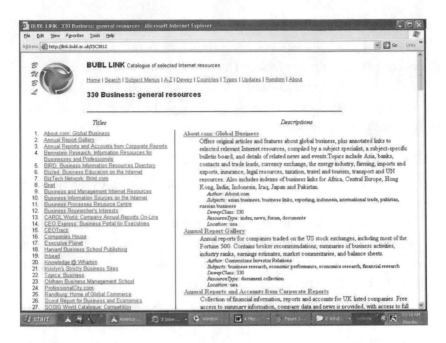

Figure 2.12 BUBL LINK

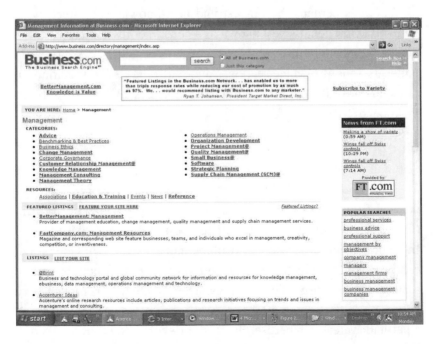

Figure 2.13 Business.com

Discussion Groups

The Web's various discussion groups are important information-finding tools (note that Chapter 7 provides tips on how to evaluate the credibility of those who offer their opinions through these groups). If you belong to a good discussion group, you may be able to get advice regarding the reliability of a particular Web site by asking another member of the group. See Appendix B for a list of sites where you can search for a discussion group that covers your particular topic of interest.

Although you'll probably want to join a discussion group (or groups) in your own industry or area of research, there are other general, yet high-quality business research discussion lists that are worth considering. These would include BUSLIB-L, a lively, active group of business librarians; SLABF-L, the business/finance division of the Special Libraries Association; IRE-L, a resource for investigative reporters; and STUMPERS-L, a networking resource for reference questions that essentially stump people. One nice thing about STUMPERS-L is that you don't need to subscribe to it to ask your questions.

After a few weeks on a good discussion group; you can usually figure out who posts most often and intelligently, is helpful to others, and knows a good amount about the given topic. You can usually even e-mail those on the list who are in the best position to answer your questions or just point you in the right direction.

Weblogs

Weblogs (blogs) are a form of personal journalism in which an individual who has knowledge of or interest in a particular topic provides his or her views on the field, usually on a daily basis, and often with lots of recommended links (see Figure 2.14). Normally the visitors to a Weblog also participate in these forums, where they can chat and debate current issues. Again, like the general Web discussion groups, these blogs help you to find experts, both the person who runs the Weblog (a "blogger") and participants who prove to be

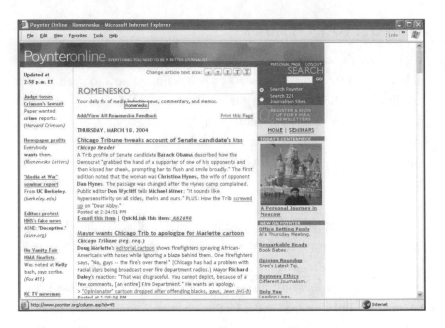

Figure 2.14 *Jim Romenesko writes a popular blog covering media news.*

credible sources. (Chapter 7 also discusses how to evaluate blog-gers as well as those who participate in them.) Though you need to be careful when using Weblogs, they can serve as useful sources for identifying emerging trends, tapping into grassroots opinions, and identifying hot topics.

See Appendix B for some useful Weblog resources.

While there are thousands of Weblogs, the table that follows includes general news and information Weblogs that I'd like to point out for special consideration. They have proven themselves to be a source of valuable information and represent some of the most pop-ular blogs within their field.

One other site worth mentioning—though it isn't a discussion group or Weblog—is About.com. Here you can find experts and expert advice on topics ranging from Attention Deficit Disorder to XML. Some subjects covered that relate specifically to business include human resources, logistics/supply chain, management, marketing, and

Weblog	Subjects Covered
Jim Romenesko	Journalism and the Media
Gary Price's The ResourceShelf	Information resources, Web searching
The Shifted Librarian	Cutting-edge librarianship that provides information anytime, anywhere
Librarian.net	Timely issues of interest to librarians
Lisnews.com	Links and some commentary to news of interest to librarians
PaidContent.org	Commentary on the digital information industry
elearningpost	Knowledge management and distance learning
Peter Scott's Library Blog	Libraries, sources, digital information
Jeff Jarvis' Buzz Machine	News, journalism, blogging, public issues
Marylaine Block's Neat New Stuff	New useful online sources
Gwen Harris Internet News	Internet usage and searching
Gurteen Knowledge Log	Knowledge management, learning and creativity
Guardian Online Blog	News, technology, media politics
Jupiter Research Analysts	Industry commentary from Jupiter Research's industry analysts

purchasing. Specific industries with About.com's expert guides are agriculture, biotech/biomedical, composites/plastics, construction, firefighting/emergency services, insurance, metals, power/energy, retail industry, and telecommunications (see Figure 2.15).

RSS Feeds

A new and increasingly popular addition to the kinds of prefiltered information resources available on the Internet is what are known as "RSS feeds." An RSS feed is an XML-based specification that allows a Web site to instantly and automatically widely distribute its latest news or other timely content to other sites. These news feeds are made available at no cost to those who choose to subscribe to the feed.

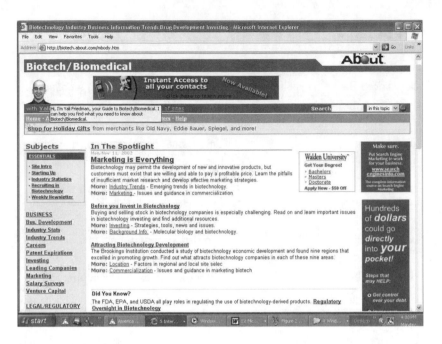

Figure 2.15 *About.com*

In order to sign up and obtain these news feeds yourself, you will need to utilize a special piece of software called an "RSS news reader." Some readers are downloads that you can run off of your desktop, while others are Web-based. Some are free, and some are fee-based. A few of the most popular ones are Amphetadesk, NewsIsFree, NewzCrawler, NewsMonster, NewsGator, and Radio Userland.

After you select a reader, you then "subscribe" to the desired RSS feeds you want to receive by entering the URL of those sites. Your reader then automatically checks those URLs at set intervals to search for the latest news headlines. It retrieves them and displays the headline, a short abstract, and a link to the full story right on your PC. You can then browse the headlines and click on any for which you'd like to view the full article.

Why would you want to use RSS? The benefit is that rather than hunting down the latest news and postings from all of your favorite bloggers and news sites, RSS delivers their latest headlines to you directly. See Figure 2.16 for a sample of incoming headlines and abstracts collected by an RSS reader.

As for which sites offer an RRS feed, there are thousands of sites that produce RSS feeds, ranging from large, well-known online news sites like BBC, CNN, the New York Times, Forbes, and Fortune, to niche Web-based journals, and countless individual bloggers. As RSS has become more popular, the number of news and bloggers that create an RSS feed continues to grow. I have posted the names and URLs of dozens of what I feel are qualified business-oriented RSS feeds on the companion Web site to this book.

Signing up with and reviewing prequalified, filtered RSS feeds is another way that you can ensure that the sources that you use on the Web have been predetermined as reputable and will provide you with sources where you already have chosen to place your trust.

Figure 2.16   *An example of an RSS Reader, NewzCrawler, displaying headlines collected from news sources like BBC News, Sloan Management Journal, Forbes, and BusinessWeek.*

Summary

- Before using the Web for business research, consider previously screened, reliable business sources.
- Use your library to take advantage of the librarian's expertise and to locate books, directories, news archives, and primary source documents.
- Be aware of Web sites, discussion groups, and Weblogs that have already proven themselves as potential sources of business information.
- Keep up with and utilize Invisible Web sources to create your own compilation of reliable business sources.
- Use hand-selected directories and hierarchical indexes as guides to locating prescreened quality sources.

CHAPTER 3

Precision Business Searching

©Cartoonbank.com

"First, they do an on-line search."

Yes, it *does* seem that *everyone* relies on Google these days! But no matter how accurate, well-sourced, and authoritative a Web page may be, it won't do you any good if you haven't retrieved pages relevant to your search. This chapter focuses specifically on finding good sites and offers precision Web-searching strategies to help you locate exactly what you need.

Figure 3.1 *Google remains the leading search engine.*

We will look at search engines—and one in particular—to show you how to do a precision search. Although there are other ways to find business information on the Web (as discussed in Chapter 2), a search engine is the tool that's most commonly used.

There are of course many search engines. Some of the most popular include Google, AllTheWeb, AltaVista, and Teoma. There are also metasearch engines like Vivisimo, IxQuick, and QueryServer—these search *other* search engines simultaneously. There are also specialized engines that focus on a certain type of information (such as phone listings) or cover specialized subject areas.

Though the other engines are good, I'll spend most of this chapter discussing just one of them: Google (see Figure 3.1).

Why Only One Search Engine?

So why cover just one engine in detail, and why Google? First, I believe that you can become most proficient at Web searching when you know the ins and outs and all the special features of a single search engine. The more you understand an engine's features, its search protocols and rules, *and* its little quirks and flaws, the better it will work for you.

This isn't to say that I think you should use only one search engine. That wouldn't be a good strategy, for a few reasons. First, no single engine covers the entire Web. Greg Notess, a Montana State University professor and author, has demonstrated that not only does no single engine index the complete Web, but there are large areas where coverage does not overlap. In other words, each search engine will turn up many pages not found by the others. For this reason, when you need to be comprehensive or locate as many pages as possible, you do in fact need to use more than one search engine. No search engine—including Google—is perfect. Each has its flaws, so in certain cases you may wish to use another search engine that has the particular capabilities you require to perform the search you need.

But if you can become expert at using one search engine—and make that your "default" tool—you may often find that it serves your needs. You can still retain a passing knowledge of a few other search engines, should you need them.

Why Google?

I recommend that the search engine you choose to become truly proficient with is Google. I've been a loyal Google user since shortly after it was released. Before Google, my preferred search engine was AltaVista. I liked AltaVista at the time because it seemed to cover more of the Web than other search engines, and because its advanced search features allowed for more precise searching.

Unfortunately, no matter how well I constructed a search on AltaVista, the most relevant Web pages retrieved often did not appear on the first or second results screen. Often, the initial pages listed were completely irrelevant, and the really good ones, if I could even find them, were buried somewhere deep in the returned results. While I was fairly satisfied with AltaVista's advanced search features, this was due to my low expectations at the time.

Then Google came on the scene, and almost instantly I and millions of others were most favorably impressed. The first thing I was happy to notice was what I did *not* see: lots of flashing ads, shopping features, music sites, pop-ups, and all the superfluous e-commerce stuff that crowded AltaVista's search page. This made the research experience distracting and added to a sense of clutter and information overload. Google's site was simple, uncluttered, and clean as could be. It clearly was created to serve only one audience: researchers. Yes, researchers—not shoppers, music fans, e-commerce marketers, gamers, or anyone else. What a refreshing change.

But the real payoff came when I entered my keywords and saw what Google returned. Uncannily, about 80 percent of the time or more, a useful and relevant site turned up at the very top of the list. Another 10 percent of the time there were useful and relevant sites in the first five or so results returned. Now, this was a search engine for the *Web*!

So Google was able to do the most important thing that a search engine can do: return relevant results. Later, I'll outline other compelling reasons why Google is my search engine of choice, but first I'll describe how it's able to retrieve its results.

How Search Engines Work

As you may know, search engines work by sending a bit of software, commonly called a "spider" or "crawler," onto the Web to follow links and then create an index of all the words on all the Web pages located. So when you perform a search, you're not actually searching the current Web "live." Rather, you're searching the static index created by the search engine. That index is normally updated on a regular basis, typically every 3 to 14 days. But remember that you're searching a "snapshot" of what the Web was like when it was last indexed by that search engine.

So for example, when you enter your keywords, the search engine examines its index and returns to you those Web pages it has indexed containing your words or phrases. But that's only half the story in getting you the best results, because the search engine then has to decide in what *order* you'll see those pages. Most people will look only at the first screen or two of results. Here, search engines normally apply a mathematical formula (an algorithm) to each of those matching pages, giving each a relevancy score. Those with the highest scores will appear at the top of the list.

The ranking algorithm varies by search engine, but factors considered include how often the word or phrase appears on a page, if the word(s) are near the top or title of the page, how close the words are to each other (for multiple-word searches), and how rare a word is. That is, some search engine's ranking algorithm "assumes" that a Web page that includes an infrequently used word means that it is more likely that the searcher will want to view that particular page. So that page will get a boost in its final ranking.

This ranking technique works pretty well most of the time, and it is, in fact, the method that AltaVista uses. But when Google came on the scene it added a new—and very significant—twist to this ranking method. Google decided to create a completely different "popularity" type of factor in calculating a page's relevancy. Those pages that had many *other* Web pages linking to them would get a boost in their scores.

To be more precise, Google looks at multiple levels of linking. It not only counts the number of links coming into a page (call this link-set A) but how many pages are linked to link-set A (call this link-set B), how many are linking into B (call this link-set C), and so forth. For example, say page X had 100 other pages linking to it. And say that in Google's formula this particular page receives a score of 100 for those links. Now say that page Y also had 100 pages linking to it, but that those 100 pages had 500 pages linking to *them*. Page Y would get a higher ranking. And if one of those pages linking to page Y had a huge number of pages linking to *it*, that would boost page Y's ranking even higher.

Best Diner in Town?

By now you might be thinking, okay, so Google boosts the ranking of pages with lots of incoming links—so what? Why should those pages get a higher ranking just because they're popular with other

Web sites? What makes them any better? Fair questions, but this method, in practice, really does work. Google returns relevant, useful pages much more consistently than other search engines that don't utilize this type of ranking method.

But why does this work? An analogy that's sometimes used is to imagine that you're out driving through some unknown territory. You need to stop for lunch, so you see two diners and you pull off the road. One is almost empty, with just a few cars in the parking lot. The other is jammed with people. You assume that the crowded, popular diner probably has something better to offer. And you'd probably be right. The same holds true for those who choose to frequent and recommend another Web page by linking to it. Usually, it means that it has something of value.

I should note that although Google's method of ranking Web pages has revolutionized the search process, it is not without its drawbacks. Newer sites that haven't yet been noticed by others on the Web are going to be at a disadvantage since fewer sites will have linked to them. Without these links, the new sites are essentially penalized in Google's search rankings. Those new sites might conceivably be better than the older ones, which have been around for a long time and have had a chance to gather a lot of links. So this is a kind of bias that you should be aware of when searching Google. There are, however, some strategies to overcome this, and I'll discuss these shortly.

Another reason why I believe you should become Google-proficient—even beyond its clean interface and fantastic record in returning relevant sites—is because of a set of features that it offers to make searches more powerful and precise. Later in this chapter I'll describe how to put the following Google features to use:

- Google indexes Adobe PDF, Word, PowerPoint, Excel, and other specially formatted files that have been put up on the Web, in addition to standard HTML files.
- Specified sections of a Web page can be searched, such as the title of the page, URL, and incoming links to the page.
- Searches can be restricted by specific domain and by how recently a page was updated.
- Google can find pages that link to a specific page.

- Images of a Web page can be viewed at the time that it was indexed by Google. (This is the "cache.")
- Returned Web pages (results) show your keywords in bold and in context.

At one time many of these features were unique to Google, but some other search engines have since integrated a number of them. However, Google still offers the most complete set. Note that these are not by any means the *only* special features on Google, but they're the ones I think are most important to understand and regularly use.

Google utilizes the following standard search protocols:

- You search for phrases by using quotation marks (for example, "market research reports").
- Multiple words default to AND (for example, *"market research reports" batteries* searches for both terms)
- OR is permitted between two words or phrases, and needs to be in capital letters (for example, *Fuji OR Kodak*).
- Placing a plus sign in front of a word or page will force a search on a word, even if it is a "stop" word. (Stop words are very common words such as "a," "it," and "the" that Google normally will not search on.)
- Placing a minus sign in front of a word or a page will exclude Web pages that contain them (for example, *Outlook –Microsoft* returns Web pages with the word Outlook, but not the word Microsoft).

Two other important search restrictions on Google: There is no truncation capability, and you may enter no more than 10 words into the search box. There is a workaround for these restrictions, which were suggested in the excellent book *Google Hacks: 100 Industrial-Strength Tips & Tools* (O'Reilly, 2003), by Tara Calishain and Rael Dornfest. Although Google does not allow truncation, it *does* allow a type of full word stemming, where users can input an asterisk that is used as a place marker for any word. So, for instance, if you entered *"market * reports"* Google would retrieve pages that contain *"market research reports," "market analyst reports," "market news reports," "market reports,"* and so forth. This workaround also helps get around the 10-word limit on your search keywords too, since those asterisks don't count towards that maximum word limit. (See Figures 3.2 and 3.3 for examples of Google's Advanced Features.)

Precision Searching Techniques

So how can you use Google to retrieve the most useful and relevant pages on the Web? The following is a five-step template that you can follow:

1. Prepare
2. Create
3. Run
4. Scan
5. Refine

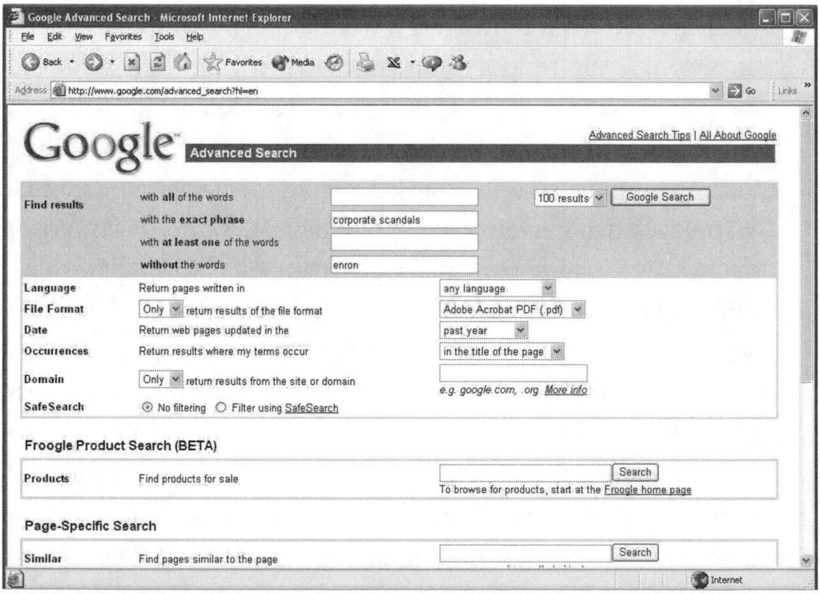

Figure 3.2 *An advanced Google search for PDF pages with the exact phrase "corporate scandals" in the title, but not the word Enron, and which have been updated during the past year.*

Figure 3.3 *An advanced search from Google's main search page.
Here I searched for pages limited to governmental Web
sites (site:.gov) in the PowerPoint format (filetype:ppt) with
the word Worldcom in the title (allintitle:Worldcom) that
had been updated in the past year.*

Prepare for the Search

As with most endeavors, the more preparation you can do ahead
of time the better your outcome. Here's what you should do before
actually beginning your search.

First, it's a good idea to set a time limit. As you know, time flies
not only when you're having fun, but also when you're online. You
don't want to realize after searching the Web for two hours that
you've hardly located anything of value. I'd suggest setting a reasonable limit on the time you'll spend on any single search engine:
perhaps 15 or 20 minutes. If you haven't found what you need in that
amount of time, then it's time to either try a different search tool or
re-evaluate your strategy.

To make your search experience as productive as possible, there are a few things to do beforehand.

First, consider how likely it is that your research query will pay off from using a Web search engine. One factor here is whether the information you are seeking is factual or conceptual.

Search engines perform best on more factual queries—in other words, when all you want is to find a Web page that contains your keywords or phrases in a relevant context. Search engines don't do as well for more conceptual-type queries, where there may be no simple *answer* to dig up on the Web; where, instead, what you're looking for is complex, involved, and requires some type of analytical response.

For instance, if you're looking for Kodak's market share of digital cameras, you have a factual query. If that information exists on the Web, you will likely find it by entering the appropriate keywords (*Kodak "digital cameras" "market share"*).

But if you are trying to find an answer to "How does the media portray CEOs?" you would have a great deal of trouble efficiently finding an answer via a search engine. Broad, conceptual queries are unlikely to return precise answers. Instead, you'll probably turn up a lot of "kind of" and "almost" relevant pages that skirt what you're really trying to find without actually answering the question.

Secondly, the Web itself may not be your best choice to get good, in-depth analysis. Instead, you may wish to research a database of scholarly or business journals, contact an association or university, find a relevant book, or interview an expert on the topic. This way you can get more detailed data, perhaps pose some of your own specific questions, and learn through your interactions with topic experts.

Conceptual queries are not impossible on the Web. In fact, with some time and experimentation, you might at least locate some good leads to expert sources to whom you might pose your question(s) directly (via an e-mail or phone interview). Or perhaps you'll get lucky and actually locate a report that examines the issue you're researching. It's just that search engines aren't really optimized to handle this type of query, and you'd probably save yourself a lot of time by going elsewhere for your research. Of course, one of the real benefits of searching the Web is that it costs you nothing—other than your time—so you can certainly at least try a conceptual query. Just don't assume that the information you *do* turn up is the best you'll find on your topic.

If you decide that your question is indeed appropriate for a search engine, then I recommend taking the following steps to prepare for your search:

- Go to Google's "Preferences" page and set the "number of results" to be displayed at the highest number: 100. You should do this because Google normally returns only 10 pages per screen, which is fine, but it forces you to click at the bottom of the page and have another screen reload each time you want to view another 10 retrieved pages. Having 100 pages displayed on a single screen saves time. If you set this preference once and then save it, Google will show you this maximum number in all future searches as well.

- Also at Google's Preferences page select your language preferences for search results. Limiting the search language can be helpful if a certain word retrieves too many foreign language pages, which can clutter up your search screen with results you can't use. (Google does offer some translation options, but these are very rough. Except for unusual circumstances, I don't really recommend them.)

Create the Best Search Statement

As librarians and serious researchers know, you can only get good results if your search statement is well done. While this book is not a primer on creating good research queries (for one thing, many readers already know the basics), I will share a few tips that are appropriate when using a Web search engine.

Most importantly, are your keywords/phrases clear and unambiguous, or are they broad and vague? Obviously, search engines do best with the former, and they especially like to crunch on hard, specific nouns. Say, for example, you were trying to confirm whether the town square of Vilnius, the capital city of Lithuania, really has a statue of the late musician Frank Zappa. Well, since both "Frank Zappa" and "Vilnius" are clear, unambiguous nouns, simply entering those terms (and avoiding the more vague ones like "situated," "town," or "square") will likely work very well for you. You'll have your answer in the blink of an eye. (By the way, there is indeed a statue of Zappa, near the Vilnius city center.)

But if you were to use a search engine to find "computer sales in the Northeast," you will likely encounter a bit of trouble. You'll need to do a good deal of experimenting and slogging through lots of sites before you find what you need, since these are common words, used in multiple contexts. Unless you can find another hidden keyword that will serve as a filter (for example, if you are actually focusing on a specific computer brand name), you may not even want to use a search engine. Instead, you might try a directory site that has compiled a pre-screened, hand-selected listing of Web pages such as INFOMINE or the Librarians' Index to the Internet (as discussed on page 33).

I've found that one of the best ways to filter out less useful and irrelevant pages, avoid information overload, and help ensure a high level of quality in the pages returned by a search engine is to consider whether there's a specific source or even a person's name that can be added to your search statement to act as a kind of expert search qualifier or filter. I touch on this in Chapter 5 when discussing the search for market research reports on the Web, but it really applies to any kind of business research.

Let me give you an example of how I use this technique in my own research. Often, I need to find information about search engines. Naturally, this is a topic that is covered over and over on the Net, and it's easy to get buried with hundreds of thousands of Web pages when doing a search. However, I do know that there are a few specific publications on the Web, as well as a few experts, whose articles and advice I can automatically and implicitly trust. When I read something from one of these sources, although I don't completely suspend my critical faculties, I do tend to trust the information (see the discussion of trust in Chapter 8). For the record, the names of the publications are *EContent, Information Today, Searcher*, and my own, *The Information Advisor*. The search engine experts I trust (and whose

Figure 3.4 *Adding the names of your most trusted experts along with your search query can help filter a search and retrieve superior results.*

writings frequently appear on the Web) are Greg Notess, Danny Sullivan, and Chris Sherman.

So let's say that I'm writing a review of a new search engine and want to see what kind of reviews and analyses have already been done. I don't just enter the name of the search engine as my search term because I would be flooded with hundreds of thousands of pages. Instead, I add those trusted experts' names as qualifiers. So, for instance, if I want to find out what these people are saying about the search engine Vivisimo, I might enter the following into Google:

Vivisimo "Greg Notess" OR "Danny Sullivan" OR "Chris Sherman."

This search would return only those pages that contained the name of that search engine, along with that of at least one of my trusted expert sources (see Figure 3.4).

I might also choose to use one of my trusted publications as an expert filter. However, limiting by publication on the open Web (as opposed to a controlled database where you can choose which publications to search) can be a bit tricky. For example, you need to be sure that the publication itself or at least some of its articles are found on the Web. Furthermore, you may get more false hits if the name of the journal is a common one that's used in other contexts. For example, trying to find *Searcher* magazine articles is tricky because "searcher" can be used in so many other contexts. If that's the case, I might use the phrase "*Searcher magazine.*" Or, since I know that *Searcher* puts some of its articles on the Web (only a selection of what's inside the complete print magazine) and has the URL "www.infotoday.com/searcher," I might use Google's domain-limiting feature to restrict my search to pages with only that URL.

There is of course a trade-off when using this expert filtering strategy—you're going to exclude certain Web pages that might very well be useful and relevant. However, for most of us, the problem these days is too many information sources, not too few. So this is a good way to winnow the sources down *and* have that smaller set be more likely to contain information of value.

Run the Search Leveraging Google's Special Features

As I have already said, Google has some outstanding features. Unfortunately, one of them is *not* a symbol that designates which pages are reliable and of high quality. There probably will never be such a Qual-O-Meter, since assessing quality and reliability of a source is a subtle, complex, and partially subjective process that can confound humans, let alone literal software programs.

The classic film *2001: A Space Odyssey* predicted that a computer would be so intelligent and human-like by now that it could even exert its will and tell a human, "Dave, I'm afraid that's something I cannot allow to happen." But not only do we *not* have thinking computers, we're still a long way away from a computer that's smart enough to say, "Yes, Dave, I can assure you that this is a very reliable and credible market research report."

Google's features and capabilities, however crude when it comes to mimicking human intelligence, do allow some leverage to at least help increase the odds that the pages it returns will be of high quality and value. Here are some strategies to follow:

- *Consider limiting a search to Adobe PDF and/or PowerPoint documents.*—Imagine the Web as an enormous vat that contains virtually any type of information you can think of. The credibility of that information ranges from, at the low end, hoax pages and wild, speculative theories to, at the high end, peer-reviewed scholarly journals and U.N.-issued international treaties. The vast majority of what's on the Web is in HTML, the standard mark-up language used to create Web pages. But many sites also load pages that are created in a different format, such as Word, PowerPoint, and PDF. Typically, a document in one of these formats reflects a higher level of care and attention. For example, in-depth government reports, consultant white papers, and academic research are often in PDF format. Conference presentations, executive speeches, and workshops are often created in PowerPoint. Specialized documents such as resumes, internal reports, or academic papers may be found in MS Word.

  Of course, there's no guarantee that limiting to one of these file types will retrieve a high-quality, reliable document. But it can increase your odds of doing so.

- *Consider limiting a search to* .edu *and* .gov *domains.*—A higher percentage of credible, noncommercial reports can be derived from academic (*.edu*) and government (*.gov*) sites than from dot-com sites. If nothing else, limiting to these domains can eliminate the most blatantly commercial material. You should note that while the body that issues domains originally reserved *.org* specifically for the use of nonprofit organizations, it later began assigning that designation to commercial (dot-com) sites as well. So, unfortunately, *.org* is no longer useful for predetermining the type of organization behind a site.

One caution on limiting your searches to academic sites: While these pages can provide some excellent information, you'll also find the personal pages of both professors and students who have space on a university server. You can typically detect this by noting a tilde (~) in the URL.

- *Consider limiting a search by date of most recent update.*—On its advanced search page, Google gives you the option of restricting the pages returned to those that have been updated within the last year, six months, or three months. Because a search engine cannot tell if an update was significant or merely cosmetic, date limiting on the Web is imperfect. However, this can be a help in eliminating pages that have not been touched at all in recent times. If your search is time-sensitive, or if you need to be sure that a source has been looked at and updated, try it.

- *Use the minus sign to eliminate pages that are clearly irrelevant.*—Say you do a search on "keyboard market," but you receive too many irrelevant references to pianos. Rather than wading through all that mess for information about personal computer keyboards, just eliminate the piano references by typing in *–pianos* on your next search. This technique works best when the word or phrase you want to eliminate is not commonly used in the context of your research topic.

Scan Initial Results

Once Google returns your initial results, your next step is to size up which pages are likely to be of most use. If you only have a handful of relevant pages, you can probably just scan them all. But where there are hundreds, thousands, or even hundreds of thousands of pages returned, you need a technique to quickly determine which are the quality sources.

Luckily, as discussed earlier, Google's ranking method does work consistently to return top sources on your first search. But you still need to be the human filter in this process and provide another level of evaluation.

There are a few techniques I find very helpful at this stage of the search. First, I quickly peruse the returned list to see which pages include a date listed to the right of the page's URL. Google only adds dates to a small percentage of the pages it indexes. According to the company, only those pages that change quickly and are very popular are dated. It also indexes those pages more frequently than other pages on the Web, sometimes multiple times a day. In my experience, those pages chosen by Google to be indexed more often and to include date designations are usually more reliable than those that are not. They are typically fresher and offer more useful data. In fact, I find this to be a more reliable way to find new and timely pages than the date-limit function in Google's advanced search.

I give these dated pages preference right away. I also scan Google's listings to view the context around my bolded keywords. This provides clues about the relevance and therefore value of a particular page (see Figure 3.5).

Figure 3.5 *The fourth and fifth pages on this listing retrieved from this Google search (the EV World and infoshop pages) include a date next to the URL, indicating that the page is likely to be freshly indexed and up-to-date.*

I also study the URL for clues about the nature of the site behind a page. This often helps me to decide whether I want to view a page. For example, a news article often has an embedded date in the URL, reflecting the date of the article. Other times you'll see certain words or clues that can tell you something about the source. For instance, you might see references in the returned page excerpts to dates or recent events to give you an idea of the page's timeliness; or, you may get a sense of the type of source the page is derived from by looking at the URL (e.g., does it contain the name of a well-known media out-let like CNN, or trade publication like businessweek.com, or a uni-versity, government agency, etc.?).

Once I've made these initial determinations, I start at the top of the list. I'll click on those pages that have met as many of these criteria as possible, but I normally don't click on the title to go to the page itself. Rather, I'll click on Google's own cache link. There are a few reasons why I like to peruse a potentially valuable Web page by click-ing on the cache, rather than going directly to the site.

First, I really like the way Google highlights my keywords and phrases in its cached copy, making it easy to scroll to the relevant por-tions of the document and see the full context around the keywords. Not only are those words and phrases highlighted, but Google assigns a different color to each word or phrase, making it even easier to zero in on just the term you want to check out (see Figure 3.6). Also, there are no pop-up advertisements!

Another reason why I normally click on Google's cache is that I find it to be a faster and more reliable method for quickly bringing up a site. This avoids running into a problem when the page is currently not available, and Google's server is so fast that it typically brings up the copy of that page more quickly than if I went to the page itself.

One caution when bringing up the cached version: It won't include changes made to the page since it was indexed by Google. In many cases, this won't matter to you at all, but if having the most up-to-date page is critical, then you should go directly to the page after giving the cached version a quick once-over to ensure it's the type of site you're looking for.

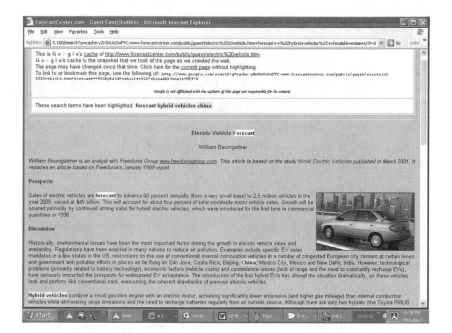

Figure 3.6 *Clicking on Google's cache makes it easy to find your keywords on the page, as Google highlights each on the Web page in a different color (here the keywords were: forecast, "hybrid vehicles," and China).*

The final step in this scanning portion of the process is to consider using your browser's "Find" button (Control+F) to locate other important words or phrases in the document. Naturally, this is much faster than trying to read through the full page or document. You might use the Find function to locate the keywords or phrases that you entered in your search (particularly if you are on the actual page, and not on Google's cached version that has the terms highlighted). Or you can use Find to search for new words and phrases that you did not enter in your search statement. (For example, if you reached the 10-word maximum in Google's search box, you can still search the pages Google turned up for another word or phrase by doing this Control+F search.)

Refine Results as Necessary

As experienced researchers know, the search process is a repetitious one, and what you learn from your initial search should help to improve your subsequent searches. If at this point you have learned a bit about your topic after scanning the best sites, you've probably found some new terminology and jargon that are associated with it. At this point you may want to go back and redo your searches using these new terms.

For instance, say you were searching for how new sources of energy are being developed to fight global warming and reduce greenhouse gasses. During your search, you may have discovered several relevant sites from which you learned that the term most often used to discuss global warming and greenhouse gasses is "climate change." You've also discovered that the standard way to describe new sources of energy is "alternative fuels." And you have also noted that the best results seem to be in government-produced PDF reports. To take advantage of this new-found knowledge, refine your search in Google to read: *"climate change" "alternative fuels" filetype:pdf site:.gov* (the latter is the protocol for limiting to PDF and government sites in Google's regular search box).

You can go even further in narrowing your search to the best sites. Say, for instance, that not only did you find that the best pages were governmental pages but they were from a particular government agency, such as the Office of Transportation Technologies, under the Department of Energy. You can tell the URL of all pages from that agency by its specific string: ott.doe.gov. You can next search just the pages in that specific site with the following terms: *"climate change" "alternative fuels" filetype:pdf site:ott.doe.gov.*

This search then returns a set of PDF documents from that agency's Web site that contain both "climate change" and "alternative fuels."

This technique can be a great way to add yet another filter on your search. In a sense, you are cordoning off a section of the Web—a section that you've determined to be reliable and relevant—and then conducting a search of its pages.

So why can't you just go to the home pages of the sites you've selected and search for what you need right there? It's possible, but only if that site provides a complete search mechanism, and then only if it's powerful and intuitive. I've found that too many site search engines are only poor to fair. It is the rare site that offers a top-notch search system for its visitors. For this reason, 99 percent of the time I prefer to search a site's pages using Google.

Alternatives to Google

Although I'm a regular user of Google, no search engine is perfect. I recommend that you become proficient with Google's ins and outs, but to do quality research on the Web you need to know when to use the most valuable features on various search engines. Gary Price has said that even if all search engines covered the same portions of the Web (which they do not), it would *still* be important to know how to use more than one of them. Each engine would rank the same set of Web pages differently, so what you'd see on the first screen or two of one search engine would not be identical to the others.

You should, then, be aware of other leading search engines, and have an idea of their unique features and capabilities. There is good news and bad news when it comes to your options to Google alternatives.

The bad news is that as of March, 2004, two highly regarded search engines—AltaVista and AllTheWeb (see Figure 3.7), while still available and active, no longer offer their own unique search engine. Instead, both merely use a version of their corporate owner Yahoo!'s search engine instead. (Both AltaVista and AllTheWeb are part of Yahoo!'s "Overture" division.)

This is too bad, since both of these search engines had offered several unique and special features. For example, only AltaVista allowed the use of the "NEAR" proximity operator, which allowed searchers to specify that the search engine should retrieve only Web pages where the keywords were separated by no more than 10 words. Also removed was its truncation feature, as was the user's ability to limit a search to a particulare geographic region or to a few segments of a Web page. In the case of AllTheWeb, this search engine had been the only one that could retrieve pages in the "Flash" format, but is no longer capable of doing so. It also had offered an FTP search, and

Figure 3.7 *AllTheWeb news search.*

previously had no maximum limit on the size of a Web page that it could index. The new Yahoo! version of AllTheWeb ceases indexing Web pages at 500KB.

On the positive side, good new search engines are still appearing, and new versions of older search engines have been relaunched. Here are the ones I think are worth trying as good complements to Google:

- *Yahoo! Search*: While searchers are disappointed that Yahoo! has standardized AllTheWeb and AltaVista to its own search engine, on the positive side, when Yahoo! launched its own search database in February, 2004, it really did create a good one. Yahoo! Search offers a clean interface, Boolean searching, includes a cache (like Google), and has lots of options for limiting a search to specific fields (title, site, language, domain, and more). It also indexes many different file types on the Web: HTML, PDF, Excel, PowerPoint, Word—and even RSS/XML.

So the good news is that although Yahoo! used to be only a directory site that had to rely on a third party for actual Web crawling, it has now launched its own solid and useful search engine that can be a good alternative and complement to Google.

- *Teoma*: Teoma is owned by Ask Jeeves. Although I have not been a big user of Teoma myself, some searchers like it because of its interesting "refine" and "resources" feature. The "refine" feature offers users suggestions on how to narrow a search into smaller segments. The "resources" feature offers links to recommended sites, created by subject specialists that provide links with advice, reference, and answers to whatever topic you've searched on.

  However, not all searches will result in refine suggestions or resources, and from my experience, the "resources" suggestions are hit and miss as to how helpful they turn out to be.

- *Gigablast*: Gigablast is not as well known as these other search engines, and was created and is still operated by a single individual by the name of Matt Wells. I have found that this search enging is getting better all the time, and has now become my default alternative to Google. I find that it consistently retrieves relevant, substantive results, is less cluttered with ads, is extremely fast, and has a pleasing design. And while I've never been all that much of a fan of the automated suggestions that some search engines make to help searchers narrow their search, in my own testing of Gigablast, its "GigaBits" suggestions for related concepts and narrower searches that it displays at the top of the screen after a search actually have often been on target and quite helpful!

- *Vivisimo, IxQuick, QueryServer—For scanning more of the Web*: To cover a greater portion of the Web, metasearch engines search multiple search engines. As mentioned earlier, no single search engine can index all the pages on the Web. In general, I'm not a big user of metasearch engines, because typically you can't perform a lot of advanced searches and set special limits. Since the search terms you enter must be understood by all the search

engines that the metasearch engine utilizes, your search statement needs to be reduced to the lowest common denominator
that's understandable by all.

Given that we discuss precision searching in this chapter, using a
metasearch engine will expand and broaden your search, rather than
narrow it. So using one might put you at cross-purposes to that goal.

That said, there are three outstanding metasearch engines:
Vivisimo, IxQuick, and QueryServer. You might wish to use one of
these metasearch engines when you have some truly obscure or
unusual search term and Google does not provide you with many
responses (or not enough for your purposes). Such terms might, for
instance, include a CEO's name, the name of a lesser-known product,
a rare disease, a small town in Ireland, and so on (see Figure 3.8).

To keep up with all the changes in search engines, I highly recommend regularly checking Greg Notess's "Search Engine Showdown"
site, which provides news, updates, and feature comparisons for all of
the important search engines.

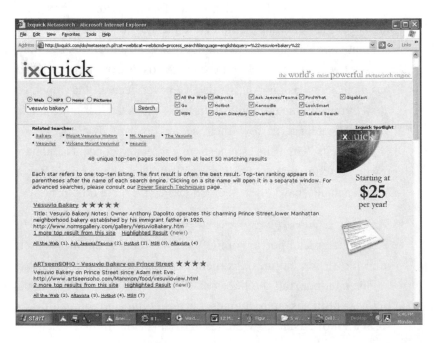

Figure 3.8   *IxQuick*

CHAPTER 4

What to Do with Questionable Sites

So far we've talked about how to use the Web's various tools to locate reliable sites, as well as how to precisely use a search engine to increase the odds of finding relevant, useful sites. There's no way around the fact that when doing research on the Web, you're going to come across new sites of unknown reliability. It's at this point that you'll need some specific, practical strategies to determine whether or not you should really trust a site, or move on.

The strategies provided in this chapter are largely derived from my own experience as well as that of some of my colleagues in the library and information fields. I've supplemented these sources with advice and input from a different type of expert: investigative reporters (especially those who are particularly skilled in evaluating information sources on a regular basis).

Librarians and investigative reporters actually have a fair amount in common, and their skills and knowledge are complementary. They are alike in that they both trade in information and knowledge, and they are trained—whether through schooling, experience, or both—in how to ferret out facts. In addition, both must evaluate the credibility of their sources, turn complex and technical data into information understandable by laypeople, and use the language skillfully.

The two professions are also different, of course. Librarians typically deal with textual materials (whether in print, online, or on the Web) and know where to locate relevant factual data. They are often expert online searchers, skilled in classifying and organizing information, and able to serve clients' needs with a quick turnaround time. Librarians and information professionals typically deliver the results of their work in some kind of summarized package that highlights the key points of their research, perhaps adding some commentary and guidance on how to best use the information.

Investigative reporters, while frequently utilizing textual material, also regularly gather information from other people, are trained to be careful and rigorous interviewers, and typically have a "beat" that makes them a specialist in a particular subject area. In most news organizations, these complementary sets of skills are put to good use during a potential news story's planning and research stage. Librarians may suggest sources and perform the more sophisticated searches, and reporters cull those sources for useful nuggets to pursue as part of the story they are writing.

Like virtually all modern researchers, investigative reporters have moved to the Web to do more of their research. They have learned to apply their well-honed journalistic skills of assessing print and human source credibility to sources found on the Web. I interviewed a few investigative reporters for this chapter, and posed several questions: How has Web research changed the way you verify source credibility? What are the red flags that tip you off to a questionable Web site? Conversely, what reassures you about a particular Web site? When you want to dig up information about a potentially useful, but unfamiliar site, what steps do you take? How do you discover any hidden agendas? What active steps do you take to verify the data you've found on the Web?

How Journalists Use the Web

Before getting into the nitty-gritty of how they evaluate particular Web sites, it's worth noting how investigative reporters use the Web in their work. All of the journalists I spoke with said that using the Web has become both a common and invaluable part of their information-gathering process. There's no question today that going to the Web to perform research and gather data has become an automatic, accepted part of the journalist's job. In fact, reporters—like librarians and other researchers — are almost uniformly thrilled about how the Web has opened up such an incredible wealth of easily accessible information from around the globe.

But journalists are also extremely careful about how they use the Web as source material. There is a preference for putting more stock into non-Web sources. And when reporters *do* go to the Web, they prefer the more "official" sites that are created by government agencies. The journalists I spoke with told me they will almost never quote a fact that they found on the Web, let alone a remark made in a discussion group. Many of them view what they find on the Web as an excellent source for *leads*: If they discover something intriguing they will then turn to other sources to get to the bottom of it.

Journalists know that it is all too easy for incorrect information to propagate via the Web, and that a "fact" noted on a site may be nothing more than the repeating of some hoax or a twisted version of the original piece of information. Today because print and broadcast reporters regularly track and scan the Web for story leads, if something incorrect is posted it may then be repeated not only by other Web sites, but in the traditional print and broadcast media as well. There have been several cases where bad data has made its way from a lesser-known Web site to one that's "branded," such as a major daily newspaper's or broadcast media's companion Web site. That data then becomes "legitimized" and may even be picked up by the traditional print and broadcast media. At that point, the bad data acquires a life of its own, and it becomes almost impossible to undo the damage done. (For some examples, visit the site of Columbia University journalism professor Sreenath Sreenivasan, who collects some of the more infamous hoaxes and flawed stories that make the rounds. See Appendix B, page 250.)

Interestingly, while the Web is a source that frequently needs extra scrutiny, in some cases it is being used as a verification tool. Mark Ingebretsen, writer of "The Daily Scan" on The Wall Street Journal Online, says he uses the Web to locate links to primary sources that are referenced in print news articles. For example, if a newspaper story mentions a press release, association report, or government document, he might then go on the Web to find and access that original document to do additional checks and verifications. He might also use the Web to identify the contact person associated with the publication of the document, whom he could then interview.

There is no question that the Web has quite dramatically altered the ways in which journalists collect, gather, and verify information. But the question remains: How do they assess Web sites they don't know?

Reporters say there are some red flags including the following:

- *It's a "personal" page*—Pages not affiliated with an organization should be given the highest scrutiny. Often these are personal home pages, identified with a tilde (~) in the address, or with the URL of a Yahoo!, GeoCities, AOL, or other consumer ISP. These pages may represent a single individual who hasn't made a serious commitment to establishing credibility on the Web.

- *The site lacks contact information*—It's a bad sign if a site does not reveal how the individual or organization who created it can be contacted. Or even who that entity is.

- *E-mail contact only*—Just a notch up from sites that offer no contact information are those with no physical address or telephone number, only an e-mail contact. This isn't reassuring at all for users, who want to know that there is a legitimate person or organization behind a site. The worst type of e-mail-only contact is one that doesn't even have the person's name or title, just a generic address like "webmaster@xyz.com."

- *Spelling and grammatical errors*—If a site is notable for poor writing and many errors, it's a sign that the creator is sloppy and careless, and possibly incompetent. This should not inspire confidence in the quality of the information provided on the site.

- *No evidence of recent activity*—A site that hasn't been updated recently won't be of use for any time-sensitive research. Furthermore, it's an example of a site that's not being maintained. Lacking a clear reference to its last update, it is sometimes possible to find clues on the site. For example, does it list area codes that have changed or mention a company executive who is no longer in the position noted?

Also, if you're on a company's site, you can often view a listing of the most recent press releases. If you find a long string of press releases but nothing from the last several months, it's a red flag. Does it mean there's been no company news? Could it mean the company has opened a newer site and you're looking at an older one they haven't bothered to remove? Has the firm gone out of business? You will want to investigate.

- *Outdated look and feel*—A site that displays no graphics but, rather, features 1990s-style HTML headlines and body text is one that hasn't kept up with the times. The data on the site may be stale as well. This is not a hard and fast rule, because there are some sites on the Web that contain good information but have a poor or old-fashioned design. When you encounter a site that looks outdated, just be sure to do the checks (as outlined later in this book) to verify the data is current.

- *Outlandish or peculiar claims*—If a Web site provides information that just doesn't sound believable, it should raise your suspicions. You can best detect this if you're already versed in the subject you are researching, but common sense plays a role too. Michael Bass, director of research for the Associated Press, recounts one such example. When a Washington State university newspaper published an article in commemoration of Filipino American History Month, it casually noted that Filipino immigrants arrived on the California shores in 1587 in a Spanish galleon named *Nuestra Señora de Buena Esperanza*, which (according to the article) loosely translates to "The Big-Ass Spanish Boat." Apparently the writer had lifted the translation from a satirical Web site, because *Nuestra Señora de Buena Esperanza* actually means "Our Lady of Good Hope."

Reassuring Signs

On the other side of the coin, the investigative journalists I spoke with agree that the following Web site characteristics are reassuring and inspire some level of confidence:

- *Complete contact information*—The best sites provide extensive contact information: not just e-mail, but a physical address and phone and fax numbers. This information is easy to find (either on the home page or immediately visible under a "Contact Us" link) and lists people's names along with their phone numbers and/or e-mail addresses.

- *An "About Us" link*—The sites that inspire the most confidence allow the visitor to immediately learn something about who is behind them, typically through an "About Us" link. Here visitors can find out who or what is behind a site, as well as its mission and agenda. It may also include information about various people involved in the site and their backgrounds, any publications or reports issued, mentions of the site that have appeared in the news, and details of its affiliations and associations.

- *Elegant, intuitive design*—While a pretty site certainly does not guarantee an accurate site, attention to detail in graphic design and navigation indicates astuteness about what makes a site "work." Such a site demonstrates savvy, and suggests there is a quality entity behind the scenes. Chris Barton, senior editor of Hoover's Online, says, "If the site is well-designed, I'm much more comfortable with getting information and trusting this site. This is based on my experience—it takes a lot of organization to collect and update information and you won't have that sense of organization and presentation with poor sites. So if it is amateurish, sloppy, or rife with copy editing errors, or difficult to use, it makes me skeptical."

- *Indication of timeliness*—One of the biggest frustrations about information found on the Web is a lack of any kind of date or other indicator of the page's freshness. The best sites will indicate when the site was last updated and be clear about what was updated. Dates can be hard to decipher—does "Updated Jan. 1, 2004" mean that a new piece of information was added, some design elements were changed, the site was overhauled, or something else? For this reason, sites that contain references or links to items recently in the news can be reassuring as these are clear indications of recent activity.

If you know something about the topic that the site is covering, you should also be able to scan it to see if recent important developments or news are covered or mentioned. If they're not, it's a potential red flag. When I'm examining pages that discuss the effective use of search engines and I run across one that doesn't mention Google, it's a pretty good sign that the page is outdated. Unless it's retrospective coverage I'm after, I'll quickly move on to other pages.

- *Cites primary sources*—Patrick Ross, Associate Managing Editor of Washington Internet Daily, says that the sites he likes best are those that not only present their own information and views, but also include references and links to primary source documents. This allows for additional verification.
- *Philosophies, approaches, methodologies outlined*—The best sites don't just give you information: They tell you why it was collected, explain the methodologies or approaches used in collecting it, identify any assumptions, and note limitations to the research. This type of information helps to provide an understanding of what goes on behind the scenes, and can be very reassuring.

For annotated listings of business sites that have already been screened for quality, see Chapter 9.

Ferreting Out the Facts

There will be occasions when you won't dismiss an unknown site completely, but you will want to take as many additional steps as you can to understand exactly who is behind the site, its mission, and agenda—and whether you can trust what you're reading. When encountering an unfamiliar site, reporters and experienced researchers switch from the more passive mode of reacting to what they see on the page to a more active strategy of ferreting out the facts behind the site.

The following section features some practical, proactive techniques for pulling up the curtain on potentially useful sites that you don't know enough about.

Understand How to Read URLs

The first thing you need to do is to understand what makes up a URL. Let's take a detour for a second and analyze the different parts of an Internet address, also called the Uniform Resource Locator (URL). For example, let's take the URL:

http://www.infotoday.com/newsbreaks/nb040426-2.shtml

This URL links to a news article published by Information Today, Inc.'s "NewsBreaks" section, breaking news on its home page. This URL, like all URLs, can be broken down as follows:

Transfer Protocol/Domain Name/Directory and Subdirectories/ File Name

- *http*: This is the "transfer protocol" that indicates that the text being transferred is hypertext, or the standard format found on the Web.

- *www.infotoday.com*: This is the domain name of the server, or computer, where the information resides and also includes the important domain suffix, .com. The fact that this domain suffix is ".com" indicates that the server is associated with a commercial entity. The two other most used domain suffixes are .edu for educational institutions and .gov for governmental entities. Another commonly encountered domain is .org, which originally was assigned only to nonprofit entities, but today may be used by commercial ones as well. There are other domains too, such as .mil for military sites, .net for computer networks, and a slew of newer, but lesser encountered, ones like .info, .biz, and .kids.

    If the server is in another country, then the URL will typically have a two letter country code attached to the domain as well. Domains from other countries may use different abbreviations to indicate the type of entity (for example, in the U.K., the suffix "co.uk" is equivalent to the U.S. ".com" and academic institutions in New Zealand use .ac.nz).

- *Newsbreaks*: This is a "directory" on the server that keeps related pages together and organized. Many URLs have one or more subdirectories (just as you may have folders within folders in your computer).

- *nb040426-2.shtml*: At the very end of the URL, you see the actual file name, representing the specific Web page. File names can end with a variety of extensions including a few different types of html files: html, htm, shtml; pdf (for PDF documents), doc (for Word documents). Image files might end in .jpg or .bmp, and so on.

Consider the Type of Site You're Viewing

Each source on the Web needs to be carefully examined on a case-by-case basis to fully gauge its reliability. However, if you know a little something about the kind of site and source you are dealing with, you can make an initial assessment about its potential value.

The quickest way to do this is to consider whether the site you're viewing is a commercial (*.com*), educational (*.edu*), or governmental site (*.gov*). At one point in the Internet's history, .org indicated a non-profit site; however, today there are no limitations on who qualifies for the .org domain. There are other top-level domain suffixes too, like .mil for military sites or .kids for sites oriented to children, but the vast majority are .com, .edu, .gov, or .org. Generally speaking, I have found the *.edu* and *.gov* sites more trustworthy than the dot-coms. Within those broader categories, there is also a hierarchy of reliability, depending on the type of source behind a site.

Following is a rather informal trustworthiness ranking of various types of organizations and sources, based on my own experiences. I've identified the common kinds of organizations and entities that put information on the Web within the three major domains, and ranked them with a very high, high, medium, or low level of confidence. Those that are rated "very high" I implicitly trust; those that are rated "high" are preferred sources that get a lower level of scrutiny. Those that are rated "medium" require further verifications and checking before using their information. Sites that are rated "low" are used as possible leads, but I don't rely on their data.

There are exceptions, but this can be used as a general guideline when encountering these kinds of sources on the Web.

Dot-Com Sites (Overall Confidence Rating: Low to Medium)

Very High

- Articles/special issues of magazines I already know and trust
- Archives of public media Web sites, such as BBC, NPR, and C-SPAN
- Sites created by journalists for other journalists

High

- Web versions of print-based newspapers and journals
- Web versions of traditional broadcasters
- Public-service organizations (sometimes these are dot-org sites)
- Academic scholarly articles
- Educational/instructional sites created by economists

Medium

- Advocacy groups/associations/special-interest sites
- News wires
- Individual experts associated with an established university
- Company-issued white papers
- Company home pages

Low

- Bloggers I don't know
- Directories/links to other sites
- Company directories (Exception: Hoover's Online, which is Medium-High)
- Company pages designed for marketing or sales purposes
- Personal pages
- Industry portals
- Individual experts unknown to me

Dot-Gov Sites (Overall Confidence Rating: High)

Very High

- Federal statistics agency sites
- Recognized international organizations that supply research and statistics

High

- Federal government information clearinghouses
- Public-service pages and services

Medium

- State/local public records collections (information may be older)
- Departmental/agency home pages (subject to more political pressure)
- Embassies/consulates (varying levels of attention to site)

Dot-Edu Sites (Overall Confidence Rating: Medium-High)

High

- University administration pages
- Faculty home pages (links, lectures, and syllabi)
- University-sponsored research center's findings and reports

Medium

- Graduate papers
- Social science data collections (need to check data currency)

Low

- Undergraduate papers

Special Category. The following are a few specific entities that inspire a very high level of confidence when I search the Web (these can be found in the dot-com, dot-org, dot-edu, or dot-gov categories):

- Traditional online databases that have migrated to the Web (e.g., PubMed, a Gale research journal database, etc.)
- Organizations that are specifically focused on the issue of enhancing information quality (e.g., COPAFS, *American Demographics* magazine)
- Pages created by a library that's affiliated with a university, association, government, or company

• Any site that has been referred by other sources I know and trust

When you come across an organization or entity that is not clearly deserving of a high confidence level, consider the following two questions:

1. What is at stake for this organization or person if he or she posts inaccurate or misleading information? For example, the ramifications of an erroneous report going out over BusinessWeek.com will be more severe than for an individual consultant with incorrect data on his or her Web site.

2. What incentive does this entity have to be accurate?

Remember, these ratings guidelines are just to help you form an initial impression. If you decide to assess the reliability of a site's information in earnest, then the hard work of digging and verifying really begins.

Interestingly, the Web itself can be placed in a hierarchy of trust. Richard Behar, a reporter for *Fortune* magazine, says that the facts tend to get more "loose" with the following mediums, from best to worst: magazines, newspapers, television, books, and the Web.

Behar believes that, with some exceptions, magazines are most reliable. Many of the larger, better-known publications employ researchers who fact-check before an issue goes to press. So, when you do find a legitimate magazine on the Web, you can feel more confident in trusting what you have located.

Run a "Whois" Search

After you've determined the type of site you're dealing with, you can then actively research who or what is behind it.

One of the best tools for finding a site's true creator is a Web utility called "Whois." This can identify who the site is registered to as well as provide the administrative and technical contact information. Also found is information on when that record was created and expired, along with domain server identification. This is the type of data that needs to be provided when someone registers a new domain.

There are a number of sites you can use to run a Whois search, and the URLs are listed on page 251 in Appendix B. One interesting investigative site is SamSpade.org, which also performs more technical functions such as running a "tracer route." According to the site, this function "maps out the path a packet takes from the server at SamSpade.org to the target machine. It can give some idea of how the target machine is connected to the network, who its service provider is, and often where in the world it is located."

The following is an excerpt of a sample Whois search run on *www.kmart.com*:

Domain Name: kmart.com
      Created on...............: 19 Dec 1994 10:00:00
      Expires on...............: 18 Dec 2004 10:00:00

Registrant Info:
      Kmart Corporation
      Kmart Corporation
      3100 West Big Beaver Rd
      Troy, MI 48084
      US
      Phone: +1.2484631000
      Fax..: 1
      Email: domainnames@kmart.com

Administrative Info:
      Kmart Corporation
      (Personal name eliminated for privacy purposes)
      3100 West Big Beaver Rd
      Troy, MI 48084
      US
      Phone: +1.2484631000
      Fax..: +1..
      Email: domainnames@kmart.com

Technical Info:
      Kmart Corporation
      (Personal name eliminated for privacy purposes)

> 3100 West Big Beaver Rd
> Troy, MI 48084
> US
> Phone: +1.2484631000
> Fax..: 1
> Email: *(Personal email eliminated for privacy purposes)*

Billing Info:
> eBrandSecure LLC
> Billing Department
> 3550 Wilshire Blvd, #430
> Los Angeles, CA 90010
> US
> Phone: +1.11112133870070
> Fax..: +1.12133872270
> Email: billing@ebrandsecure.com

Note that Whois can be extremely helpful, but it's not perfect: information can be missing or outdated. However, it is an excellent starting point when you are looking for information about the entity behind a site.

Taking the Next Steps

Once you have some information about the organization that operates a given site, you can employ additional, active strategies to learn more. This can include researching the entity itself as well as contacting a person behind the site to ask your own questions. Although this book doesn't teach you how to research or perform competitive intelligence, I will suggest a few things you can do to learn more about the person or organization behind a site.

One useful technique to learn more about a Web site is to check what other sites link to it. This is of particular value when you are having difficulty finding any useful information about the site or its creators and are looking for others you can turn to for assistance. Google will return a list of Web pages that link to any site you specify. This can be done by either going to Google's advanced search page and entering the Web site under the pull-down box that reads "Find Pages that Link to the Page" or using Google's standard search box and preceding the URL you are checking with the prefix "link:website." So, for example, to view all pages that link into the Information Today, Inc. site, you would enter the following into Google's search box: link:www.infotoday.com.

The simplest and sometimes most effective way to dig up some information is to go and "Google" that entity. In other words, just enter the name of the person or organization into Google and see what comes up. If either is at all prominent in the area you're researching, says Patrick Ross, you are likely to find a good deal of relevant information, such as newspaper articles, conference presentations, and affiliations with other institutions.

You should also query Web discussion groups. This can be done simply by clicking Google's "Groups" tab, which allows you to search over 700 million individual postings to thousands of Internet newsgroups, going all the way back to 1981! (Technically these newsgroups are part of what is known as the "Usenet" system of global discussion groups.) The advanced search option in Google Groups also allows you to limit your search just to a particular author, or someone associated with a particular organization (if you know how their standard e-mail address ends). For example, to find messages from Microsoft employees, you could enter *@microsoft.com* in the author field.

Caution: Although you can learn something about people by finding what they've said and done in the past on the Web, don't assume that this information in any way defines who they are now—or even were then. Bits of postings and data on a Web newsgroup can easily be taken out of context and create inaccurate assumptions about others. (For a full treatment of this hazard, I highly recommend Jeffrey Rosen's *The Unwanted Gaze: The Destruction of Privacy in America*, Random House, 2000.)

Besides searching Usenet groups for past postings, you can also include your own query about the entity in a group. In this case, you'd want to find a Usenet group or mailing list (listserv) that seems appropriate for your query, since those who subscribe might have some knowledge of the organization or person you're interested in. (See page 251 in Appendix B for some sources that will help you locate the names of these groups.)

In addition, there are also a whole host of research tools and resources—including phone books, reverse directories, e-mail lookups, and the like—that can help you with your informal research. For example, Google has its own phone book search that you can invoke by entering the organization name, city, comma, and state abbreviation to retrieve a full address and phone number.

What's the Real Agenda?

It is tempting to think that it's possible to focus only on those sites that are purely factual and don't have a point of view, but as Barzun and Graff put it, "Facts very rarely occur pure, free from interpretation or ideas. ... In reality, most of the facts we gather come dripping with ideas" (*The Modern Researcher*, p. 134).

It is nearly an impossible task to locate unbiased information. Every decision by any entity—whether a news organization, association, or market report—focuses on collecting one set of information and disregarding another to make a certain assumption, thereby reflecting some set of values.

Still, there is bias and there is *bias*. A Gallup public-opinion survey on smoking will suffer from the unavoidable human biases of determining what's worthy to be measured, what the important questions are, and what isn't important to ask. On the other hand, a survey on the same subject from Phillip Morris might reasonably be expected to suffer from the more pernicious bias of having a vested interest in a particular outcome. In other words, some points of view are so strong and overriding that the resulting data can only be properly seen within that context. And if that context includes a powerful ideological, commercial, or social agenda, the information must be scrutinized carefully.

This can certainly be accomplished, and the good researcher doesn't necessarily disregard information that's coming from a particular point of view. Rather, the researcher ensures that it is evaluated within the proper context. A problem can occur if the entity's interests are somehow obscured, making it more difficult to discover the real agenda and mission. For example, an advocacy group with a particularly strong view and philosophy can create a very neutral-sounding name that sheds no light on its true agenda. For example, it would not be obvious that an organization called the Center for Consumer Freedom is funded by the Food and Restaurant Industry to work to oppose government laws that would regulate those industries.

So while evaluating the reliability of a particular site and deciding who or what is behind it, it's also wise to determine the mission of the person or group. This is very important, as you'll need to account for bias as well as subtly disguised political and social leanings.

As any investigative reporter will tell you, determining what an organization is all about can take a lot of work and digging. Often this means reading reams of primary documents, conducting scores of interviews, and following connections—and, of course, following the money. Who funds the organization?

You can do some of this investigation yourself. The following are steps you can take without embarking on an extensive investigative project:

- Find out why this organization exists and why its Web site was created. Read as much as you can on the site itself to get some feel for an agenda. If you have access to a newspaper archive database (most libraries offer this), search on the name of the organization and see what's been written about it in the past.

- Look for the name of the company's CEO, executive director, or principal and check his or her past affiliations and jobs. Sometimes you can find the person's biography or a resume. What companies did the person work for, and what were their missions?

- Of particular importance when researching nonprofits and associations is finding out who funds them. Where does the money come from? If it's not stated on the site itself and the entity is a tax-exempt nonprofit organization, its tax returns (Form 990) are public information and may be examined.

You can even do this online by linking to GuideStar.org, a nonprofit organization that makes such tax returns available.

- Read the Web site carefully to detect loaded phrases and propaganda techniques. Does the site try to push a particular position or stance? Does it do so outright or is it more subtle in its choice of words and presentation of facts? (See Figures 4.1 and 4.2.)

It should be noted that advocacy groups—even those that are not completely upfront about who they are—can sometimes be useful information sources. But remember that they are special interest groups, and that whether on the left or right their mission is to persuade, not simply to provide the facts. Once you understand the true nature and mission of a group you can use its information in the

Figure 4.1   *The Center for Consumer Freedom is produced by an anti-regulatory organization called the Center for Regulatory Effectiveness.*

Figure 4.2 *The Center for Consumer Freedom*

proper context, seek confirmation or challenges from others, and ultimately make informed decisions about what to believe or not.

Of course, you should be aware of your own biases when conducting research and choosing which sources to pay attention to and which to disregard. This relates to one of the virtues outlined in *The Modern Researcher*: self-awareness. The authors examine the matter of bias in the researcher himself, explaining that all researchers naturally have what the authors call a reason for doing their work—some impetus for the project that is driving them to perform research. The authors call that force a "guiding idea":

> Since guiding ideas affect both search and selection, let us call the researcher's temperament (that is, the whole tendency of his mind) and his present intentions and hypotheses, his total *interest*. We may say without implying any blame that his interest will determine his discoveries, his selection, his pattern making, and his

exposition. This is unavoidable in all products of the mind.... "Bias" is an *uncontrolled form of interest.* (*The Modern Researcher*, p. 186)

It is possible, say the authors, to control that interest while researching. The authors quote Italian educator and political figure Gaetano Salvemini, who said, "Impartiality is a dream and honesty a duty. We cannot be impartial but we can be intellectually honest" (p. 187).

Public Information Sources Available to Online Researchers

Becoming an effective investigative reporter means learning how to detect and follow leads, interview subjects, seek out truths and detect lies. This only comes with years of hard work and lots of practice: You can't expect to gain the hard-won insights and develop the instincts of a true investigative reporter by reading a few pointers and tips in any book, including this one. However, what you can do is, first, be aware of the types of records and databases that are available to you and, second, know where to access some of the research tools investigative reporters use in their background research on individuals, organizations, and corporations.

The following is a sampling of the kinds of public information sources that are available on the Web to researchers:

Federal Government
- Department of Transportation accident reports
- OSHA violations
- EPA toxic/hazardous waste releases

State Government
- Department of Motor Vehicles (drivers licenses, vehicle registrations)
- Department of Corrections (prison records)

- Secretary of State/Department of Corporations (When incorporated, names of directors and officers, business licenses)
- Uniform Commercial Code (UCC) Filings
- Bankruptcy records

Local Government
- Board of Elections (voter registration records)
- Court Clerk (criminal charges, civil suits)
- Tax Collection Office (personal and business property listings, tax paid, tax abatements, property maps)
- Register of Deeds (ownership of property, liens against business or personal property)
- Building Department (building permits, building inspection records)

The good news is that the tools for locating public records data are becoming more common and easier to use. Increasingly, they are available to anyone via the free Web.

Today there are several searchable databases available—at no charge—that include details on who funds and contributes to what organizations or political candidates. These sites are often produced by groups on the left that want to expose the interests of large corporations and right-wing entities. They're also produced by groups on the right that wish to identify sources of funding for left-leaning organizations. In addition, politically neutral entities established by the government and public accountability groups are moving their databases directly to the Web.

The main beneficiary of all this activity is you, the researcher. These databases are a boon to those who need to dig for information on all types of entities. (In the section that follows you'll read about some of the best of these investigative tools, as well as resources for obtaining additional sources and advice on conducting investigative research.)

Searching public records is a discipline unto itself, and there have been numerous books written on this topic alone. One of the best sources for learning more about searching public records is BRB Publications of Tempe, Arizona, which produces a series of guides and fee-based online sources for finding public records.

Note that the availability of public records has become a contentious issue. The ease with which so much information about people can be found on the Web has caused some legislatures to make public documents (such as motor vehicle records) less accessible. These records have always been public, but in the past someone who wanted to find them would have had to visit (or at least write to) the proper office and have a manual search done. As governments make their publicly available information more easily accessible on the Web you can expect the outcry from individuals and privacy advocates to grow louder.

Sources of Organizational Funding Information

Capital Research Center (CRC) GreenWatch

Political Orientation: right

According to its Web site, the CRC, founded in 1984, is a watchdog group that reports on the activities of tax-exempt charities, philanthropies, and other not-for-profit organizations.

Databases: *GreenWatch*—Lets users search funding sources for progressive, left-of-center organizations. (See Figure 4.3.)

GrantMaker—Lets users search grants from companies and organizations. (See Figure 4.4.)

Center for Science in the Public Interest

Political orientation: left

For 30 years, the Center for Science in the Public Interest has been a strong advocate for nutrition and health, food safety, alcohol policy, and sound science.

Databases: *Integrity in Science Database*—According to the organization, the purpose of this database is to surface "corporate ties of scientists, academics, and nonprofit organizations in the fields of nutrition, environment, toxicology, and medicine." (See Figure 4.5.)

Nonprofit Organizations with Ties to Industry—Not really a database, but a listing of nonprofit organizations that have financial or other ties to industry.

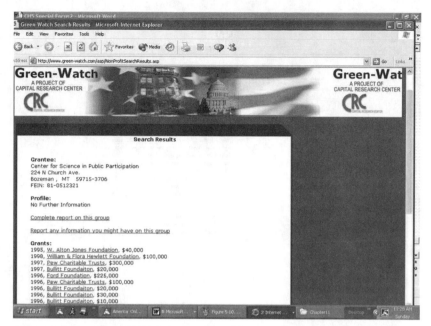

Figure 4.3 GreenWatch is produced by a conservative organization that identifies sources of funding of left-of-center entities and activities.

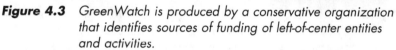

Figure 4.4 Grants given by Gap Inc. as identified by Capital Research Center's "GrantMaker."

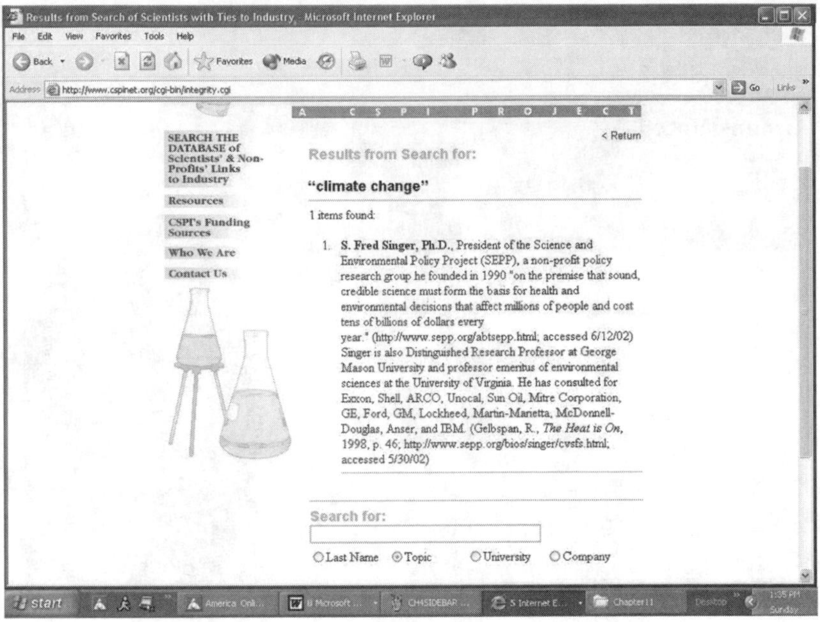

Figure 4.5   *A search on the left-leaning Center for Science in the Public Interest's "Integrity in Science" database retrieves a biography of the climate change skeptic S. Fred Singer.*

GuideStar

Political orientation: neutral

Database: *The National Database of Non-Profit Organizations—* Allows searches for IRS Form 990s from over 850,000 IRS-recognized nonprofits. According to its Web site, GuideStar is produced by Philanthropic Research, Inc., a 501(c)(3) public charity founded in 1994. GuideStar's mission is to "revolutionize philanthropy and non-profit practice with information." (See Figures 4.6 and 4.7.)

Common Cause

Political orientation: reformist/neutral

According to the Web site, Common Cause is "a nonprofit, non-partisan citizens' lobbying organization that promotes open, honest, and accountable government. Supported by the dues and contributions of over 200,000 members in every state across the nation, Common

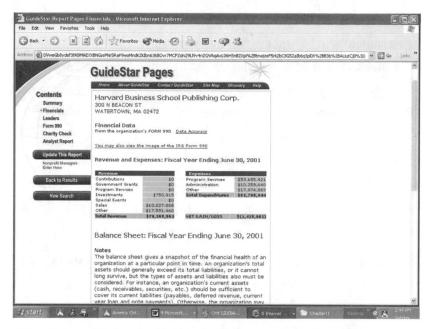

Figure 4.6 *GuideStar displays the financial information it has collected on the Harvard Business School Publishing Corporation, including a link to its IRS Form 990.*

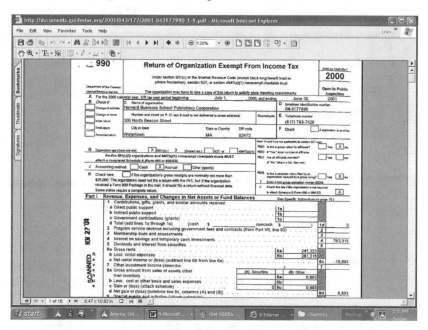

Figure 4.7 *The full image of Harvard Business School Publishing Corporation's Form 990 filing with the IRS.*

Cause represents the unified voice of the people against corruption in government and big-money special interests."

Database: *Soft Money Laundromat*—A free, searchable database of special-interest soft-money contributors to the Democratic and Republican national party committees. (See Figures 4.8 and 4.9.)

Public Records Web Sites

The federal government makes several databases available that can shed light on companies, industries, and organizations. Following are some of the most useful.

Occupational Safety and Health Administration (OSHA)

Database: *Statistics and Data*—Enables users to search OSHA inspections conducted at a certain establishment or within a particular industry group. The text of accident investigation summaries can also be found here. (See Figures 4.10–4.12.)

Office of Thrift Supervision (U.S. Department of Treasury)

Includes the following searchable databases:

- *Institution Directory*—Searchable database of institutions that are regulated by the Office of Thrift Supervision.
- *Holding Company Database*—Searchable database of active, proposed, organized, and FRB holding companies.
- *FDIC Institution Directory*—Provides the location and deposit information for more than 82,000 FDIC-insured banking offices as well as the latest comprehensive financial data for every FDIC-insured institution.

Federal Election Commission

Database: *Transaction Query System*—Allows searches for individuals who contributed more than $200, contributions received or made by a certain committee, and contributions received by a specific campaign. (See Figure 4.13.)

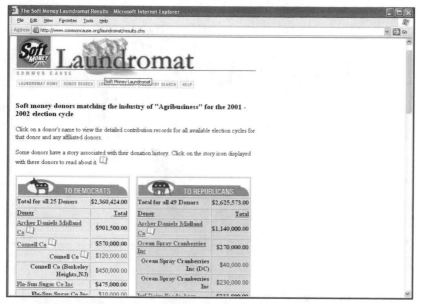

Figure 4.8 *Common Cause's "Soft Money Laundromat" database identifies an individual's business, union, and industry contributions to both the Democrats and Republicans.*

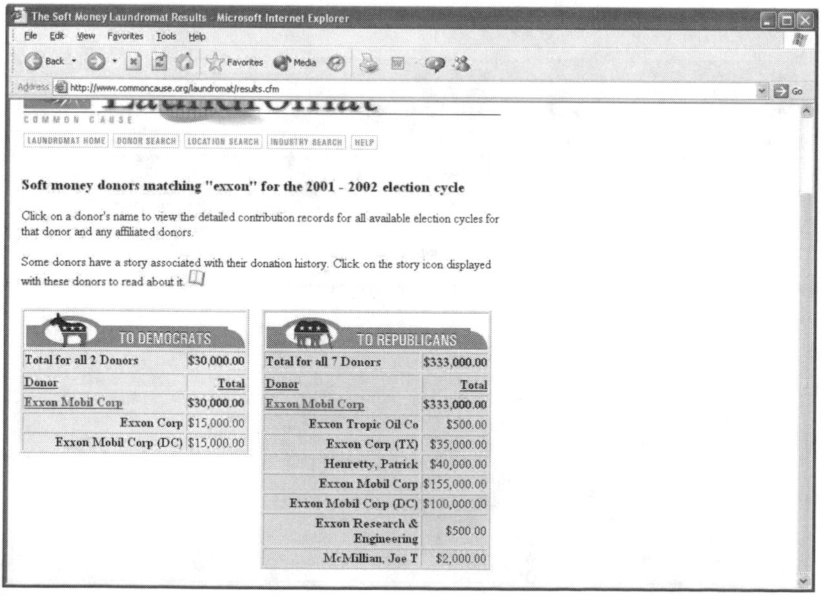

Figure 4.9 *The Soft Money Laundromat also identifies contributions to the political parties by a specific company.*

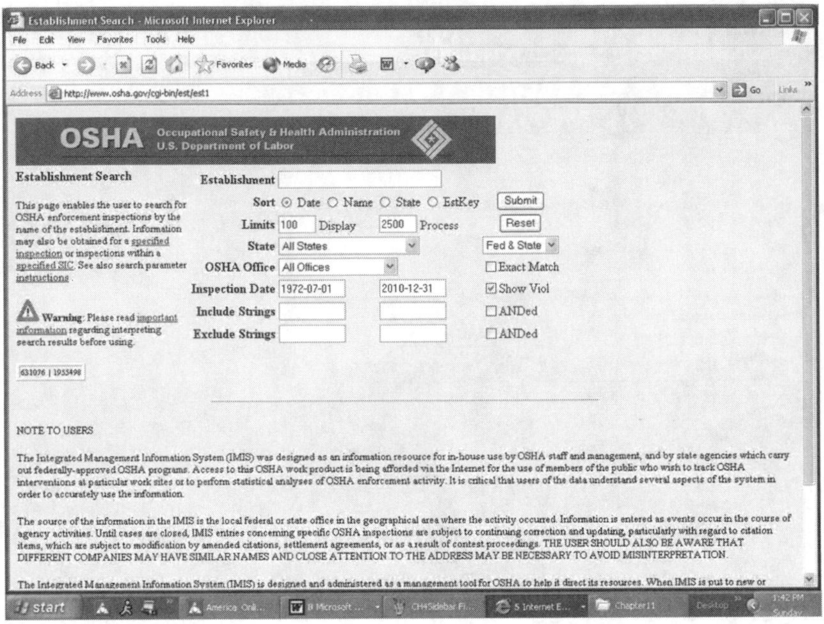

Figure 4.10 *The U.S. Occupational Safety and Health Administration's (OSHA) "Statistics and Data" provides details on companies where accident investigations have occurred.*

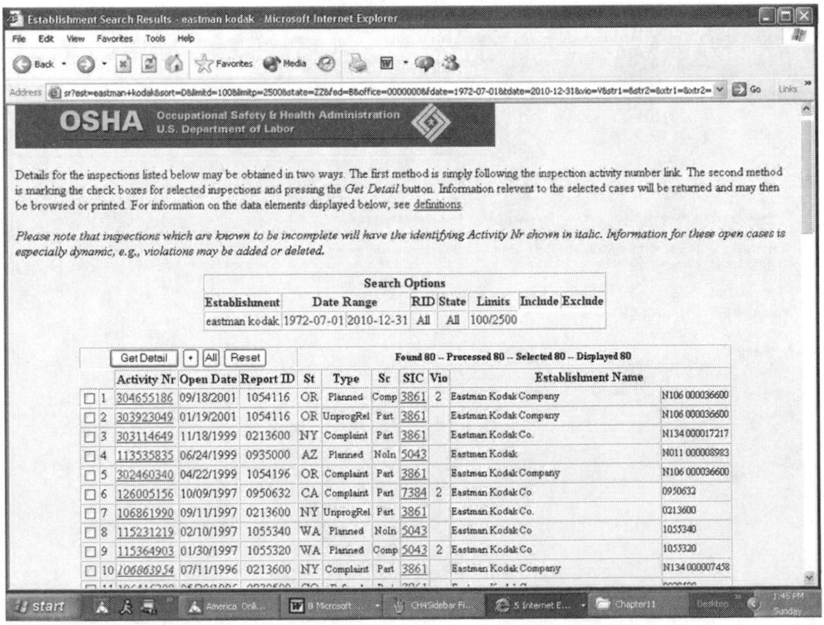

Figure 4.11 *A listing of investigations conducted by OSHA on Eastman Kodak's facilities.*

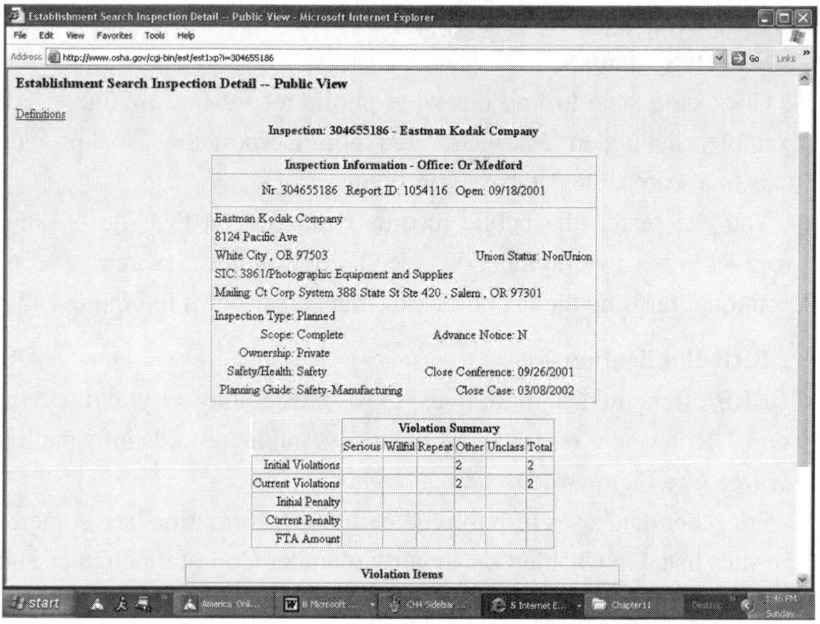

Figure 4.12 Detailed results of an investigation of a specific Eastman Kodak case.

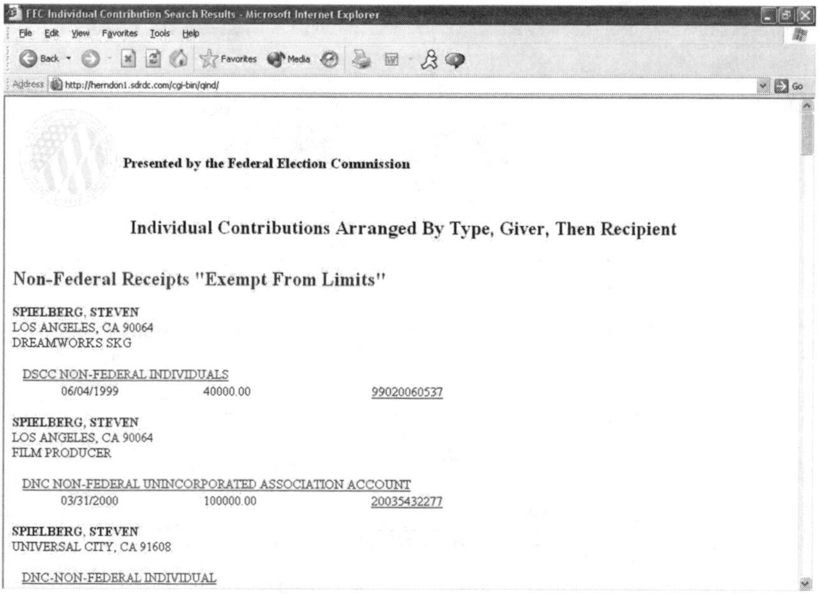

Figure 4.13 A search of the Federal Election Commission's Transaction Query System for political contributions by Steven Spielberg.

State and Local Public Records

Search Systems

Click on a state to find out what public records are available. For example, clicking on "Maryland" and then "Corporations" will provide links to a searchable database (see Figure 4.14).

You can search the public records databases on this site by keyword—a very powerful function indeed. For example, a search on "contributions" turns up the list of records databases shown in Figure 4.15.

BRB Publications

BRB offers links to more than 1,330 state, county, city, and federal court URLs where researchers can access public records information for free (see Figure 4.16).

For other databases of publicly available information, see some of the sites listed in Chapter 9, categorized under Corporate Finance and Corporations—History and Management.

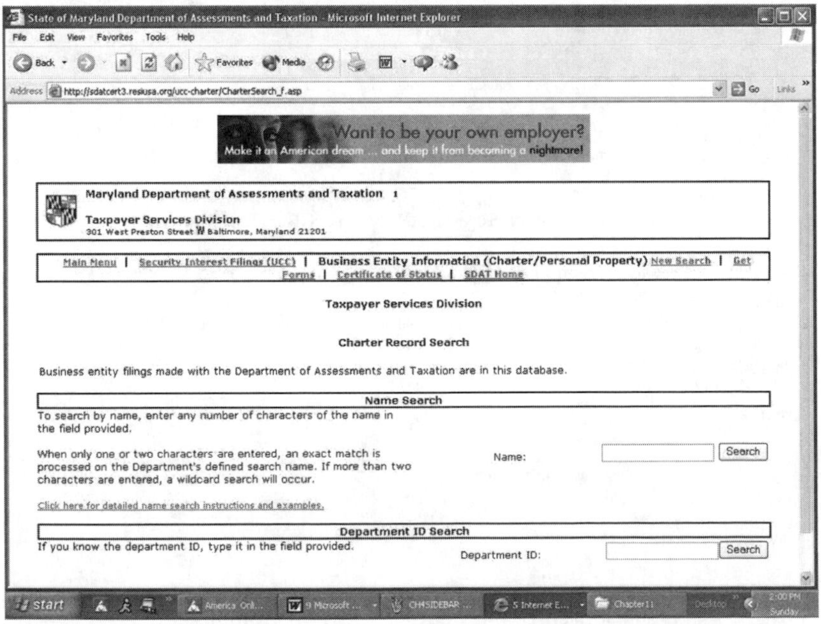

Figure 4.14 *The Search Systems site identifies what public records are available from each state.*

Figure 4.15 *A search on the Search Systems site "Public Records Locator" identifies sources of public records matching the keyword: "contributions."*

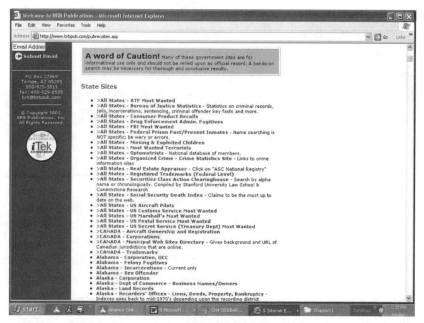

Figure 4.16 *A listing of states' public records Web sites can be found by browsing BRB Publications.*

Additional Investigative Research Resources

The best resource to learn about investigative research techniques is the Investigative Reporters & Editors Association (IRE), a top-notch organization dedicated to educating and enhancing the skills of investigative reporters. Two excellent sections of this site that are open to the public are IRE Resource Center and IRE Tip Sheet.

Another recommended source for tips, strategies, and tools is "Virtual Gumshoe: Investigative Resources Available on the Web." For business-specific filings, I recommend LLRX's "Business Filings Databases."

PR Watch, a quarterly publication of the left-leaning Center for Media & Democracy, has published the very useful Web page called "How to Research Front Groups." This lists and describes several tools for research funding as well as the connections of large corporations and right-wing organizations.

These resources are listed in Appendix B, beginning on page 251.

On the Web: Verify, Don't Trust

Once you know who's behind a site and what its mission is, you'll be in a much better position to examine its data and claims, and thus to begin the critical process of verification.

According to *The Modern Researcher*, verification "is conducted on many planes, and its technique is not fixed. It relies on attention to detail, on common sense reasoning, on a developed 'feel' for history and chronology, on familiarity with human behavior, and on ever-enlarging stores of information" (*The Modern Researcher*, p. 99). One becomes accomplished at the skill and art of verification primarily by practice, over time, rather than by following a set of rules.

Nevertheless, the authors do outline the basic principles that go into the scholarly practice of verifying information. One critical aspect is "collation," the careful comparison of different sources covering the same topic to look for discrepancies and "oddities and the legwork that's needed to get to primary source documents to inspect them for oneself. Eventually the researcher arrives at truth through *probability*," which is "a firm reliance on the likelihood that evidence which has been examined and found solid is veracious." And what ultimately constitutes true evidence is information that "not only confirms your view, but excludes its rivals."

Verification is imperative for reporters, who must always check and confirm their facts. The following are steps that should ideally be taken to verify anything you find on the Web, especially when you get it from an unknown Web site. The first two rules are particularly important.

1. Always try to find the original source. Don't rely on someone who is quoting from a report, a newspaper article, government document, or any other source; get to it yourself, if at all possible. The Web makes this much easier than in the past, when getting to a primary document would mean a trip to a library, government agency, news archives, or wherever it was stored. Since so much published material (especially prominent reports and news stories) is available on the Web, sometimes all it takes is entering the source's name into Google and looking at it yourself.

2. If you can't verify something from an original source, then at least try to find someone who will confirm the facts for you. Getting a confirming source is a very important rule for journalists—in fact, many news organizations have a policy whereby they will not publish sensitive information without at least one additional, confirming source. The Web makes it easy to search for and find names and contacts of experts— book authors, writers, or prominent bloggers, for instance— who could confirm information for you. But it's good to broaden your research and go beyond the Web to find experts too, so ideally, you should try to obtain your confirming source by a means other than searching the Web (for example, by using a library source such as a hard copy reference directory, or by telephoning an expert at a university or governmental office).

3. Use traditional, non-Web reference sources as verification tools. Have you found a quote on the Web that's supposedly

attributed to a well-known person? Before reporting it yourself, check a copy of *Bartlett's Familiar Quotations* or another established hard-copy reference work. If someone mentions the budget of a government agency, check the U.S. government's manual. If an association's budget is claimed to be $100 million, look it up in the *Encyclopedia of Associations*.

4.   Don't forget the fee-based online services, which offer databases of newspaper and journal articles that you can search to verify what you've found. For this purpose, I use the Dialog database and often search its newspaper files, as well as the ABI/Inform journal database and Trade & Industry Database.

5.   If you need to verify statistical data related to demographics, public policy, or a social issue, you may be able to find a federal government site that will at least provide you with some assurance that the data is the official version. (Try FedStats or one of the other government clearinghouses described in Chapter 6.)

Verifying Uncertain Information

If you're unable to verify something you've found on the Web, either do not use it, or use it with a disclaimer. For example, below are two cases where I used the Web as the medium to track down experts and locate confirming sources to some unverified information.

Case #1: Checking an Unverified Claim about Micro-cars

I recently had to do some research on an interesting and quirky topic—why is it that the teeny little cars that are so popular in Europe are not available in the U.S.? In searching the Web, I came across an online forum called Allpar, which describes itself as a site that "serves Dodge, Chrysler, Plymouth, DeSoto, and Jeep owners and enthusiasts."

Members of this group discussed developments, trends, and issues that affected owners of those cars. I noted that the site owner posted a tip that was passed along from a couple of its members, informing the group that DaimlerChrysler was going to be bringing its tiny "Smart Car," which has been quite the rage in Europe over the last few years, to the United States in 2006, and would be doing so by using a manufacturing plant in Juiz de Fora, Brazil. This was interesting news and relevant to my research—if it was true. I then went about making an effort to use that tidbit as a lead to try to verify. Here are the few simple steps I took:

1. Because the posting identified the names of the members who passed along that tip, I did a search on the two person's names to see what I could learn about their background, and to assess their credibility. It turned out that both people were actively involved in the automotive industry, and were cited on other sites as good experts on various topics related to automobiles. A good sign—but not enough!

2. I then took the most specific/obscure phrase that was in that three paragraph posting and did an additional search on the Web. I searched on "Juiz de Fora" and added "Smart Car." This then led me to another car forum called "Automotive Intelligence" that repeated this same information. Another good sign. Additional searches retrieved several "name" publications with a presence in the Web that repeated the same bit of news. Those sources included Motor Trend, Forbes, Business Week, and Bloomberg.

3. By now, I was convinced that this was very likely to be accurate information, which then gave me additional confidence in that intial auto forum, as well as in the two individuals who made that first posting. These people, I felt, might be interesting experts to track down and interview if I needed to do so.

4.   Although I did not pursue this step in this case, the next and final step would be to contact the automotive firm itself to confirm the accuracy of this information.

I could have approached this confirmation process differently. For instance, I could have immediately called the automotive company to try to confirm the unverified data, but given that it seemed that this was rumored information at the time, I was not confident that I could get a good answer. I could also have tried to track down the e-mails or phone numbers of the two forum members who posted the tip, and ask them my own questions to try to gauge their credibility. But ultimately, it was pretty easy to find several reliable confirming sources right on the Web, giving me a high degree of confidence that this was accurate information.

Some of this confidence also comes from the fact that several of those sources I used—Bloomberg, Business Week, and Forbes— would be considered of the highest level of trustworthiness for business researchers. For the names of other "core" news and information sources, see Chapter 9.

Case #2: Is This What the Buddha Said?

In this case I had to employ even more persistence and off-the-Web digging to try to get to the expert I needed.

While doing research for this book, I came across the following quote on the Web, which was attributed to Buddha:

> *Believe nothing, no matter where you read it or who said*
> *it, no matter if I have said it, unless it agrees with your own*
> *reason and your own common sense.*

This was a nice quote for use in this book—but was it true? I searched all over the Web to see if I could find some kind of authoritative confirmation or citation of an original source, but the only Web pages my searches turned up were those where an individual or small business used the quote, but did so without any attribution or sourcing. Nobody cited a reference or original document. I wanted—and needed—to find out if this was something that Buddha had reportedly actually said.

One initial strategy was to check various print and Web-based quotation dictionaries, but none of the ones I reviewed included that quotation, so I was beginning to get a little skeptical. My next strategy was to see if I could find an authoritative work on Buddha. I ran some searches on Amazon, and turned up what seemed to be an on-target book, titled *The Sayings of Buddha*, written by a gentleman by the name of Geoffrey Parrinder, and published by Ecco Press, November, 1998.

My next step was to try to track down this author to ask him if this was indeed a quote that he included in his book, or that he had ever heard. A search on his name on the Web to try to find him eventually led me to a site that mentioned that Parrinder taught at the Theology and Religious Studies department at a university in London called Kings College. I then linked to the Kings College Web home page, clicked on the links to the individual departments, and called up the departmental Web page. However, I could not find any reference to a Professor Parrinder. What I did then was to note the name of a key faculty member of the department whose e-mail was also listed, and sent him the following e-mail note:

Dear Professor Byrne,

Good day. My name is Robert Berkman, and I am an editor and author living in Falmouth, MA in the United States.

I am contacting you because I am currently working on a book where I am trying to get confirmation of a quote, reputedly said by Buddha. I have found that there is a book titled "The Sayings of Buddha" published in 1998 by Geoffrey Parrinder, who according to my information, is currently Professor Emeritus of Comparative Study of Religions at King's College London.

I wonder if you could confirm this for me, and perhaps let me know if he can be reached as I am looking for an authoritative source to confirm this quotation.

Thank you very much for any assistance. If you have any questions about my project, I'd be happy to answer them.

Sincerely,
Robert Berkman
17 Dillingham Avenue
Falmouth, MA 02540
508-540-5185

I received back the following e-mail reply from Professor Byrne:

Dear Robert Berkman,

I have no contact address for Prof Parrinder. It is many years since he came into the Department. I can find no trace of the book you mention in the KCL library catalogue, which is not to say that the book does not exist.

I will try to make some inquiries.

Have you thought about getting the book on interlibrary loan?

Peter Byrne

I replied back to Professor Byrne, thanking him for his e-mail and asked if he knew where Professor Parrinder could be found. He replied in another e-mail that listed "the last address" the school had for him, but added: "But I can't be sure he is still alive! If he is he would be about 90."

I then called the U.K. directory assistance, to see if there was a Parrinder in the town that Byrne mentioned, and there was indeed a listing. I called the number in Britain, and a very elderly sounding man answered the phone. After I explained my question, he asked me to put my query in writing to him, which I did.

After a few weeks, I received a blue airmail letter back in the mail from the U.K. Inside was a note, obviously composed on an old manual typewriter, that read in part:

The statement that you provided is not known to me...I have checked this in Early Buddhist texts, Buddhist texts, and Early Buddhist Scriptures, but it sounds more like a modern statement than an authentic early text...on the face of it, this quotation reads like a literary phrase, and therefore not a spoken phrase...the reference to "common sense" sounds more like a modern version than an ancient tradition.

Kind regards
Yours sincerely,
Geoffrey Parrinder

So my conclusion is that if a foremost scholar on the sayings of Buddha had not come across the quote—it was not something that I could use with any certainty!

Note that in both these cases, the key was to go beyond the original source, look for confirming sources and experts that I could pose my own questions to, and where needed, go off the Web completely to get an authoritative source to verify my information.

Talking to Your Source

If you're unable to track down primary sources or other confirming data, you should try to contact the source yourself and ask him questions in order to get a better feel for his knowledge, agenda, and capabilities. Send an initial e-mail to introduce yourself and explain what you are trying to find and that you have some questions. If the person is receptive to your questions and you can set up a telephone appointment, that would be an excellent way to start a dialogue.

How do you determine whether the person is a reliable source? A lot of this comes down to you. You'll be surprised how reliable your instincts can be in guiding you (more on this in Chapter 8). However, there are some specific questions you should ask yourself, namely:

- **How did you encounter this referred source?**—It's an excellent sign if you were referred from another source, as the best way to find reliable experts is to be referred by other trustworthy experts. That other trusted source might be a person who is affiliated with an organization, association, or publication that you've come to rely on.

- **Does the person know what he or she is talking about?**— What is the basis for this person's opinions or statements? Is it research, personal experience, observations, or something else? Sometimes business reporters and researchers are referred to a press officer who answers questions. This is fine in some cases, particularly when you want to find out about a company's history, background, philosophy, or other official data. However, if you have detailed operational questions, you have to consider whether the person is really capable of answering your questions. If you feel that the person isn't fully qualified, you should politely request to speak with someone who has more intimate knowledge of your topic.

- **Is the person recognized in his or her field?**—Find out if the person has published in any prominent journals, spoken at conferences, or is recognized by any prominent institutions. If it's an organization, where else is it cited on the Web or in other sources? This helps prove credibility. Be flexible in applying this guideline. Some people, especially if they're younger, may have valuable insights to offer, but their work or views may not be widely disseminated. Similarly, just because you may not have heard of a Web site, don't dismiss it out of hand. There are many smaller sites that are considered credible leaders in their niche areas.

When talking to your source, also ask yourself the following:

- **Does he or she know what you already know?**—Ideally, when you talk to a potential expert, you have already developed some knowledge about the field. You should see if that person is familiar with what you've learned. You might even ask a question to which you already know the answer to check his or her knowledge.

- **Is he or she attentive to your questions?**—Does the person attempt to answer what you've asked, or ignore your question and discuss some other matter altogether? A good source will listen carefully to your question and respond directly.

- **Does the person express points and opinions clearly and convincingly?**—Someone who speaks in dense technical jargon or cannot express his points clearly will not only be hard to understand but may be less than credible.

Can't Get a Date?

There's nothing more maddening than reading a Web page and not having any idea if it's new or old. Surprisingly, this happens even with documents and other sources that you'd expect to always show a date, such as a press release or news story. Here are some strategies for determining when a page was posted:

- If there is contact information for the author, send him or her an e-mail and simply ask.

- If the page in question seems like it may have made the rounds elsewhere on the Web—such as a news article, company press release, etc.—look for a unique or unusual phrase. Enter the phrase into Google and see if you turn up any other pages that include it. These pages may provide a date, or some additional clues.

- If the item does look like it was previously published, use a search engine such as AllTheWeb's News Search that indexes and retrieves news and magazine articles. You'll retrieve an actual news story, which almost always includes a date.

- The WayBack Machine might be able to help you. It has created a snapshot of what the Web looked like on specific days over the last several years. If you enter the name of a site and a particular date, you can see if the information you see now was on the site at that past date. (Note that the WayBack Machine's collection, while fascinating and quite a bit of fun, is a bit spotty.)

- Finally, if you simply want to ensure that you know what's new on a particular Web site, you can use one of the Web page watch and notification software programs. These can help you discover when a certain page changes and specifically what new information is contained on it.

Final Do's and Don'ts

The following is a summary of what you should and should *not* do when you run across information from an unknown Web site.

Do	Don't
Have pre-existing knowledge on the topic	Build your topic knowledge from only a Web site
Get a confirming source on any factual data	Use anything directly from a Web page
Go to any original source mentioned	Assume "it's all there." Rather, ask "What's missing?"
Try to find official sites to confirm the data	Assume an organization is exactly what its title says it is
Remain skeptical	Assume that a Web site isn't credible just because you've not previously encountered it

CHAPTER 5

Company and Industry Sources

The Web has revolutionized the process of obtaining information directly from companies. Before the Web, your options were limited: You could ask the business for an annual report, hire a specialist to conduct a search of the SEC's database of public filings, consult a print-based company directory in a library, read the business press, or perhaps sign up with a news-clipping service to keep up with press releases. Needless to say, these are neither comprehensive nor particularly time efficient ways to keep up with company news and developments.

But as with everything else where the Web is concerned, that was then and this is now. Today, your choices seem almost limitless. Now you can download or read annual reports on the Web (often on a company's own site), browse public company filings from the SEC's EDGAR system or on one of the EDGAR spin-offs, search a Web-based company directory like Hoover's, and search for current press releases on a company's home page.

In addition, because so many companies use the Web as a primary method for disseminating their data, you can now find information that was difficult, if not impossible, to obtain just a few years ago, including:

- Company history and background
- Company philosophy, outlook, and broad strategic direction
- Names, titles, and backgrounds of key executives
- Market focus and priorities
- Employment opportunities
- Organizational structure, subsidiaries, and divisions

- Detailed product catalogs and brochures
- Technical documentation
- Links to recent articles about the company
- Recent company news and announcements
- Recent multimedia presentations
- Stockholder information
- Recent financial filings

Because of a ruling by the SEC called "Fair Disclosure" (Regulation FD), which requires that public firms reveal "material" information in a nonselective manner to all parties at the same time, more companies comply with this by broadcasting Webcasts of important announcements. Typically, Webcast conferences include earnings reports, dividend reports, new-product releases, merger/acquisition news, announcements of management changes, and shareholder meetings.

Sources for Locating Company-Provided Data

The first place to look for company information is a firm's own Web site. Although there are many Web-based company directories, I've found that the most effective method to find a company site is simply to enter the company name (in quotation marks if it's more than one word) into Google. Ninety-five percent of the time the company's Web site will appear at the top of the search results listing. (Sometimes Google won't return the main home page but an interior page—such as the "About" page. Then it's a simple matter of either "backing up" the URL or following a link to the main page.)

A sample company home page is displayed in Figures 5.1 and 5.2. Clicking on the "About Us" link in Figure 5.1 uncovers various useful information: a company overview, client list, career opportunities, international operations, press releases, partners, investor relations (which typically has the company's financials and other important data), and corporate brochures. Clicking on "Investor Relations" brings up more details, as illustrated in Figure 5.2.

Other key sources for getting information directly from a company include one of the EDGAR public filing sites (see Appendix B) or from

Figure 5.1 *As with many company home pages, background information on the knowledge services firm FIND/SVP can be found under its "Investor Relations" link.*

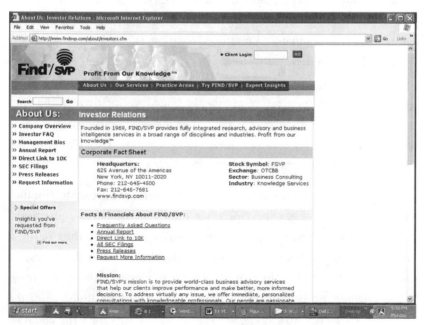

Figure 5.2 *Facts and background data on FIND/SVP are displayed after clicking on "Investor Relations."*

a news aggregator such as Yahoo! News, which includes press releases and allows you to search by company name.

How Credible Is Company-Supplied Information?

Can you trust company-supplied information? Sometimes, but you need to approach press releases, financial statements, and other company-generated documents with skepticism. Until recently, you would have thought you could at least rely on a public company's financial filings, since such data is legally required to be accurate. But as the Enron debacle revealed in 2001, even supposedly unimpeachable data can be suspect.

Although the Web often gets a bad rap when it comes to data quality, one researcher found more reliable and complete company information by searching the open Web than was provided by the company itself. In this case, an investor who filed a suit against Global Crossing reported on a popular investor message board his frustration at not being able to obtain relevant, critical information from the firm's own financial filings. The researcher claimed he was able to find much more about the company's condition, business relationships, and operations on the open Web.

Whether you can trust company-supplied data ultimately comes down to two issues. One, of course, is your level of trust in the specific firm you are researching. The other is based on the specific *type* of data you are relying on. Following are some questions to consider in respect to various types of data issued by a company.

Press Releases—These are issued for a variety of reasons, including personnel changes, new-product releases, mergers/acquisitions, earnings reports, and more. Are they credible? Although they're often written optimistically in the hopes of influencing potential investors and they always contain a measure of self-aggrandizement, most press releases are helpful and legitimate sources of intelligence for the business researcher. You just need to know how to spot the hype and read through it to get to the facts.

Sample Press Release

FOR IMMEDIATE RELEASE
CONTACT:
Anne Jones
Director of Public Relations
Wisdom, Inc.
123 Main St.
Pronda, VT 02220
Phone: 814-555-1234
E-mail: ajones@wisdom.net

WisdomWizard Software Upgrade Now Lets Staffers Gain Deep Insight into Markets

Pronda, VT—June 10, 2004—Wisdom, Inc.'s (http://www.wisdomnow.com) Wisdom-Wizard version 3.5 knowledge management software now offers users the greatest insights yet into how to effectively tap into their markets by turning raw data found on the Internet into deep insights of actionable intelligence. According to company CEO John Thomson, this upgrade provides features unmatched by any other knowledge management software and provides users with the kind of competitive advantage never before available.

"WisdomWizard 3.5, scheduled to be released in the third quarter of 2003," says Thomson, "is the result of our analyzing what our customers have asked for and delivering what the market needed."

Thomson says that the product will be available at no extra price than the current version 3.4. Purchasers of this new version, however, will need to be sure that they have upgraded to the latest version of the accompanying server software.

With a reputation for excellence and quality, Wisdom, Inc. has become the leader in the insight category of knowledge management software, with a 500-percent increase in sales over the last three years. Launched in 1999, Wisdom, Inc.'s product line has expanded over the last five years to include knowledge management software. Founder Helen Smith, born in Westfield, N.J. and previously known for her pioneering work as a designer of pet snowshoes, is today heralded as the leader in insight software.

Smith serves on the faculty of the MIT Sloan School of Management and sits on several executive boards. She has written books and numerous scholarly papers on the role of knowledge in modern organizations.

Wisdom, Inc. is a publicly held company that was founded in 1999, with head-quarters in Pronda, Vt. It has over 500 clients and three other offices in San Jose, Calif., Houston, and Boston. The company has 125 employees.

What can you actually learn from this press release?

- Basic directory data—Company address, phone number, Web URL, CEO name, location, number of employees, office locations
- Basic CEO biographical data
- Name and contact information of PR person
- Company is involved in the knowledge management software field
- New product will have more features than the previous version
- Sales are apparently growing quickly

The unverifiable claims in the press release would best be ignored.

Of course there are examples of totally fabricated press releases, so be wary. In August 2000, a fictitious press release was sent out on Internet Wire (a Web newswire) that falsely reported, among other things, that the firm Emulex was being investigated by the SEC, its earnings were to be restated, and its CEO had resigned. The news went around the Internet and was eventually picked up and posted on several major business news outlets, including CBS Market Watch, Bloomberg, and CNBC. This fake press release caused Emulex to temporarily lose more than $2 billion in market value, and caused individual traders to lose money when they sold their shares at a price lower than the stock's true value. In this case, the business wires were fooled because the information had come to them from a known, legitimate source—Internet Wire. But the fake release was written and posted by a former employee (who created the

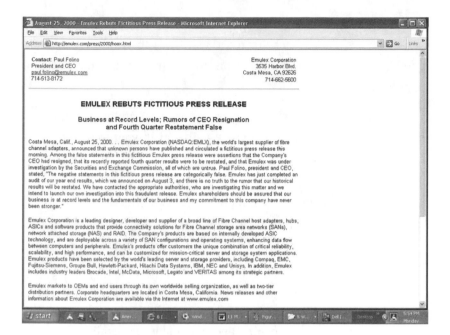

Figure 5.3 *Emulex's rebuttal of the fictitious press release*

bogus release to try to make a financial gain) who knew how to get Internet Wire to pick up and distribute a press release. So this information, though false, was coming from a "known source" and presumed to be true by the recipients. While Emulex issued a prompt rebuttal, the damage had already been done (see Figure 5.3).

As a business researcher, what can you do to protect yourself from falling prey to bad data? The Emulex hoax was an especially harmful one—to the firm, certainly, but also to researchers—since the bogus press release was accepted as a legitimate company announcement and circulated on the Web as well as by reputable business sources like Bloomberg. One of the best ways to protect yourself is to rely on sources whose brand and reputation you trust. However, as this case illustrates, even such trusted sources can be led astray. It serves as a reminder that you should never let your guard down completely. Always question the credibility of information.

Suspicious Company Data—When reviewing any type of company-supplied data, watch for red flags. Does the information seem odd? Does it seem incomplete? Does the writing sound amateurish or unpolished?

If the answer to any of these questions is "yes" and you plan to utilize the information in a significant way, you'll want to take the following action steps to further check the data:

1. Get on the phone and confirm the data directly with a company spokesperson. If it's a larger firm, try public relations, the press office, investor relations, or corporate communications. A small company's spokesperson could be the CEO, marketing director, or human resources manager. A human source such as this is your best bet. Be sure you know with whom you are speaking and document the details.

2. Find a reliable secondary source to confirm the information.

3. Go to the company's Web site and see if the information is posted there.

4. Ask a knowledgeable person within your own organization to review and comment on the information.

For information on recognizing and dealing with Web hoaxes and misinformation, I recommend Anne Mintz's *Web of Deception: Misinformation on the Internet* (CyberAge Books, 2002).

Financial Results—It has generally been accepted that if a company is privately held you need to be skeptical in regard to its financial figures, since such firms are under no legal obligation to provide numbers to the SEC. Conversely, it has been largely accepted that you can rely on financials taken from documents filed by public firms, because the law demands accurate accounting from these companies. Of course, revelations about accounting practices at firms like Enron, WorldCom, and Adelphia have shown that even public companies' financials can't always be trusted.

Business researchers often need an accurate assessment of how a company is performing. So how can you *really* measure a company's performance?

Nell Minow is founder and owner of The Corporate Library, an information clearinghouse and Web site that focuses on corporate governance. She says that researchers can use indicators other than reported earnings to understand a company's capabilities and performance. Specifically, she advises using the following types of sources:

1. **Credit Reports**—Minow points out that, unlike earnings data, a company really can't fudge its credit report. It's created by another entity altogether and relies on data provided by other companies.

2. **Composition of the Board of Directors' Audit Committee**—The composition of a company's board of directors (particularly the board's audit committee) is one of the very first things Minow says she scrutinizes as a way to determine the reliability and quality of its numbers. Minow says there are companies that have family members and sports superstars sitting on the board who know little or nothing about U.S. financial reporting practices and requirements.

3. **The *Wall Street Journal*—**Minow says that because the *WSJ* assigns a beat reporter to cover individual companies, its articles contain a great deal of knowledgeable, trustworthy insight about those firms' performance and outlook.

Another good indicator of a company's true financial health is cash flow, since this data is also difficult to fudge. Other analysts suggest examining "softer" indicators of a company's health and outlook, such as employee satisfaction, customer loyalty, inventory levels, or whatever metric is critical for firms within a particular industry.

Standard and Poor's (S&P) has developed its own approach to solving the problem of unreliable earnings data. The company believes that earnings should remain a legitimate performance indicator, but the definition of "earnings" needs to be refined. S&P has introduced its own measurement, called "core earnings." According to S&P, its core earnings measurement changes the composition of earnings by treating stock options as regular compensation, excluding pension gains, including restructuring charges from ongoing operations, excluding gains and losses from asset sales, and by other adjustments.

These rules are currently *not* the standard in corporate financial reporting which, in fact, is cause of much of the criticism of how companies currently calculate their earnings.

Whether or not S&P's new methodology will become a standard with official corporate financial bodies like the SEC or the Financial Accounting Standards Board (FASB) is still an open question. To date, the two institutions have not embraced it, though the issue of expensing of stock options has been examined by the FASB. (For more information on S&P's core earnings initiative, see the Web site listed on page 252 in Appendix B.)

Annual Reports—Many companies are now posting their annual reports in Adobe PDF format on their Web sites. As business researchers know, these reports provide a wealth of useful information on a company. This is a boon to the researcher, but be aware that sometimes a company will post only a portion of its report online— and those sections may include only the most positive information. Furthermore, if an annual report on the Web does not include the footnotes, you'll be missing those all-important qualifiers that often provide the most revealing details.

Data Disclosed on the Web—Because company financial news typically is disseminated in the form of a press release, there's always the potential for hoaxes and misinformation. However, because of the SEC's Regulation FD, companies are moving to disclose more on their Web sites. In fact, one Web site called LeFile, which is devoted to best practices in corporate Web site communication, has been pushing for

the SEC to allow companies to make their Web sites the *primary* disclosure medium. As this trend continues, company home pages can
increasingly be used to verify suspicious data you've come across.

You can also use the Web to tap into company announcements
live as they happen—getting the word right from the horse's mouth,
so to speak. Some company sites announce when they are planning
a Webcast, and there are several third-party sites—Webcasters—
that aggregate official company Webcasts. These include BestCalls
and CCBN.

Not all Webcasters are alike, though. If you're going to use one to
keep track of company announcements and calls over the Web you
should know how they differ. When considering a Webcaster, try to
get answers to the following important questions:

1. How long has the Webcaster been broadcasting company
   events?

2. How many companies are covered?

3. What types of events are covered?

4. How timely are the broadcasts? Are they in real time? If
   not, how long is the delay?

5. Do you need to listen to the entire broadcast or can you
   zero in on specific short segments?

6. Are written transcripts made available?

7. Is there a searchable archive?

Other sources where you can go to confirm company financials are
the various public-disclosure sites such as EDGAR and the EDGAR
spin-offs. These are official sites and you can be sure that they are
getting the information directly from the official SEC EDGAR site.

**Organizational Structure, Market Focus, Share, Strategy, and
Other Information**—Besides press releases and financials, companies provide a great deal of "softer" information about themselves
on their Web sites, such as history, mission, organization, corporate

focus, and so forth. Before the Web, most of this information was found primarily in the annual report. Today, it's also found—and often in greatly expanded form—on company Web sites.

Typically, you'll find such detailed information under "About Us" or "Investor Information," both of which are normally accessible from the company's home page.

How much stock should you put in this information? Purely factual data is certainly more believable than anything that can be categorized as opinion. Factual data would include the following statements:

- Our company was founded in 1976.
- Our CEO previously worked for company XYZ, and then moved on to ZYX.
- We employ 250 people in six offices worldwide and are headquartered in New York.
- We merged in 1988 with ABC and changed our name to XYZ.
- We began our business as a publisher of aviation trade journals.
- Today we have 25 divisions that serve 13 industries in 15 countries.

These types of statements can pretty well be taken at face value. But you need to be more careful with opinion-type statements. These are often claims that herald a product breakthrough or rave about a product's supposed capabilities. They may also be self-aggrandizing statements about the firm itself. Examples might include:

- Our line of do-it-yourself plaque-removal kits is one of the most respected in the industry.
- Our revolutionary new copiers provide an unprecedented ease of use for equipment operators.
- These features provide unsurpassed capabilities.
- We at Zinkers, Ltd. are dedicated to continual quality improvement.
- Companies that implement our new knowledge-management software see an immediate increase in efficiency.

Your best bet is either to disregard such unverifiable, opinion-based claims or to confirm them with neutral third parties.

There is also a gray area: statements that are purportedly fact-based, but need additional verification. This information might relate to market share and growth, both of which may be subject to some exaggeration or manipulation. The following are a few examples:

- Our company continues to maintain its position as the world's largest supplier of pizza boxes.
- Our market share has grown 20 percent per year for the last 5 years.
- Of those who use our product, 88 percent said they would buy from us again.

In these situations, you'll want to track down the original source data so you can check it for yourself, see the full context, and make your own judgments. Or you might want to do some independent research to see if there's other data that confirms or contradicts these statements.

The Web hasn't created all the puffery and exaggeration—this has existed since the dawn of commercial enterprise. What the Web *has* done is provide us with more of everything: more good, useful information as well as more questionable data. The net result is positive for business researchers, since so much potentially valuable information is available. The key is to know how to read and analyze the opinions and claims you encounter, work with the reliable information, and dismiss the less credible. If you can do that, you should wind up with company information you can use.

Market Research Reports and Data

At some point, most business researchers need to find market data or conduct market research. While definitions of market research (or "marketing research," as it's sometimes called) vary, it's designed to help a company learn about an industry or opportunity, enter a new market, or expand its capabilities. A more detailed definition can be found in my book, *Finding Market Research on the Web* (Market Research.com, 2001). Market research can encompass research of the following (excerpted from page 16 of *Finding Market Research on the Web*):

- Buyers in a specific market (demographic characteristics, behaviors, opinions, habits)

- Industry supplying the market (statistics on size, structure, growth, trends, distribution, outlets)
- Regional demand (country/regional demographics, economic trends, establishments, business climate)
- Key products found in the market (by category, shipments, production, sales trends, market share, product leaders)
- Regulatory environment (laws, regulations, business practices, social mores that constrain the market)
- Company research (company names, rankings, profiles, competitive strengths and weaknesses, market shares, strategies, etc.)

While this kind of information can be found here and there throughout the Web, the most commonly sought-after source that pulls together much of this detailed market data for selected markets or industries is the prepackaged (or "off the shelf") company and industry research report. These are detailed reports published by market research firms and investment brokerage houses.

Technically speaking, there are actually two different types of off-the-shelf reports. There are those published by market research firms, simply called "market research reports," and there are those written by Wall Street investment firms, which are usually called "investment research" or "brokerage research reports." Both types of report contain detailed data and analyses on companies, industries, and markets, and both are of interest to those doing market research.

Another way these research reports vary is that some focus on a specific company (typically called "company reports") while others focus on a particular industry or market.

Although the contents of each report varies, the following are some elements you'd typically expect to find:

- Key measurements of the industry (size, growth, trends, etc.)
- Forecasts of industry and specific sector growth
- In-depth profiles of key companies/competitors, including their sales, financials, history, key executives, and strategy
- Quantitative breakdown of company sales, sometimes by product line and segment
- Profiles of consumer groups and demographic breakdowns

- Leading products and market-share data
- Analysis of outside forces that might affect market growth
- Quantitative data on consumer buying, based on surveys or direct measurements (such as by supermarket scanners, shipment data, etc.)
- Analyst views and insights of key companies' strengths/weaknesses
- Analyst views of future market potential
- Analysis of likely impact of new government regulations
- Analysis of international market and competition (export/import possibilities, global market potential, etc.)

Market reports are generally a pricey information source. Typically, they cost anywhere from a low of about $500 to well over $10,000. A common price tag is in the low four figures.

There are several reasons why business researchers find market reports particularly valuable. One is the expert analysis by an author or analyst who has studied the market and key companies closely over a period of time. Another is the amount of quantitative data supplied, which may be finely segmented and difficult to find at that level of detail from other business sources. Also, though these are considered expensive business information sources, buying an off-the-shelf market research report is still far less expensive than conducting your own custom market research study.

Business researchers also like these reports because many online vendors and Web aggregators allow the purchase of a single page or other portion of the text. Thus, if you are looking for a certain piece of company data or a specific element of market information, it can often be obtained without having to purchase the entire report.

Where on the Web?

Before the Web, off-the-shelf market reports were available online via professional online services like Dialog, LexisNexis, and Dow Jones. But the Web has proven itself a boon to business researchers by making such reports available, and from more publishers. It has made them easier to find, reduced their costs, and led to improvements in search interfaces and design. It has also brought about free viewing of tables of contents and executive summaries, which has now become the norm.

Today there are several leading Web aggregators that provide access to thousands of market research and investment research reports. These providers can be broken down into two groups. One group includes those that were "born on the Web" and requires no up-front paid subscription fees. The second group is comprised of traditional online information services that preceded the Web, but have since migrated to it.

BORN ON THE WEB

- MindBranch
- MarketResearch.com
- Reuters Research On-Demand
- Thomson Research
- Research and Markets

TRADITIONAL ONLINE SERVICES THAT MIGRATED TO THE WEB

- Dialog (MarketFull)
- Profound (ResearchLine)
- LexisNexis

It should be noted that these aggregators aren't the only places where market research reports can be found on the Web. There are industry-specific sites that aggregate reports within their respective fields. Also, some individual market research publishers have their own Web sites, through which you can search for and purchase reports directly.

Basic Credibility Issues

As you might suspect, concerns about how to adequately assess the overall credibility and value of an off-the-shelf market research report precede the Web. The problem has always been that purchasing one of these reports (or even buying just a small slice of one) is like getting a "black box"—you don't know what you've got until you see what's inside. It's rather tough to pin down precisely what makes for a quality report, since so much of it is intangible and subject to the abilities of the people who prepare them.

That said, there are some rules of thumb for making judgments about these reports. Following are the key issues to consider before buying an off-the-shelf market research report. Some may require you to review portions of the report in advance of purchase.

CREDIBILITY OF COMPANY

- How experienced is the company in covering this particular market and/or industry?
- Who is the primary analyst? What has he or she previously written on this market or industry?
- Does the firm use in-house analysts and writers, or does it employ freelancers?

DATA SOURCING AND METHODOLOGIES EMPLOYED

- What is the source of the numerical data provided?
- How was any quantitative data collected? (through interviews, phone calls, or mail surveys?) If a questionnaire was employed, you should ask to review it.
- What is the size of the sample of any surveys used? What was the methodology?

ACTUAL DATA PROVIDED

- To what level is the data broken down?
- Besides quantitative data (which is always sought after and important), is textual data also provided? You must be able to get some context for the data as well as commentary about the information that's provided.

CUSTOMER SERVICE CAPABILITIES

- After buying the report, can a buyer speak to the analyst and ask questions?

TIMELINESS

- When was the report completed? Keep in mind that several months to well over a year can elapse from the time a report is commissioned to when it's finally published. If you're studying a fast-moving industry, be sure to take this time lag into account.

POTENTIAL BIASES

- Does the report seem to contain a lot of hype and excitement about an "exploding" market? Be very careful about this, since most research firms have a built-in bias about looking to a fast growing market. Such hype can drive more sales of a report, since companies naturally have a greater interest in learning about an expanding field.

Steve Heffner is an acquisitions editor for Kalorama, Inc., a New York-based life sciences market research publisher (and a division of MarketResearch.com). He advises buyers to consider the following factors when making an evaluation:

- Is the scope and methodology clearly laid out at the beginning of the report? This is critical. A report that does not do it well, or at all, is suspect.
- Is most of the data primary research, or secondary? There's nothing necessarily wrong with secondary data, but if there's a lot of it, it may create the problem identified in the next item.
- Is data used from many different sources? Heffner says this can cause major difficulties since different sources will use varying market definitions, different assumptions, and various methodologies. An analyst who tries to combine multiple approaches can end up with a hodgepodge of data and ultimately invalid results and analyses.
- How much of the data is supplied by the companies themselves? If it's a great deal, be careful: Company-supplied data may be overly optimistic and numbers could be inflated in an attempt to influence the market.
- When viewing a forecast (which is simply an educated guess), be wary of one that takes a current trend and simply projects it into the future in a linear fashion. This might mean the analyst has not looked at more subtle factors that can impact current

trends, such as the emergence of new competitors, new technologies, or possible government regulations.

Another newer issue surrounding trustworthiness has surfaced, related mainly to investment analyst research reports. In recent years, certain Wall Street research firms and individual analysts have been caught up in the widespread corporate financial scandals. Several have been accused of writing glowing, yet clearly undeserved recommendations for companies with existing business relationships to their investment firms.

In a high-profile case, Merrill Lynch agreed to pay a $100 million fine after admitting that its research analysts were unduly influenced to write positive analyses of companies that they were supposed to be covering objectively. This wasn't necessarily done because of existing (and clearly conflicting) business relationships: There were also reports of individual Wall Street analysts providing positive analyses of Internet and telecommunications companies in which they held stock.

So where does the Web fit in to all this? As mentioned earlier, the Web has been great for market research buyers. It has opened the pipeline for more reports from more niche publishers, and has even helped to bring down prices. Steve Heffner does note that there's a flip side in that the Web has increased the amount of competition among market research report publishers. It may be causing some—even certain large, established publishers—to cut corners and reduce the time and investment in their reports, thereby reducing their overall quality.

By being a smart comparison shopper, you can take advantage of the increased level of competition among market research report aggregators on the Web. The following section includes the features and capabilities you should look for to ensure you're using the provider that's giving you the most for your money and providing the best market research report services.

Clues to Report Relevancy

One of the problems in locating the right market research report online is the difficulty in determining ahead of time whether it will contain the information you need. Sometimes you don't discover until after you've purchased a report (or a section of one) that what you thought would be inside isn't there at all.

One provider does include a feature, at no extra cost, that can be of help here. The report aggregator MarketResearch.com informs you of the number of times your keywords appear on various pages in the initial listing of returned reports. This can be very useful for getting a sense of how relevant the report may be for you. Figure 5.4 demonstrates MarketResearch.com's "Search Inside This Report" feature that provides this function. (Note that it's necessary to register with MarketResearch.com in order to utilize this feature.)

You should have the option of viewing, at no cost, a table of contents and executive summary of the report you're considering. Often the executive summary provides valuable top line market statistics and other summary data of real use to business researchers. If the provider doesn't offer this service, find one that does.

In some cases, you should consider contacting the aggregator or publisher to ensure that a report will contain the data you need. For instance, Heffner advises buyers who are unsure of the usefulness of a particular table to ask an aggregator for assistance in getting a copy of the page, which will have the actual numerical data blocked out from the publisher. Having this can be very helpful because the column and row headings should indicate whether the information the potential buyer needs will be included in the table. Heffner says many publishers will provide such samples in order to make a sale.

Because it's so difficult to gauge the quality of a particular market research report, such reports would seem to be ideal candidates for Web-based reviews. Amazon.com, in fact, does include a section called "ebooks and edocs" in its "Books" section. A subsection here called "Research Reports" sells market research studies from well-known market research and business information providers like D&B and The Gartner Group. And, as with Amazon's books, electronics, and other products, buyers of market research reports can rate them

Figure 5.4 *MarketResearch.com's "Search Inside This Report" helps users identify which pages of a report are likely to be most relevant.*

on the site. Unfortunately, since relatively few buyers get their market research reports from Amazon, only a small percentage of the listed reports include user reviews. Those that do typically contain only a single reviewer's comments. Unfortunately, there is no "consumer reports"-like rating service that evaluates, reviews, or ranks market research reports. To get feedback from other buyers, though, on a report you are considering purchasing, you might try going to an online discussion group or Web forum where there is an audience of likely buyers, and ask the group if anyone has purchased the report, or used reports from the publisher, and what their opinions were. For example, if you're thinking of buying a report that covers an issue in the Information Technology (IT) industry, a discussion forum of IT professionals can be found at the TechRepublic IT portal. (To locate an Internet discussion group relevant to your interest area, you can either just browse through the Google Groups or Yahoo! Groups site, or search a directory site like Tile.Net or CataList.)

Investment Research Reports

As mentioned earlier, reports issued by investment firms are a separate type of research report. Designed for investors, these typically emphasize analysis of companies including their financials, competitiveness, market position, and management structure, but also include some information that is not of great interest to business researchers, such as buy/sell/hold stock recommendations. Still, because investment research reports include nitty-gritty company and industry analyses and consumer/demographic data, they can be of great value to business researchers. Many reports can be purchased through the online services and aggregators as listed in the section of Market Research Reports and Data. Also check out Reuters, an aggregator that focuses specifically on the distribution of investment research reports.

Most of the guidelines provided to help you evaluate pure market research reports will also apply to investment research reports. But an additional consideration when using these reports revolves around the question of credibility. As noted earlier, some well-known firms and specific analysts have been accused of writing biased recommendations about certain companies. This bias usually takes the form of an overly optimistic forecast when an analyst recommends a stock in which he or she has some interest. While business researchers typically are not too concerned about stock-picking when doing market research, it is wise to steer away from reports produced by any firm that has a problem with credibility and objectivity. Note: To prevent future abuses and as a result of the suit against Merrill Lynch, that company and others like Credit Suisse First Boston, Inc. and Salomon Smith Barney, Inc. have revamped how their analysts are compensated and how they interact with other parts of the company.

So how can you avoid potentially biased investment data? If you already use reports from an institution you've come to trust or you prefer reading the work of a particular analyst, you might just stick with those known entities. On the Web, it's especially important to stick with those sources you can trust.

Of course, it's not likely that you'll be able to obtain *all* of your reports from a company that you're already familiar with. Still, given the aforementioned biases of many of these investment firms and analysts, if you plan to purchase a report from an investment firm with which you haven't dealt before, you might want to obtain your analyses from completely independent firms. Companies such as Value Line or Morningstar have no other relationship with the firms they cover—they simply write analyses. It should be mentioned that the biggest dangers in relying on the biased reports were related to their buy/sell/hold recommendations, and not the basic factual company data such as its balance sheet, executive profiles, market shares, and other information not related to buying or selling stock in the firm.

There are a few places you can check for the results of surveys that rate and rank various analyst firms. These can be useful guidelines to determine which studies to purchase. *Information Week* conducts regular surveys that measure user satisfaction of analyst firms' research, and *Institutional Investor* magazine releases an annual list of its choices for top individual analysts and analyst firms. Investars is another site that ranks brokerage firms' performance, and has a special focus on independent research firms.

What about white papers? A white paper is a treatment and discussion of some problem or issue, and in the business arena, they are typically written by vendors, particularly information technology vendors, to describe how its product or service can help solve some business problem. White papers have become very common on the Web, as more IT and other firms see writing them as a way to establish credibility in their industry, and promote their products as a business solution.

Because these white papers are created by vendors, whose primary goal is to promote themselves and position their own products, they obviously cannot be seen as a neutral, objective source. You need to be particularly skeptical about the particular business problem that the vendor has identified that needs solving (since the vendor may have a solution that is in search of a problem), and of course be skeptical about whatever claims are in the white paper regarding the particular product.

White papers can still provide some useful data for business researchers such as an overview of the industry, industry statistics, and the names of key players and competitors. If you are actually researching the company itself, the white paper can provide good information on how the firm is positioning itself in the market, as well as provide detailed product specifications and details not available from other sources.

If you do choose to use a white paper for industry information, market statistics, consumer demand, and so on, be sure that the origin of that information is properly sourced so you can confirm it yourself.

To find white papers you can either simply use a search engine and enter your topic along with "white paper" to see what turns up, or you can go to one of the various leading white paper portal sites that focus on aggregating white papers from vendors. Leading portals include BitPipe, TechRepublic, and ITPapers for the IT industry, and BNET for broader business white papers.

Finding and Evaluating Discrete Market Data on the Web

So far, I've discussed how to evaluate market research that comes prepackaged in a report created by a known research publisher and that's accessed through a known aggregator. But how do you evaluate market data that you turn up in a search on the open Web? After all, while it can be a tricky endeavor, you *can* find market data on the Web.

Evaluating the reliability of what you find in your open-Web searches will depend largely on the nature of the specific source. Market research sources on the open Web can include all of the following:

- Vendor sites
- Online media sites
- Newsgroup postings
- Press releases
- Home pages of market research publishers
- Reference sites
- Consultant sites
- Industry portals

Some of these sources—such as company home pages, press releases, online media, and newsgroup postings—are important

Figure 5.5   *Inputting keywords and phrases commonly associated with market research like "units shipped" and "forecast" helps create a more focused market search.*

enough to have been given a separate treatment in this book. When doing market research, you can apply the strategies outlined for evaluating the reliability of those sources.

You can also improve the quality of your market research by being careful in your initial search. Follow the Google-search guidelines in Chapter 3, and when you get to the step of creating a search statement, consider a specific strategy for finding market research data.

I'd advise that you employ specific words and phrases in your search statement that are regularly found in the context of a market research discussion. Such keywords and phrases might include, for instance, units shipped, forecast, market share, shipments, projected, and outlook (see Figure 5.5).

The idea is to use one or more of these terms in your search along with your specific industry/company. For example, if you wanted to find market research data on the outlook for cable modems you might enter the following in Google:

"cable modems" outlook forecast

Naturally, you'll need to experiment a bit with these or other terms, but doing this will help Google retrieve pages that are more likely to be market research related. Try to avoid using common words like "sales" or "trends," because they're frequently used in other contexts.

Another term worth adding to your search statement is "white paper," as these reports are typically free but often contain detailed data and analyses of a given subject. You might also try the phrase "press release" to uncover press releases that excerpt some top-line data from a recently published market research report.

Similarly, if there are certain trustworthy research publishers that regularly cover the field you're researching, append their names to your search statement. This way, you might find reports that they have published, excerpts from a report that's quoted in a trade magazine article, a Web site that quotes from the report, that publisher's press release, a conference presentation, or other forum.

In addition, if there are experts in the industry whom you respect, and these individuals are sometimes quoted by name, try appending that person's name to your search string as well. Doing so can serve as a qualifier to filter your search to return only those Web pages that include that person's name.

Company Directories

One of the most common forms of business research is simply looking up facts about a company. Business researchers were doing this for years before the Web by scanning popular print directories (such as D&B's Million Dollar Directory or S&P Register), and eventually by searching company directories on the fee-based online services. Directories provide a wide range of company information, including address, phone numbers, number of employees, sales, earnings, detailed financials, history, executive bios, and more.

Today there are many company directories available for free on the Web. Probably the best-known company directory on the Web is Hoover's, based in Austin, Texas. Hoover's began as a publisher of inexpensive print directories (called Hoover's Handbooks), and eventually migrated its products to the Web (see Figure 5.6). (Note that although Hoover's makes some company information available for free, more in-depth reports are only available to paid subscribers.) Other popular company directories that are free and available on the Web include D&B Small Business Services, Kompass, Yahoo! Finance, Thomas Register, and Corporate Information, a site owned by Wright Investors' Service.

The primary factor in evaluating the quality of company directory sites is to determine how they differ, since there *are* significant differences. Examples of these differences include the kinds of sources used, the number and type of companies covered, and the level of detail provided on each. Specifically, you should ask the following questions:

- **What is the source of the data?** Does the data come from the company itself? Does it come only from public filings? Are many secondary sources used, such as trade publications, phone books, and news stories? Is some data estimated by a

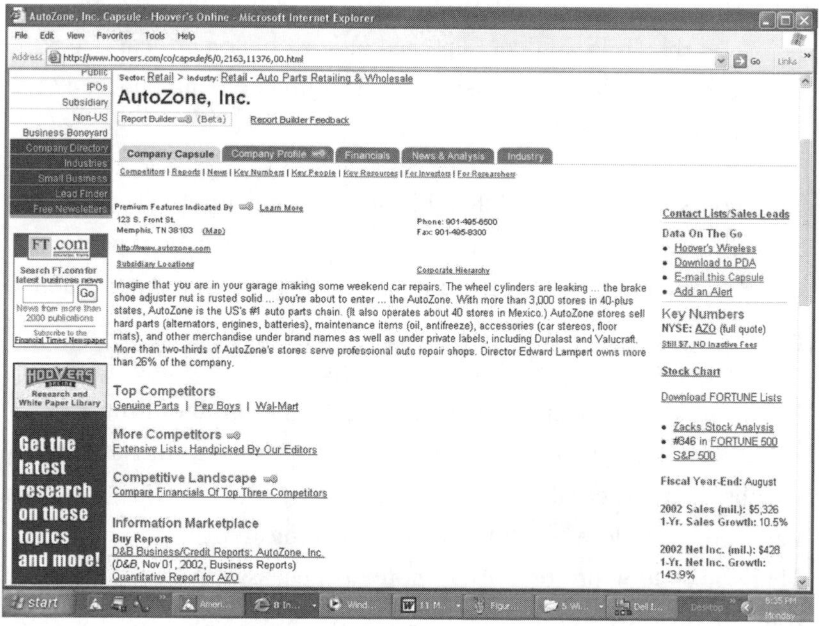

Figure 5.6 *A search on Hoover's will retrieve a good amount of detail on a company at no charge.*

formula created by the directory publisher, or is it all hard and verifiable?

- **What kinds of companies are covered?** Are they in the U.S. only? North America? Global? Public companies only or also private? Large firms and small firms? What is the cut-off if based on size?

- **What information is provided on the listed companies?** Directories vary not only in provided information, but also in how complete its listings are for the companies it does cover. For example, a publisher might claim that a directory includes earnings information on companies, but then you may discover that this is only true of the larger public U.S. firms. Or it may say that the number of employees is included in the directory records, when in fact such data is spotty and available only for a small percentage of all listed companies.

- **How often is the data updated?** Each company's record should be reviewed and updated at least once per year. Does each listing indicate when it was last updated and checked? If not, it should be!

Of course, keep in mind that this discussion is limited to free company directory sites on the Web: We can't necessarily expect these sites to embody or present any kind of gold standard when it comes to comprehensiveness and quality. The best company directory data is still available from the fee-based services and databases. (For example, Hoover's offers more information about the companies it covers, and more advanced search options, to those who pay to subscribe to its Hoover's Pro service.) Still, with free sites, you have nothing to lose (except time) by checking more than one to find what you're looking for. Furthermore, as necessary you should see if you can verify the information you've found on one site with information from another. (For a list of free company directory Web sites, see Appendix B, page 254.)

A good company directory will have the following characteristics:

- Explains where the information comes from
- Covers as many companies as possible (public and private, U.S. and international, large and small)
- Offers advanced search functions, including Boolean searching and the ability to screen and filter your search by various criteria (geographic location, size, etc.)
- Includes, along with contact data, some historical, financial, and organizational information
- Updates its listings regularly and—importantly—indicates when updates were last completed

Other Sources

Along with the sources we've already covered, the Web has made it easier to find reports, news, and analyses from a wide range of organizations such as chambers of commerce, associations, and think tanks. While these can be excellent sources of research, white papers, and reports, you have to be particularly careful to determine the agenda and purpose of each organization.

Chambers of Commerce

Chambers of commerce have always been useful for learning about smaller companies located in a particular region, industries with a large presence in that area, and characteristics and statistics about the town or city. It seems that virtually all chambers of commerce today have their own Web sites, and often provide good quality, free data. To locate a particular chamber, you can simply plug the name of the town and "chamber of commerce" into a search engine, or search an online directory such as the World Chamber of Commerce Directory.

Each chamber of commerce, of course, has a very specific mission: to improve the image of the town or city and attract more business. They typically include recent news and developments that paint the town and local businesses (particularly those that are members) in the best possible light. So, be aware of the potential for bias.

Associations and Think Tanks

Associations and think tanks can be excellent sources for business researchers. An association's Web site usually provides statistics and analyses, and may have additional resources such as its own online publication, excerpts from conference presentations, and other back-up data. The Web has made it easier than ever to tap into associations, as there are searchable free directories that make it simple to look up and link to one. You need to be cautious, however. It's important to find out who is on the board, and what its overall mission is. Don't assume that a neutral-sounding name means that the organization has no ideological or political purpose.

In addition, the Web can make a small two-person "association" with a $2,000 budget look as important and prominent as one with 10,000 members and a $10 million budget. If you're not sure whether a particular association you've located on the Web is significant, I'd recommend you take a trip to your nearest library and check *The Encyclopedia of Associations*, published by Gale Research. This guide identifies legitimate associations and provides relevant details about each, including year founded, a synopsis of its mission, and other useful data.

Think tanks can be another excellent resource for in-depth reports and analyses, usually on some social issue or public policy matter. The tricky part is not just finding them, but understanding their mission and political leanings. There are conservative and liberal think tanks, as well as those devoted to specific causes. To find out about particular think tanks, you can first read a general description by consulting a Web directory like NIRA's World Directory of Think Tanks (which is freely searchable on the Web). You should then determine the think tank's mission and goals by studying its Web site. Consider the affiliations of those on the board. Browse past papers or press releases to detect a consistent political or ideological point of view.

For more on evaluating who or what is behind any site, be sure to read Chapter 4: What to Do With Questionable Sites.

CHAPTER 6

Statistics, Polls, and Surveys

Statistical Data

All business researchers need statistical data of some kind. Whether it's statistics that measure market size or share, data that measures industries or company performance, economic trends, or population and demographic information, numbers are to business as sunshine is to plants.

There are just as many ways that businesses use statistical data as there are types of statistics. Companies need statistics to decide whether to enter a market, detect emerging trends in its current market, understand broad industry trends, spot competitors, understand the current economy, identify emerging overseas markets, discern consumer buying habits and trends, break down the market into niches, help create internal forecasts, select new retail location sites, and more.

Business statistics cover a huge area. The following are among the most commonly sought-after business statistics:

- **Marketing statistics**—Market size, market share, market growth, marketing segments
- **Industry statistics**—Industry size, shipments, trends, geographic breakdowns
- **Company statistics**—Sales, revenue, balance sheet, earnings, growth, ratios, valuation
- **International statistics**—Worldwide markets, imports/exports, demand, trends

- **Economic statistics**—Overall economy (GDP), inflation/ unemployment, manufacturers' shipments, retail sales, consumer purchasing, housing starts
- **Product statistics**—Product sales, growth, trends, imports/exports
- **Social/demographic statistics**—Population trends, ethnic breakdowns, health and welfare indicators
- **Consumer surveys and polls**—Buying habits, consumer preferences, opinion surveys

This section discusses issues surrounding the quality of the business statistics you'll find on the Web, especially those from the government. Note, though, that this book cannot serve as a complete primer for how to use and evaluate business statistics; that's another book entirely. In fact, I can recommend two other CyberAge Books that are all about finding and using statistics, both written by information expert Paula Berinstein. One is *Finding Statistics Online* and the other is *Business Statistics on the Web*.

U.S. Government Statistics

The U.S. government is actually the largest publisher in the world, and a great deal of its published information consists of statistical data. Whether it is demographic or social indicators from the U.S. Bureau of the Census or international market data from the U.S. Department of Commerce, the federal government is an enormous supplier of numerical data. Much of the government's information is made available from its central clearinghouse, the Government Printing Office (GPO), though an enormous amount is also made available directly from the individual issuing departments and agencies.

Increasingly, the federal government has embraced the Internet as the most cost-effective and comprehensive way to disseminate its information. It has transferred a great deal of its print, CD-ROM, microfilm, and other media to the Web. More and more, those who wish to locate and search for government data are turning to the Web. You can go to one of the clearinghouses established by the government, or to a particular agency's Web site.

Businesses use statistical data from the U.S. government for countless applications. For instance, financial professionals may rely on the U.S. Department of Commerce's Bureau of Economic Analysis forecasts to align their own industry and company's budgets and forecasts. Companies use the U.S. Census population breakdowns by variables like age, ethnicity, and income for target marketing and for new retail store site selection. Export and import data collected and analyzed by the U.S. International Trade Administration can be used to assess international competition or find new, untapped markets overseas. And whether it's air travel statistics from the Department of Transportation or water usage trends from the EPA, there is a seemingly endless amount of discrete data that can be put to use by all researchers.

Perhaps the most commonly used statistical agencies for business purposes are the U.S. Bureau of the Census, which produces mountains of social and demographic data, and the U.S. Department of Commerce, which generates the lion's share of business-oriented statistics. However, all of the individual government agencies—from the Department of Agriculture and the FCC to NASA and the Department of the Treasury—churn out reams of their own statistical data on the seemingly infinite number of topics and subtopics that fall within their realms (see Figure 6.1).

Where on the Web?

Because of the huge amount of government statistical data that is generated, and the number of agencies involved, locating just the information you need can be a tremendous challenge.

Appendix B lists a selection of some of the best federal government sites for locating statistics. However, there is one particularly excellent statistics clearinghouse, FedStats (see Figure 6.2), which is created by the government and serves as a single gateway to data produced by over 100 federal agencies. On FedStats you can find the statistics you need by browsing an alphabetical index on topics, a list of the federal government's major statistical program areas, or the names of specific

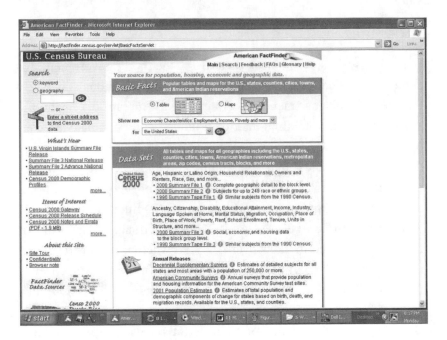

Figure 6.1 *Bureau of Census American Fact Finder*

agencies to find their statistical sources. You can also conduct a keyword search of 70 statistical agencies directly from the site.

Quality/Credibility Issues

The U.S. government has traditionally been seen as an authoritative, reliable source of high-quality information. For example, the *Statistical Abstract of the United States*, a single compilation of key statistical data gathered by all the federal agencies, has long been considered the bible of statistics. It includes not only authoritative data but a full description of the various methodologies used by the various agencies to gather data.

Each individual statistical agency has data-quality guidelines that its information must comply with, and the agencies are staffed with professionals who are scrupulous about the integrity of their data. Determining the factors that underlie reliable statistics is a technical area that statisticians and experts are continually refining. For those who want to learn how the federal government's statistical agencies

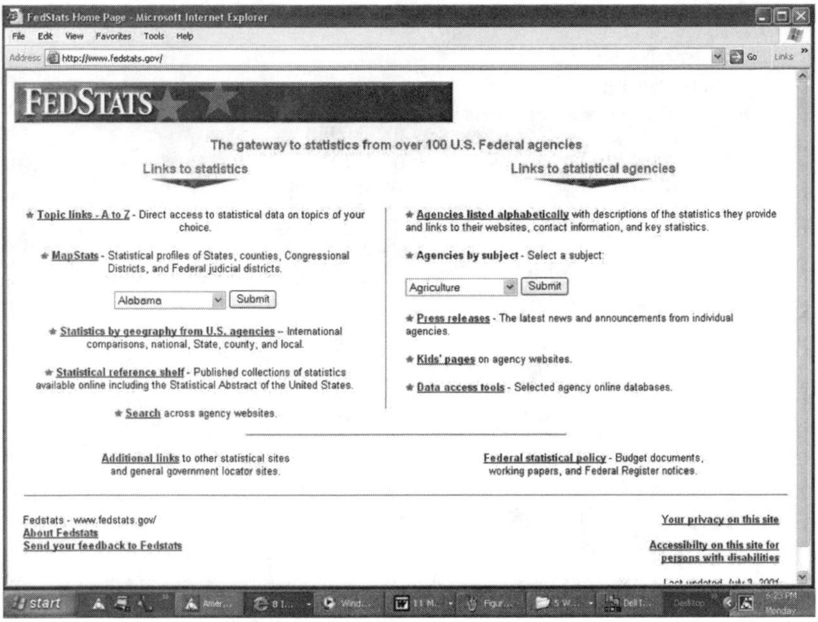

Figure 6.2 FEDSTATS Home Page

operate, I would highly recommend reviewing the latest annual edition of *Statistical Programs of the United States Government*, available from the Office of Management and Budget.

Canada's federal government is another respected source of quality statistics on data about its own country. Statistics Canada (see Figure 6.3) has put together a very useful, concise definition of what makes for "quality" in statistical information. See Appendix B for information on how to download a PDF of Statistics Canada publication: Statistics Canada's Quality 2002 Assurance Framework (Catalog #12-586-XIE). See in particular the section called "Statcan: The Elements of Quality."

Web Concerns

Although the creation of reliable statistics is a mathematical and statistical endeavor that is not inherently related to the Web, and though official governmental statistics are generally considered to be of high quality and authoritative, there are some specific issues to keep in mind when accessing statistical data on the Web. Some are

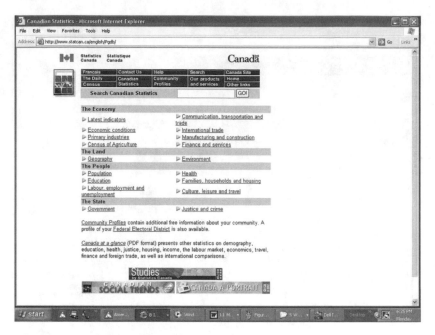

Figure 6.3 Statistics Canada

older concerns and others have been raised more recently. The following are some potential problems to consider when accessing federal statistics on the Web.

TIMELINESS/CURRENCY

One long-standing concern surrounding a wide range of government data, including statistics that precede the Web, is timeliness. When using government data, you need to check for a date. Sometimes many years elapse between certain statistical series, and the "latest" data available may be several years old. For example, the Economic Censuses are conducted once every five years, and it can take quite a while for the most recent of this data to be compiled and disseminated.

On the Web you especially need to check dates when you find some government data via a search engine. It's always possible that your search has retrieved an older page with outdated data that is still up and available on the Web. It's better to find the original issuing agency that is the source of the data. You may be able to do this simply by going to the root of the page's URL and trying to retrieve that data set directly from the home page. Doing this will help ensure that you've ended up with the newest data available.

This hazard of accessing older data can be particularly true when using Google, my recommended search engine. However, because Google ranks pages so heavily by "popularity" (how many other pages have linked to the site), an older government page that has garnered many links may very well outrank a newer page just placed on the Web that's updated its data series.

For example, some time ago I ran a search on Google to find a link to a popular governmental booklet, and the top results listed older versions of that guide (see Figure 6.4). Because I knew that a more recent one had been published, I then added the year (2002) to the search, which then resulted in Google pulling up the more current one to the top of the list.

Figure 6.4 *Google's top-ranked page is an outdated version of a federal government booklet—the newer version is ranked third.*

COMPLETENESS OF ARCHIVE

As more statistical data migrates to the Web, you must be sure that all of the original archival data, footnotes, and other elements that were in a pre-existing print, CD-ROM, or other previous series are included in the Web version. Unless you actually have a copy of the original it can be hard to determine.

DOCUMENTATION AND METHODOLOGY

It's critical that accompanying any statistical report is complete documentation that includes the methods employed for conducting the research, the initial assumptions, survey methodologies, limitations of the research, margins of errors, and so forth. Ed Spahr, executive director of COPAFS, says that documentation on the Web not only should always be available but "in your face" too. In other words, it should be made nearly impossible to be missed by the user.

EASE OF USE/INTUITIVENESS

Just because an agency has migrated its data to the Web doesn't mean that it will be easy to dig out specific information. Some government agencies do very well in presenting and organizing data, and some do a poor job. If you're having trouble navigating a site or trying to find the specific data you require, the best thing to do is simply look for a "contact" link and telephone or e-mail the person listed and ask for technical help. The best way to quickly find what you need is if you can manage to be simultaneously on the phone and online at the site at the same time.

INCONSISTENT/VARYING ASSUMPTIONS

A downside to so much good data on the Web is that users can run into trouble when trying to reconcile varying measurements and analyses created by different agencies. For example, Spahr says that if you were trying to find average household income for a particular state, you would find one set of data from the Bureau of the Census' decennial system, another from the current population survey, and yet another from the survey of income and program participation—and these surveys would all be conducted from divisions within the same agency (the Bureau of the Census)! Surveys from different agencies are likely to use even more varying assumptions and methodologies.

ISSUES OF ACCESS

Access is another concern of researchers using the Web to find government data, even though one of the traditional benefits of information available on the Web has been easier access.

One aspect is how to find what you need from among the numerous agencies and plethora of data. The government publishes so much information that it can be nearly impossible to keep up with all of it or even to know the best places to look. A strategy to help ensure you are tapping into the most complete collections is to use all of the various "one-stop" clearinghouses set up by the government to help users find what they want. (Naturally, it seems a misnomer to have more than one "one-stop" clearinghouse.)

Another, more recent access-related trend regards the removal of data from certain government agencies. This has been done out of post-9/11 security concerns and worries about certain sensitive information falling into the wrong hands. For instance, some data related to transportation, energy, chemicals, and public utilities have been removed. On other sites, it has become harder to access certain data. For example, the Department of Energy restricted access to its EnviroFacts database, which contains information on potential environmental hazards around the country. You can keep up with what's being removed from government Web sites by checking OMB Watch, a watchdog site that maintains an ongoing list of these deletions (see Figure 6.5).

In addition to the removal of previously available government data determined as sensitive, the government has recently taken other measures related to information access that have alarmed some observers. These concerns have specifically focused on policies, new regulations, and actions taken by the Bush administration that have affected the availability and, to some, the integrity of data emanating from the government. Among the concerns are:

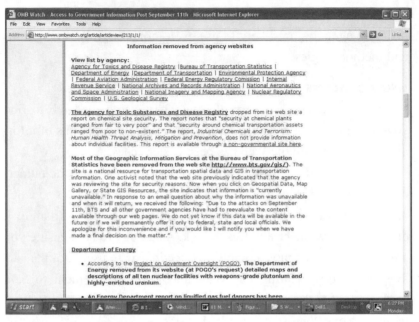

Figure 6.5 OMB Watch

- A "Data Quality Act" directive issued by the White House Office of Management and Budget (OMB) in January, 2002, that specified a set of data quality criteria that all agencies were required to meet. This has caused concern in some quarters because requiring federal agencies to adhere to a new definition of data quality has opened the door to challenges by industry advocacy groups who want to delay or forestall new regulations (e.g., clean air rules, worker safety, etc.) that were based on surveys, research, or other data collection activities. One active industry lobbying group, called the Center for Regulatory Effectiveness (CRE), has challenged data published by the EPA, focusing primarily on its reports and findings that relate to climate change.

- A move by the Office of Management and Budget (OMB) to have government agencies use private sector printers for their publications, and move away from using the printing services of the centralized Government Printing Office (GPO). The GPO is the largest disseminator of U.S. government publications and information in the world, and its Web site has been the GPO's primary method of distributing government information on the Web. Library associations raised concerns that this move would mean an increase in "fugitive documents"—government publications that are hard to track down because they are not available from a central clearinghouse like the GPO. A June 2003 agreement between the OMB and GPO has set up a pilot print procurement project, which is seen as a compromise that will permit private sector printing but still ensure that copies of agency publications will be made available for library archives. It is not clear yet what the impact this new printing arrangement will have on government document availability.

• A directive from the OMB that requires a new level of peer review before government agencies may release data that could be used for creating new policies relevant for regulatory practices. As with the data quality act, there are concerns that this represents an unnecessary new burden on agencies that will result in delaying the release of important information and will be used maliciously by certain industries as a strategy to forestall new regulations.

• A September 2003 decision to discontinue a pilot project whereby the public was able to obtain access to an index of Congressional Research Service (CRS) reports. CRS reports are highly respected, detailed, and objective studies of a wide range of current issues, performed by researchers for members of Congress.

In addition to these issues surrounding access, serious charges have also been made that the Bush administration has not respected the integrity of data, and has injected far more politics than previous administrations. A statement issued by the Union of Concerned Scientists, titled "Scientific Integrity and Policymaking" and signed by 60 leading scientists voices alarm over how the Bush administration was misusing science. According to the organization:

> when scientific knowledge has been found to be in conflict
> with [the Bush administration's] goals, the administration has

often manipulated the process through which science enters into its decisions. This has been done by placing people who are professionally unqualified or who have clear conflicts of interest in official posts and on scientific advisory committees; by disbanding existing advisory committees; by censoring and suppressing reports by the government's own scientists; and by simply not seeking independent scientific advice. Other administrations have, on occasion, engaged in such practices, but not so systematically nor on so wide a front. (From Union of Concerned Scientists, "Restoring Scientific Integrity in Policy-making" http://www.ucsusa.org/global_environment/rsi/page. cfm?pageID=1320)

See page 255 in Appendix B for the URL to the executive summary and full PDF report.

INTERNATIONAL STATISTICAL AGENCIES

Business research also involves locating statistical data on the economies, trade, and population of other countries. One of the best ways to ensure that the international statistics you find on the Web are authoritative is to use "official" statistics, which are generated by national statistical agencies. You can find an up-to-date listing of these agencies, with links, at the United Nations site on its page "National and International Data Sources and Links." One example is Finland's national statistical agency, Finland Statistics, which offers a free, excellent database of statistical data called WebStat.

The federal government is not the only place to go to find statistics, though it is a primary source. Statistical data is also generated by other entities: associations, chambers of commerce, market research firms, polling organizations, publishers, and miscellaneous marketing portal sites on the Web. Here's a quick checklist of key concerns to keep in mind when obtaining data from one of these sources when you encounter them on the Web:

Source: Associations, chambers of commerce
Typical Data Generated: Economic and industry statistics

Key Quality Concerns: Watch for PR agenda of the organization and any positive spin placed on how the data is interpreted

Source: Market/Brokerage firms

Typical Data Generated: Market, industry, company data including market share, market size, product segments, sales, financial data.

Key Quality Concerns: Methods/sources for data collection; potential conflicts of interest

Source: Survey and Polling organizations

Typical Data Generated: Consumer behaviors, actions, and opinions

Key Quality Concerns: Survey methodology, questionnaire integrity

Source: Newspapers, wires, journals, media sources

Typical Data Generated: Reports on results of other polling organizations, findings from universities and other research entities. Some media outlets also conduct and report on their own surveys.

Key Quality Concerns: Over-dramatizing significance of finding; not reporting all data in context; reporter not understanding the subtleties of the meaning of the numbers. If the survey was done by the publication itself (e.g., an industry or reader survey), check for basic survey matters such as definition of universe, size of sample, sampling method, representativeness of sample to universe, precautions against self-selection bias, and wording of survey instrument (questionnaire).

Source: Company directory database (e.g., D&B, Hoover's, infoUSA, Disclosure, etc.)

Typical Data Generated: Company data: number of employees, revenue, earnings, financials, market share

Key Quality Concerns: Primarily the source of the data. For example, was the data derived from public filings, secondary sources, or via primary data collection methods? And, importantly, is any of the data not "actual" data but simply "modeled" data based on using a particular rough formula? (For example, companies in a certain industry with this range of employees typically have a revenue of $xx.)

One Strategy: Use Preferred Statistical Sources

You will often come across an unknown source on the Web that cites statistics, but since you don't know anything about who's actually behind the site, you won't be sure whether you can trust it as a credible source. One strategy then is to have a handful of reliable, trusted sources that you regularly turn to when you want good statistical data. Following are the names of a wide range of specific sources that I have used and like very much for all types of statistical data. The URLs for these Web sites can be found in Appendix B.

— U.S. Government Statistical Agencies
  • Principal statistical agencies
  • Statistical Abstract of the U.S.
  • Bureau of the Census: Economic Census
  • Bureau of the Census: American Factfinder

— International Statistical Agencies
  • United Nations: Links to Official Statistical Agencies
  • United Nations: Millennium Country Profiles
  • Global Statistical Finder: Finlands' WebStat
  • OECD (Click on "Statistics")

—Survey Organizations
- Pew Internet & American Life Project
- Pew Research Center for the People and the Press
- Comscore (Consumer Behavior) "News"
- ACSI Index, scores by industry
- PollingReport (to compare survey results)

—Publishers/Marketing Portals/Miscellaneous
- ClickZ (online marketing, demographics)
- Statistics.com (portal to global data sources)
- NationMaster (fascinating, creating graphs to compare countries on hundreds of data points)
- Fortune, Forbes Lists and Rankings

(A good way to keep up with recommended sources of other business statistic sites on the Web is the free e-mail newsletter I edit every month, called "Best of the Business Web." See Appendix B for the URL.)

A Primer on Understanding Statistics

Quality in statistics is a matter that transcends the Web, and a basic education in what to look for when using statistics is valuable for researchers that use quantitative data and figures from any medium.

The following information is from the "Statistics Basics" chapter in Paula Berinstein's *Finding Statistics Online*, and serves as a general primer on the fundamental considerations to keep in mind when coming across most types of statistical data.

- *Normal Range.* What is the "normal" range for the thing being counted? Are you counting something that normally occurs in high or low ranges?

- *Starting Point.* When dealing with increases and decreases, consider the location of the "starting point" or the original data point.

- *Possible Rates of Change.* What is the possible or likely rate of change for the thing being counted?

- *Factors Behind the Numbers.* What are some other, hidden forces that may be impacting large changes?

- *Self-Reports.* Remember that any time people report facts or opinions about themselves or others, there may be distortion.

- *Specious or Biased Sources.* Consider the source of any study or report.

- *Authority.* Consider whether the source is authoritative for the thing being measured.

- *Flabby/Trick Words.* Watch out for undefined terms, half-truths, incomplete or misleading comparisons, and words that editorialize (e.g., "only," "just," "but," and "fully").

- *Using different types of base numbers or assumptions.* Watch out for apples-to-oranges comparisons.

- *Flawed analysis.* Be sure that causality is not being attributed where none exists.

- *False Extrapolation.* Can one set of data truly be extended to accurately apply to another?

- *Lack of Context.* Check that graphs start at zero and are proportional, so as not to over exaggerate a rise or fall.

Polls and Surveys

In the course of your research, you are likely to come across surveys and polls. These might include surveys of consumer preferences and buying habits, employee satisfaction surveys, market research surveys, and product evaluation surveys.

Using survey data always requires an extra level of skepticism and caution, mainly because conducting a valid survey is a true science. If a survey is not performed correctly, it can provide completely invalid and/or inaccurate results. Furthermore, complex areas such as beliefs, expected future actions, and even opinions can be quite difficult to obtain reliably through a quantitative approach like a survey.

Creating a valid and accurate survey means following a strict scientific approach. It includes critical areas such as defining the universe to be measured, using random sampling techniques, avoiding self-selection bias, and carefully constructing the survey instrument to avoid influencing respondents or asking questions that people cannot easily answer. Once obtained, the data also requires calculation of a statistical margin of error and careful attention to how the final data is segmented and displayed so that it can be understood by the users.

Although the guidelines for evaluating the reliability and validity of a survey are the same whether you read it in a newspaper, market research report, or on a Web page, there are some relevant issues that involve the intersection of the Web and survey research.

An increasing number of marketers and surveyors are performing their surveys via the Web. Traditional methods, such as mail, phone, and in-person surveys, are still being used, but Web surveys have begun to look more attractive to many survey organizations because they are inexpensive to administer, offer fast turnaround times (often within 24 to 48 hours), and, in some cases, produce a higher response rate. In addition, several companies, such as Zoomerang and SurveySite, have created software that make it easy to perform a Web survey.

But Web-administered surveys present some potential hazards. Is the surveyed sample indeed representative of the entire population ("universe") that is being studied? Although the demographics of Web users have become increasingly similar to the general U.S. population, there are still unrepresentative aspects of the Internet-using population. For example, according to surveys conducted by the Pew Internet & American Life Project, Internet access is still less common among those who live in rural areas, and among the elderly, and the less affluent. For this reason, if you rely on a survey organization that used the Web to reach people, you have to consider how results could be skewed by the nature of those who have Internet access versus those who do not.

Another concern with Web-based surveys is that unless they're carefully designed, they can be prone to self-selection bias. This occurs when a population to be surveyed is not randomly selected (through methods like randomly dialed telephone numbers in a phone survey) but when it's primarily up to each person to decide if he or she would like to participate. Two examples of surveys that suffer from self-selection bias are magazine surveys and those where you call an 800 or 900 number.

The problem with self-selection is that those who actively make an effort to participate in a survey usually have some characteristic that makes them unrepresentative of the full universe under study. For instance, those who choose to call in to an 800 number may wish to make this effort because they feel more strongly—possibly in a negative way—about the issue at hand than the average member of the surveyed group who wouldn't feel so motivated to make the phone call. (This would be even truer for a 900-number survey where one actually has to pay to take part.)

Web-based surveys may be conducted in various ways: by e-mail, via an e-mail invitation to a Web site to fill out a form, or via a pop-up window. If there's no effort to gather a random sampling, then that Web survey will suffer from self-selection bias.

Another concern for those who administer Web surveys is preventing people from responding more than once ("ballot stuffing"). Another is to assuage privacy concerns in order to get honest and reliable results. These are certainly not insurmountable problems, but you need some level of confidence that these issues were handled by the survey organization whose data you're relying on.

No matter what type of survey data you're planning to use, the following are basic questions you need to ask in regard to the quality and reliability of the survey.

Sponsoring Organization

- Who sponsored this survey? Was it an organization that has a vested interest in achieving a certain outcome?
- Is it a more neutral organization whose interest is primarily data gathering (such as The Bureau of the Census or a publication like *American Demographics*), or is there an interest in a certain social policy or commercial result?
- Who paid for the survey?
- What past surveys has this organization conducted? Are you allowed to see the results of these surveys? Do they all come to the same conclusion on a contentious topic?
- What are the qualifications of those who administered the survey? Did the organization employ or use experts in statistical methodology? Are their biographies available on the Web site?

Survey's Goal

- What is the survey trying to measure? Is it something that is quantifiable, measurable, and countable (such as the number of computers or VCRs in U.S. households, etc.)? Or is the survey trying to pin down something more complex, such as people's behaviors or values? The former is much easier to measure than the latter.
- Who is the target universe? Is there a clear definition for this target?

Methodologies

- How were the respondents to this survey selected (phone, mail, in-person, or the Web)?

- What is the size of the sample surveyed?
- What was done to ensure that a random selection was employed so that respondents would be representative of the target universe?
- What kinds of safeguards were taken against self-selection bias?

Survey Questionnaire (Instrument)

- Can you examine the questionnaire used in the survey?
- Are the questions open- or close-ended (forced choice). If the latter, do the choices provided artificially limit or influence the respondents?
- In reviewing the questionnaire, did it suffer from any of the following flaws:

  1. Were hidden and implicit assumptions made that served to narrow the respondents' potential range of answers?

  2. Did it use loaded phrases and terms that could influence respondents?

  3. Does the order of the questions present any biases? For example, could the raising of a certain issue in one question influence an answer to a later question?

  4. Were the questions clear and unambiguous, or could they be read more than one way?

  5. Were the questions simple or complex? (People have trouble with complex questions.)

  6. Did the questions ask for memory recollections? (These are difficult for people to answer accurately.)

  7. Did the questions ask the respondent to admit to some behavior that is socially disapproved of? Many people will not admit to behavior or views that they feel are unpopular with others.

Survey Results

- All surveys have a plus/minus margin of error. Is the survey's margin of error published?
- What *is* the margin of error?
- Do any conclusions that are stated as a result of this survey actually follow logically from the data revealed in the survey?

Finally, because survey data can be so doubtful, to increase your level of confidence in a particular survey's results you might check to see if other surveys, created by other sponsoring organizations, came to similar, confirming results.

CHAPTER 7

News, Talk, & Blogs on the Net

Online News and Media Services

In the course of a business research project, the searcher typically will need to access news sources to find stories about a company, product, social trend, economic development, or other item. And the news sources consulted would include both business-specific news outlets, like a Bloomberg or Fortune, as well as more general sources such as daily newspapers and the major wire services.

As most searchers are fully aware, "the news" is everywhere on the Web—and almost always available for free. The Web has turned news into a commodity that can be easily found on thousands of different sites, from all across the globe. Generally, this has been a blessing for researchers. But of course, as with most Web gifts, there is a small price to pay: the sometimes confusing array of news outlets on the Web and the difficulty in knowing which to rely on.

The subject of how to be a critical reader and viewer of the news is another book in itself (although some coverage appears in Chapter 8). Naturally, you should maintain the same skepticism about Web news sources as you would with print or broadcast sources. But the Web raises new, unique concerns when it comes to news reliability and quality. These include understanding the various "types" of news on the Web and understanding its limitations.

Types of News on the Web

You need to be aware of the various forms of media that are available on the Web in order to choose the right medium for the type of research you are conducting. On the Web you can find the following types of news sources:

- Individual online news sites (CNNfn, nytimes.com)
- Breaking-news aggregators (AlltheWeb.com News, Google News, Yahoo! News)
- Searchable news databases (American City Business Journals, FindArticles.com)
- News alert services (CBS MartketWatch alerts, Google News Alerts, CNN Alerts)
- Industry News Sites (PaidContent.org, TechRepublic)
- Other/special categories (audio/video news archives, link sites, local news search, desktop news database, fee-based news)

In this section I'll give descriptions and examples for each of these types of news sites, advise when to use a particular site, and note any special issues related to source quality and reliability.

INDIVIDUAL ONLINE NEWS SITES

These are the Web sites of individual news organizations. Some popular sites that fall under this category include CNN.com, ABCNEWS.com, and nytimes.com. Typically these are free (The Wall Street Journal Online is a notable exception), employ newspaper-like graphics to display the latest news, offer links to related coverage, and, often, contain a searchable news archive.

If you already have a trusted print or broadcast source, you may wish to use that outlet's online site to get your news. One caution: You cannot assume that what is in the print (or broadcast) version will automatically appear on that organization's site. News Web sites can vary significantly from their traditional counterparts, sometimes excluding certain features (local columns and classifieds, for instance) and offering Web-only exclusives. The organization and layout of the news may be different as well.

BREAKING NEWS AGGREGATORS

These are sites that pull news from multiple online news sources (up to thousands) to create an aggregated listing of breaking news headlines. Here, you can perform a keyword search to retrieve headlines that match your terms, and then select one or more headlines to view the full text of a news story.

There are several sites where you can search a breaking news aggregator's collection. Some existing well-known Web search engines, such as Google and Yahoo!, offer a special separate news search tab, while other sites, like NewsNow, are geared specifically and solely for aggregating breaking news. Google News employs a newspaper-like graphic format including a "front page" with top news stories, along with photographs, of current breaking news. DayPop is another specialized news aggregator; its database combines both regular news items as well as thousands of recent blog postings.

News aggregators are effective when you want to find breaking news from multiple news sources, or when you need to search for slightly older news items that weren't covered by your preferred individual online news source. News aggregators vary quite a bit in certain key areas, such as in the number of sources included, types of sources (for instance, DayPop includes Weblogs), length of archive, timeliness, and the ability to conduct advanced searches.

The Google News site is unique in that the stories it displays on its front page are not selected by human editors but by Google's own algorithm, which looks at factors like a site's popularity, freshness, and other factors to determine how high it should rank. Google uses this formula in ranking its Web sites, and has now applied this successful method to creating its news front page.

SEARCHABLE NEWS DATABASES

This category is similar to the breaking-news aggregator in that you can search for news stories from multiple sources, except that these sites don't focus on breaking news but allow a search of broader archives, in the manner of traditional databases. Two sites in this category are FindArticles.com and American City Business Journals.

(See page 257 in Appendix B for the URLs of these Web sites.) Use these sources when you're interested in finding stories that were published weeks, months, or even years ago. (A more recent and less expensive entry into the archive news searching arena is HighBeam, previously known as eLibrary. HighBeam allows researchers to search either the Web or a database of popular, trade, and academic journal articles.)

The catch is that the Web is simply not the best place to do this type of archival news research. The most comprehensive newspaper and news journal archives are primarily still available through fee-based subscription services, including professional online services like Dialog, LexisNexis, and Dow Jones, or via a library-oriented news vendor like ProQuest.

NEWS ALERT SERVICES

These are similar to aggregators in that they draw from multiple news sources and provide timely, up-to-the-minute stories. However, news alert services also allow you to create a customized profile of the topics you want to track, and then alert you when one is found. Popular, free news alert services include Yahoo! Alerts, Google News Alerts, CNN Alerts, and CBS MarketWatch alerts. Some individual newspapers, including the *New York Times*, offer news alert services, but these track only news stories from that individual source.

These services are useful when you have a need to track stories that mention a particular company, industry, product, or other topic over a period of time. You have to ensure that the specific types of sources covered by an alert are the kinds of media that you prefer. For example, depending on your needs you may want to make sure they're not primarily press releases, or that they include international coverage.

News alert services vary in other important ways, such as frequency of update, advanced search capabilities, how much of the news story is displayed in your alert, and how the alert is actually delivered (e.g., via a Web site or e-mail).

INDUSTRY NEWS SITES

These are special niche news sites that provide news, advice, and commentary just on a specific industry, e.g., PaidContent.org provides news on the fee-based digital content and information industries. Some of these sites also are designed to provide additional "community"-like features and services. For instance, TechRepublic is a community for information technology (IT) professionals that not only provides news, but a discussion forum, technical advice, downloads, and other information and services of interest to that community. (One special type of niche news site is the investment related site, such as The Street.com, or MSN Money, but purely investment-type sites are not covered in this book.)

RSS NEWS FEEDS

While RSS feeds are a technology, and not a type of news, as discussed in Chapter 2, you should be aware of how this news collection and display tool can help you more effectively gather and organize your Web-based news sources.

OTHER/SPECIAL NEWS CATEGORIES

There are some other useful categories worth noting, such as sources that provide audio and video news archives. My personal favorites are the National Public Radio (NPR) and C-SPAN sites, both of which provide extensive free searching of their news archives. Some other news sites that provide audio and video include FOX News, the Nightly Business Report, CNBC/Dow Jones, and CNNfn. These sources are particularly useful for locating interviews with CEOs, although it can be tricky to zero in on just the segment of the show you need. To help you with this, NPR does an excellent job of breaking its stories into smaller segments (see Figure 7.1).

Two other special news categories that are important to know about are local news search sites and desktop news databases. Local news search sites aggregate and display news just for a particular region of the country. Although several of the leading news aggregators and search engines are working on developing a local news search feature, the best and most advanced of these local news search sites is a free site called Topix.net.

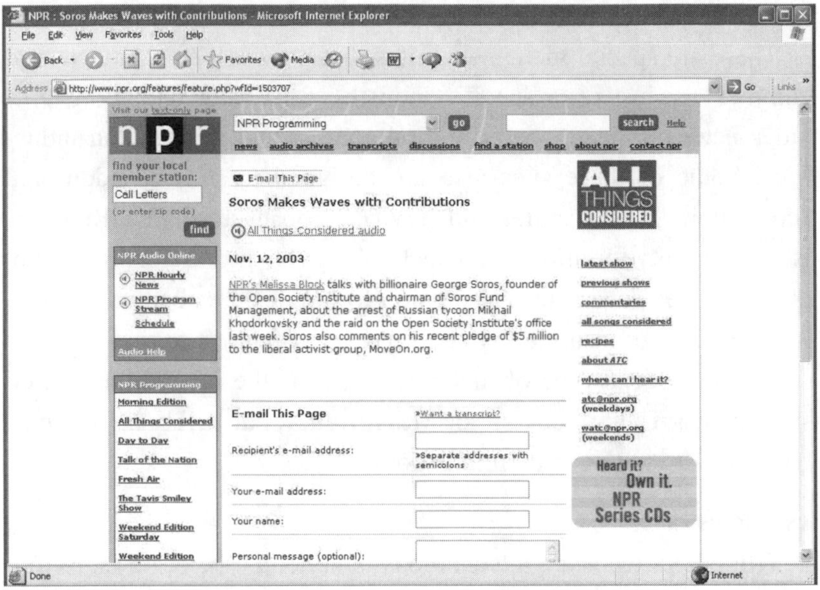

Figure 7.1 *NPR's news archive permits users to search and listen to individual segments of its broadcasts.*

Although these are not technically on the Web per se, you should also be aware of the availability of a desktop news database called Rocketinfo. This is a downloadable piece of software that allows users to simultaneously search and display a wide range of Web-based news, blogs, and other information sources from one's desktop. Rocketinfo's software works similarly to an RSS Reader but has more content, function, and features. It resembles more a traditional searchable database than a simple news reader.

Another special news category includes sites that do not actually offer news, but simply provide links to worldwide news sites. These can be excellent resources for finding both regional and international news sources. Some of the top sites include NewsLink, ABYZ News Links, NewsDirectory.com, and Newspapers.com. The SLA's news division site offers a useful site open to the public that identifies which online newspapers provide archival access and provides details on each archive (such as how far back the archive goes, if fees are charged to search it, etc.).

Keep in mind that, given the scope of this book, I've mentioned only those news sites on the Web that are available at no cost. There are some extensive fee-based news search sites that are accessible through the Web. Factiva.com is an example of a fee-based provider with an excellent reputation for providing detailed, substantive, and timely business news.

Web News Evaluation Tips

Besides understanding the types of news sources that exist on the Web, it's important to keep the following three points in mind when attempting to evaluate the quality and usefulness of the news you find online:

1. Remember the difference between a news aggregator, which is common on the free Web, and a full database offering a complete archive, which is less common. If you are conducting in-depth archival research, your best bet is to search a non-Internet database.

2. Remember that what you find on a news organization's Web site is not necessarily identical to the coverage appearing in its original print version or TV/radio broadcast.

3. Remember that on the Web anyone can call himself a "journalist" and his outlet a "news source" (Weblogs, discussed earlier, are an example). Be alert to the background and credibility of news sites you've never heard of, and of those that seem to be the work of a single individual. When encountering such a site, I recommend asking the following questions:

    -   What's the name of the organization behind the news site?
    -   Where can you find out about its history and background?
    -   Is full contact information provided, including a physical address?
    -   Does the site also publish a print newspaper? If so, is the newspaper listed in a standard newspaper directory such as the Standard Periodical Directory, Oxbridge's National

Directory of Magazines, or Katz's Magazines for Libraries? If so, that's a good sign. If not listed there, is the publication at least listed in a directory to online publications, such as Fulltext Sources Online?

- Who links to this news site? (thereby giving its users an implicit referral) (You can find out who links to the site by running an advanced Google search and entering the URL in "Find Pages That Link to the Page ..." You can also use AllTheWeb's search engine for find incoming links by entering link:www.xyz.com

- Is the site updated on at least a daily basis?

- Is there evidence of the same kind of quality control that you'd expect in a credible print news source? (Is it carefully edited and well designed?)

Web Discussion Groups, Blogs, and More: Opinions and Anecdotal Information

One of the most profound changes the Web has wrought is the ease with which we can find other people's advice on virtually any topic — from apple growing to zebra farming. For the most part, I believe that this has been an enormous boon.

Many business researchers are accustomed to using the Web to locate the opinions and experiences of others. Some do so by subscribing to one or more discussion groups where it's possible to ask colleagues for advice on a current research or business problem. For example, many business librarians rely on the excellent BUSLIB-L mailing list to get ideas and help in finding and evaluating various business information resources. Others use even more specialized discussion lists to find tips, strategies, and resources for research in a given industry.

In addition to these types of groups, business researchers can sign up with the more informal Usenet newsgroups, join Web site discussion forums, or check in with their favorite Weblogs. As mentioned earlier, the creator of a Weblog (a "blogger") uses his or her site to offer daily comments and opinions in a particular topic area, providing links to favorite sources and the latest news, and inviting readers to respond and discuss the issues being raised.

Some business researchers also scan investor message boards to learn about companies and get a feel for where they're headed, though as mentioned earlier, investor message boards can contain a great deal of misinformation.

On the Other Hand ...

The flipside of all this new and useful personal information is that we must be more careful than ever when determining who and what to believe. Much of what you'll come across on the Web will be a first-time encounter, and you'll have no prior history to help you decide whether or not the source is trustworthy.

Before the Web, there were filters that an individual had to pass through before his or her views could be widely published and disseminated. While those filters served to narrow our communal conversation, they also blocked some of the most blatantly unverifiable, wrong, or useless information. On the Web, for better or worse—though I believe mostly for the better—everything and anything goes.

While it's easy to be overwhelmed by too many views and opinions of questionable veracity, with a few strategies, tools, and some practice, you can use your own filters to reduce the "noise" and zero in on the most useful and relevant conversations.

How, then, do you go about evaluating the reliability and accuracy of some unknown views and advice you've come across on one of these freewheeling Web discussion forums? First, you can make an initial assessment based on the specific type of virtual meeting place. For example, is it a Weblog, mailing list, Usenet group, Web forum, or investor message board?

Weblogs

There are Weblogs that have become so prominent and widely read (such as SlashDot and AndrewSullivan.com) that they're widely seen as just another mainstream media source. But there are many obscure Weblogs, with new ones coming online all the time, that offer valuable

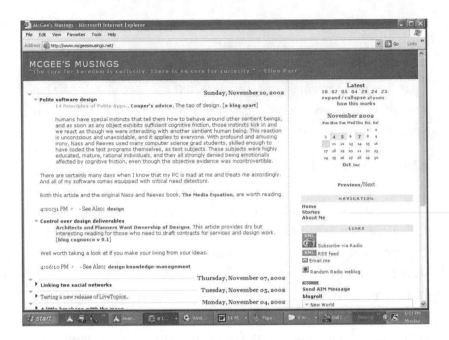

Figure 7.2 *McGee's Musings is an example of a quality blog. This one covers the field of knowledge management.*

commentary and insights and would be a high-quality source of information (see Figure 7.2).

If you get information from a Weblog, you might be finding the views of both the Weblog's creator *and* some of its visitors. If you're getting opinions from the creator of the Weblog, you should have an ample history of past blogs (writings) by this person to make some initial assessments, based on the evaluation strategies provided in this section. You can also learn more about the Weblog by using the specialized Weblog search engine DayPop, which allows you to enter the subject of your search and see which Weblogs appear most often. The DayPop "Top 40" feature is a list of the most-linked-to Web pages that's updated four times per day. It allows you to enter the name of a Weblog with the prefix *link:[name of Weblog]* to see how many other Weblogs link to it.

If you're on a Weblog and the person you want to evaluate is not the blogger, but someone who is posting messages, you might try searching the Weblog to find other postings by the same individual.

If that's not possible, you can turn to DayPop again to search on that person's name for postings on this and other Weblogs.

But use caution when using Weblog information, because breaking news and rumors are passed quickly between bloggers. Something dramatic and compelling that's posted on a popular Weblog or online news site in the morning might be mentioned by hundreds of Weblogs by that afternoon. As mentioned earlier, this can allow the quick spread of bad data and outright hoaxes. You should confirm your sources on this kind of information before putting any stock in it.

Some Weblogs employ a novel, Web-based form of journalism called participatory or "open source" journalism. Here the readers of a Weblog organically add to an original news story, which causes the story to grow and evolve based on the input. Aly Colón, Ethics Group Leader & Diversity Program Director at the Poynter Institute in St. Petersburg, Florida, told me he has "mixed feelings" about this concept. On the positive side, he feels the process lets more voices be heard. But the downside is an increased chance of getting bad data if there isn't a system for verifying news and information that's coming into the Weblog. He advises readers of these open source Weblogs to know something about the contributors before believing what they add to a news story.

Finding Trustworthy Bloggers

Is there a way to identify which bloggers are going to be trustworthy and provide the most credible information? Like any other source, you'll likely have to make this determination by spending some time reading through a blogger's site and trying to find answers to some of the questions mentioned earlier. But you might also be able to filter out the trustworthy bloggers by trying to get a feel for his or her reputation. On the Web, reputation has become the key metric for trustworthiness, and there are several ways and tools you can use to try to gauge an unknown bloggers' reputation. For example you can:

- Note if the blogger's pages are ranked highly on Google. Since one of the primary ways that Google ranks pages is by the number and popularity of the incoming links, and because links do roughly indicate Web-based referrals, bloggers who appear toward the top of a search are likely to be often read and cited by others. For example, if I do a search on librarians and wifi, the very top page returned by Google is a blog from Harvard called BloggerCon, which means that this is a very widely read blog.

- Try running a search on a search engine that specifically indexes blogs, such as DayPop or Waypath. As with Google, those blogs that have the highest ranking are those that typically have the highest readership.

- Look for mentions of specific bloggers in the mainstream print press. Journalists are increasingly quoting and citing bloggers as important sources when they are writing an article, and typically the reporters will do research to find out which ones have the most influence, and will quote that particular blogger in the article.

If you find a blogger that you trust, look to see if that blogger has created a "Blogroll," which is a list of links of bloggers that *that* blogger likes and reads. See Figure 7.3 for an example of a blogroll.

Mailing Lists

The level and quality of discourse on Internet mailing lists (commonly, though, inaccurately, called "ListServs") can be quite high, with substantive and knowledgeable contributions by subscribers. Two good sites to search for a mailing list discussion group are tile.net and CataList.

Usenet Groups

I'm not much of a fan of the Usenet discussion groups, as I've never found the quality of conversation particularly high. Although there are certainly exceptions, I tend to avoid them and don't recommend them for serious business research.

Web Forums

Some Web sites set up forums that allow visitors to chat and discuss topics that relate to that site's focus. Many newspaper and online

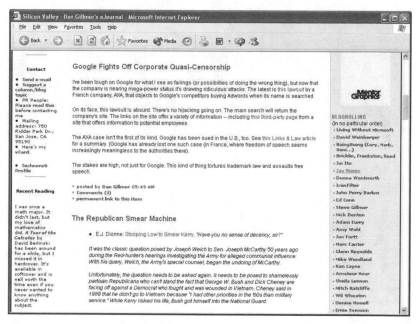

Figure 7.3 Example of a blogroll (the bar on the right side of the screen).

media sites, for example, provide a forum for their readers to discuss the latest stories and columns. The subject and tone of a site can determine the quality and level of discourse that you'll find in its Web forum. For example, a forum on a site devoted to statistical methodologies for conducting reliable surveys will likely have an audience with knowledgeable people, many in academia, who have some level of expertise in the area. On the other hand, a Web site that's simply devoted to the latest online marketing techniques is less likely to have as qualified an audience.

Spending a little time on certain Web forums will allow you to find out which members regularly post, offer useful contributions, and are respected by other members. Anything and everything cricket-related can be discussed on the Cricket Web Forum (see Figure 7.4).

Investor Message Boards

There are many investor message boards on the Web (see Figure 7.5). Though it's possible to glean good information on companies

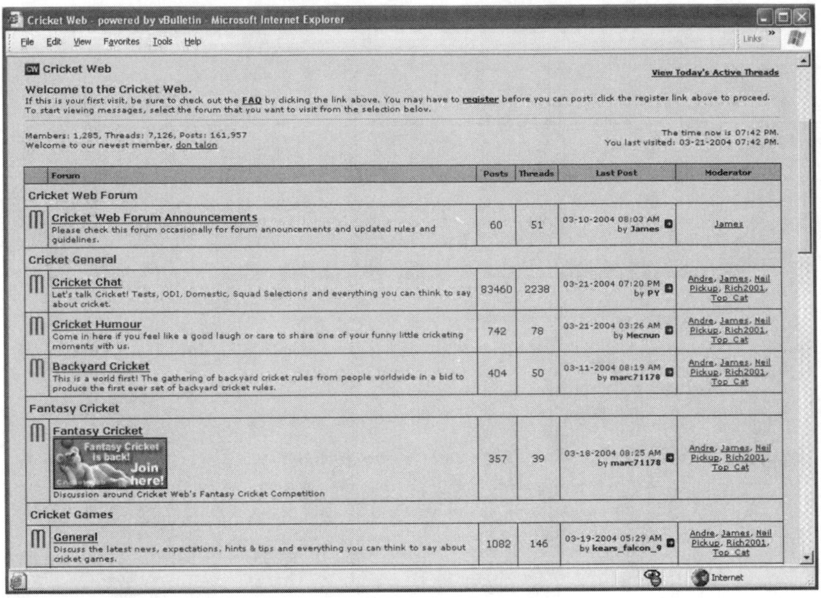

Figure 7.4   *Cricket Web Forum*

and industries from them, they can also be such minefields of potentially bad information and even deliberate misinformation that I don't
recommend their use by business researchers.

Evaluating the Messenger's Message

Besides considering the kind of forum where the individual is
posting, you also need to take a close look at the person and the
likely reliability of his or her views. The following are some questions to ask when making this closer evaluation:

- Where did you locate this person? Was he or she referred to
  you by another trusted source?
- Where else has this person presented his or her views? In
  forums other than an Internet discussion group?
- Who else has cited the views of this person? Are these considered good sources?
- Does the person demonstrate some familiarity and knowledge
  of the area? For example, does he or she know about existing
  sources and information, or others who work in the field?

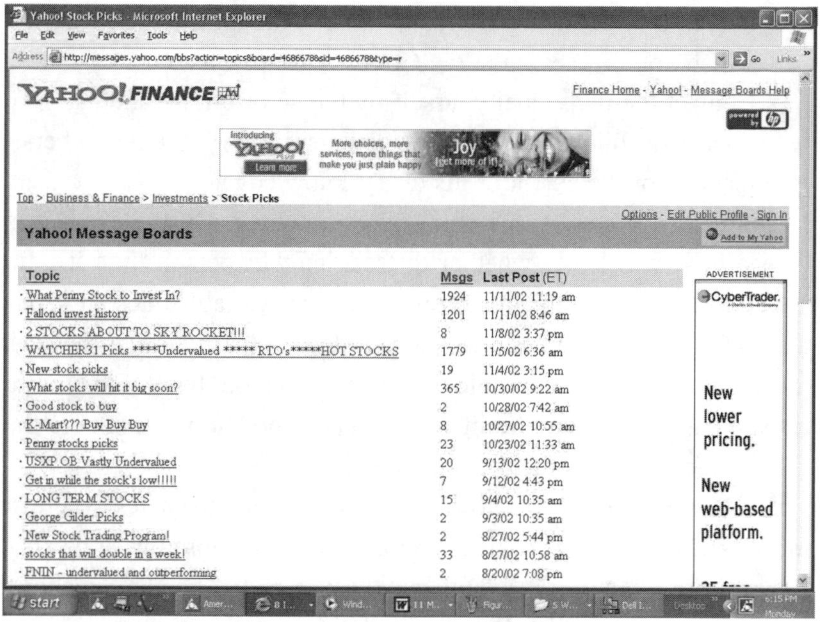

Figure 7.5 *Example of an investor message board.*

- How does the person present his or her views? Is it in a clear, logical, thoughtful, and organized manner? Or does it come across as ranting? Is he or she open to alternative views? Is he or she open about the methods used to come to conclusions? Does he or she offer back-up or evidence for claims?
- Does the person have hidden biases that you should know about? Does he or she work for an organization with a specific agenda? What could be his or her motivations for providing this information?
- Has this person kept up with changes and new developments in the field?

You can also take these proactive steps to ascertain whether the person runs a trustworthy site:

- Have some other sources confirm what the person is saying.
- Do some research: Enter the person's name into a search engine to see where else he or she has spoken or written.

Search both the general Web as well as the discussion groups, which you can search at the Google Groups link.

- Contact the individual yourself by phone or e-mail and ask your own follow-up questions. This will give you a much better feel for the extent of his or her knowledge.

Ultimately, much of this comes down to trust. On the Web, it is indeed harder to know whether to trust another person than it is in your day-to-day life because there are fewer available cues and context to help you make your decision. It does help, though, to have as much knowledge as possible ahead of time on the topic you're researching. You'll then be in a much better position to evaluate the quality and value of others' topic knowledge.

It's also important to know the kinds of circumstances where it makes sense to rely on, or be open to, nonexperts' opinions and experiences. For example, it would make sense to utilize the anecdotal reports and experiences of other people in the following cases:

- You want subjective opinions (you want to know others' views of a product or of a company's customer service).

- You want to hear from those with first-hand experiences (you want to hear how adult adoptees were first told about being adopted or you want to find out what musicians in Berlin think about the new music store that just opened there).

- You need referrals to other sources (you want to get recommended resources and sites to learn more about the topic that you're researching, such as where you can find statistics on the pet food industry).

- You're trying to understand the nature of a certain demographic/cultural segment (you're considering launching a new product to a niche market and want to observe an online discussion group geared to this population to understand their current issues and concerns).

- The ramifications of following the advice or opinion you receive are not too serious (you're looking for recommendations on useful Web sites or asking for names of upcoming conferences in your field).

However, you would *not* use anecdotal reports and anonymous postings if you were performing the following kinds of research:

- You need precise figures from a reliable source (you're trying to find statistical data measuring the growth of an industry or market or you want a trustworthy estimate of a company's market share in a certain industry).
- You need in-depth analyses by a trustworthy expert (you're trying to understand future trends in a complex industry or you need to find out the strategic direction of a new competitor).
- You need unbiased hard data, with clear sources (you're wondering about the financial health of a particular company or you need the latest figure on the GDP of Argentina).
- You need scientifically sound information (you need to know how two pharmaceutical drugs could interact or you need to know how hybrid vehicles' braking systems work).
- The ramifications of following the advice or opinions are serious (you want to know if there's a likelihood of an economic slowdown in your industry next quarter or you need to understand the organization of a firm you're considering merging with).

These are only general guidelines, of course. The great thing about the Web is that you can almost always find an expert somewhere who is a reliable source of knowledge and views, even for difficult and complex questions. The point here is to consider whether anecdotal views and opinions are appropriate or inappropriate as a source given the kind of research you're conducting.

One of the interesting things about the Web is the ease in which people can converse, comment, and advise others. And while it's true that just as in the offline world, Web users eventually determine whose comments encountered online are most trustworthy, and worth paying attention to, this can be a challenge simply because of the sheer number of unknown persons offering up their views and purported expertise. For example, if you look at an Amazon member's review of a book you're considering purchasing, how do you know whether that person is qualified to review the book or is someone who shares your tastes and values? You really don't! An even more worrisome possibility is that the person is just shilling for the author to write a positive review as a favor, or if a product review, working for the company (or conversely, criticizing a competitor).

But there are some interesting efforts underway to try to quantify and pin down how much trust you may want to place in unknown persons on the Web. On the most basic level, on the Web, you find new trusted sources by looking for other people recommended by those that you already trust. As mentioned earlier, bloggers typically do this by creating their own "blogroll" or list of other bloggers that they regularly read or recommend.

Some sites that solicit opinions and commentary try to assist its members in making a judgment on products by asking visitors to rate the quality of others' contributions. Amazon is a high profile example, since it asks its visitors to rate whether a particular reviewer's comments were helpful or not, and then displays that score (e.g., 8 out of 13 people found the following review helpful) above the review. But this approach is still subject to manipulation.

A more advanced approach has been taken by a consumer advisory site called Epinions, which allows its members to create what it calls a "web of trust." A "web of trust" is a network of specific reviewers that has been recommended by a member as providing good advice. Epinions cross-references the networks to find common trusted sources, and makes assumptions that people listed in more than one network are likely to be trustworthy. Epinions also allows its members to create a "block list" so that certain other member's reviews never appear.

Note that because of the great deal of commentary and discussion specifically about corporations and products that take place on the Web, a new field called "reputation management" has emerged that advises companies how to keep track of, monitor, and even influence its reputation on the Web. A couple of leading reputation management firms are WebFountain, biz360, and Converseon.

You can also use the blogging "TrackBack" function to find out who else on the Web has commented on a particular blogging post. For example, I recently was doing some research on how RSS Feeds might impact the role of company librarians, and discovered a potentially interesting and insightful blogger from Italy, who had coined the term "RSS Master" as a potential new role for information professionals. I was intrigued by this, but I was not familiar with this blogger (who called himself "Robin Good"). Then I noticed in the "TrackBack" feature at the end of the article that an industry analyst I knew of had linked to and commented on the piece in a very positive way. This provided me with more assurance and a level of trust in this particular blogger.

A site that helps do this on a much broader scale is a very intriguing one called Technorati. Technorati monitors and indexes over 1.8 million blogs and RSS feeds, updating its database, according to the site owners, every nine minutes. If you enter a URL in the Technorati search box, you can get a list of all the other sources in Technorati's database that are linking to that site. You can even do a "conversation search" to see which bloggers linked to a particular discussion thread or site over the last 24 hours.

While all of this tracking and following can be a dizzying exercise, it will help you evaluate and assess how widely circulated and "quoted" a particular blogger is on the Web, and make some judgments about his or her impact on the Web community.

The Wacky vs. The Fringe

One of the fascinating aspects of Web discussion groups is that you can tap into early opinion reports, and sources of knowledge that haven't yet made their way to the traditional media. Sometimes these discussions can sound rather far out. For example, in November 2002, after worried parents used discussion groups to express concern about a possible link between vaccinations and a child's autism, an article appeared in the *New York Times*' "CyberTimes" reporting that scientists and researchers were beginning to look into the correlations. In another example, a Web discussion group reported on vast increases in malformations in frogs. This story was subsequently picked up first by science journals and then reported in the mainstream media as a legitimate concern.

Of course, you may find someone who asserts that he has crossed the universe to visit Earth, and someone else who complains about an annoying robot his boss has implanted in his brain.

Are those running these groups on to something or simply just *on* something? Sometimes it's hard to tell. In a review of a book about Ralph Nader, investigative reporter Steve Weinberg, a contributing editor to *IRE Journal*, writes that "sources who seem neurotic or even paranoid should rarely be dismissed without some checking" (*IRE Journal*, November/December 2002, p. 40). Nobody seemed to believe Nader's worries that he was under surveillance while researching the matter of auto safety, and, in fact, it was shown that General Motors has hired detectives to try to discredit the activist.

How can you distinguish between someone who is, well, a bit wacky and not to be believed, versus someone else who has insights not yet accepted by others? (This person is sometimes referred to as a "fringe thinker.") You'll encounter both types on the Web, for sure, so the table that follows offers some guidance on how to distinguish between the visionary and the merely bonkers.

Remember, the following are just general guidelines and hardly represent a fool-proof formula. But I think they're legitimate guidelines to help you make your distinction.

One caution: These guidelines are admittedly biased toward a rational rather than an emotional orientation. Some people are going to be both angry—and credible! So don't be thrown off right away by a rant. Try to get to the bottom of what the person is saying, or upset about, and use the other verification techniques outlined in this book to see if you ultimately find them credible and reasonable.

Way-Out Wackos Typically...	Far-Sighted Fringe Thinkers Typically...
Use very emotional language in their postings	Present their views calmly and rationally
Have not earned any credentials in their field	Have advanced degrees and successes in their field
Cite only their opinions and nothing else	Cite others' theories and work in the field
Have some personal grudge or ax to grind	Are not personally involved in the issue
Feel passionately about their topic	Feel passionately about their topic
Have not published or presented in any forum	Have published or presented in some journal, conference, or gathering of colleagues, even if non-mainstream
Angrily reject disagreements with their views	Are open to discussing their claims
Express their views poorly in writing	Are able to express themselves clearly in writing
Are not welcome in the groups they participate in	Are welcome among colleagues, though they hold out-of-the-mainstream views

CHAPTER 8

Knowledge, Intuition, and Trust

"Education is the one thing we can't get overloaded with. The more of it the better."

—David Shenk, *DataSmog*

Some of what goes into appraising the quality of business information—or any information for that matter—goes beyond specific tools and concrete evaluation strategies, and involves more intangible or softer matter. Cultivating these qualities can provide a more elegant, longer-lasting solution to the matter of evaluating information.

This chapter offers some guidance in developing those qualities that will assist you in this area. Specifically, I'll discuss the following:

- Building your own knowledge
- Developing critical thinking skills
- The art of asking the right questions
- The use of intuition
- Whom to trust
- Determining truth

Building Your Own Knowledge

One of the best ways to avoid being misled by any type of information, on the Web or elsewhere, is to acquire as much knowledge as possible on your topic of research. Armed with some familiarity and know-how, you're in a much stronger position to judge the value of the information you come across.

This is easier said than done, of course. For many if not most research projects, the whole idea is to learn about a topic you're unfamiliar with. Still, there are some steps you can take to build up a base of knowledge and add to it as you go along, so that you're always approaching information from a position of some understanding. The following are approaches that I recommend:

1. Pre-Research Steps

Your business-related research will take place within a context of how the business world currently operates, so it's important you have a basic understanding of business realities. If you've worked in the business world for at least a few years, or if you have a degree in business, then you already have some knowledge. If you're new to the business world, you should take a crash course that teaches how business works, jargon and terminologies, and the current issues. Such a course might use some of the following resources:

- **Textbooks**—There are a great number of "Intro to Business"-type textbooks that you can find in your local library, a university library, or via an online bookseller.

- **Publications**—Speaking of your local library, go to the publications area and grab the last three to four months' worth of *Fortune, Forbes, The Economist*, and *Business Week.* You'll quickly get a handle on what the hot issues are in business around the world. I don't recommend you read these on the Web—you won't be able to access the archives easily, and you'll miss out on the serendipity that browsing offers.

- **Courses/Workshops**—Get the latest catalogs from your nearest universities, community colleges, and adult education centers. You're sure to find a wide range of beginning business courses open to anyone in the community.

Even if you're a seasoned businessperson, you should also find out where your knowledge gaps are. For example, you may know a great deal about company libraries and intranets, but do you know anything about corporate finance? You may be a proficient telemarketing supervisor, but do you know anything about inventory control or strategic planning? Of course you can't know everything, but learning as much as you can in the areas you're weak in will only strengthen your capabilities at work, and make you a savvier searcher.

You should also try to build some knowledge on the specific matter you're researching *before* venturing out onto the Web, by consulting other sources. Why? Well, although there's outstanding information on nearly any subject on the Web, there's also much dubious data. If you go to a reputable print source — such as a trade journal article, book, government document, etc. — or to a library database, you're going to get filtered information. In other words, this data had to go through a vetting process to be published and is more likely to be accurate. It's not necessarily "better" information than what you'll ultimately find on the Net, it's just less likely to be completely misleading. Build up at least a little knowledge this way and you'll be in a better position when you go onto the Web.

Similarly, if you know someone who knows something about the subject you're researching, it would be worth taking a few minutes to chat with this person to explain what you're looking for and get some pointers and advice. The questions that this person asks you as well as what he or she imparts to you during the conversation can fine-tune your approach to the research and improve the results.

There's another type of expert who can probably assist you no matter what your subject is: a librarian. Librarians are specifically trained to help information refine seekers their research questions, identify the best sources, and find the information they need. Spending as little as 10 minutes talking about your research problem with a librarian can save you hours if not days of research time. It will help you build your knowledge of where to look to uncover the most helpful and reliable sources of information on your topic.

In the ideal scenario, you'll go on the Web with some basic knowledge about business, and some additional knowledge about the subject of your research. You'll then be in a better position to assess the value and quality of what you come across. But your knowledge-building activities won't end there: You will now leverage what you find on the Web to better understand the key issues of your research.

2. Interactive Knowledge Building

Say you follow the advice given earlier in this book (but of course you will!) and begin your research with a Google search and by consulting a recommended directory, such as the Librarian's Index to the Internet.

As you refine and hone your searches, you will quickly scan some of the initial Web pages that are returned to see if they contain the information you need or contain leads to other good sources. Each time you do this, you will naturally increase your knowledge of the topic. Some areas will be reinforced as you read more logical and persuasive arguments from others, and other initial thoughts may be discarded. The more you read, the more you learn. And the more you learn on a topic, the better your ability to evaluate relevant information.

In other words, the more time you take in your research the more knowledge you'll build. Increasingly, you'll be in a better position to evaluate the quality of what you find. After reading, say, 20 or 30 different pages or documents, you will have been exposed to a large amount of information, seen the differences in how the topic is covered, applied some of the guidelines addressed earlier in the book, and slowly become somewhat of an expert. Confidence in your own judgment should naturally increase during this process.

This also means that you shouldn't rush to judgment in accepting the first relevant site you encounter. It's easy to judge relevance, but harder to judge quality. The latter often comes from a comparison of what else is out there. So until you have a fair amount of exposure to information on your topic, it's difficult to determine which pages and people have the most to offer. True, there is some "you'll know it when you see it" involved (as I discuss in the "Intuition" section beginning on page 196), but intuition works best when it's informed. In fact, one definition of intuition is our ability to tap into the knowledge that we have acquired over time, but cannot articulate consciously.

You can accelerate the interactive learning process by asking questions—typically via e-mail—of those Web site authors whose pages you find particularly compelling and relevant. Their answers will help you better understand the topic at hand, increase your knowledge, and make you a better judge of future sources. It's a "virtuous circle," the opposite of a vicious circle.

3. Staying Informed

You'll want to stay informed on the topics you regularly research, so that you can remain sharp and do a good job in evaluating the sources you come across. You can do this by reading trade journals and online newspapers, attending conferences, joining relevant Internet discussion lists, and taking classes to improve your own skills. Bottom Line: An informed searcher is a savvier searcher.

Developing Critical Thinking Skills

"All of our knowledge results from questions, which is another way of saying that question-asking is our most important tool. I would go so far as to say that the answers we carry about in our head are largely meaningless unless we know the questions that produced them."

—Neil Postman, Chair, Department of Culture and Communication, New York University, in *Teaching as a Conserving Activity* (Dell, 1979, p. 154.)

We've heard a lot over the past several years about the value of critical thinking, especially when navigating the deluge of media sources, dealing with information overload, and using the Internet effectively. But how many of us really know what critical thinking means, how we can become critical thinkers, and how to actually apply critical thinking skills in our daily lives?

M. Neil Browne, a professor and author of *Asking the Right Question: A Guide to Critical Thinking* (Prentice Hall), calls critical thinking "a virtue term" that's sometimes used to describe positive ways of thinking and problem-solving. While all the elements of what constitutes critical thinking are complex, it does refer to taking an active, thinking, and questioning orientation toward the reasoning and arguments of others. Such a critical thinking stance contrasts with a passive, nonquestioning approach.

These abilities come into play when we are presented with arguments and claims. Critical thinkers have the ability to step out of the information or conversational interchange and observe and reflect on the larger context in which it's occurring. Critical thinkers take notice of the types of evidence, reasoning, and arguments being presented, and are able to detect fallacies and flaws. They also know how to formulate probing questions, and come to valid conclusions based on the data and reasoning presented.

But how do you become a critical thinker? Are critical thinkers born or made? These are complex questions. There are mountains of research available on the topic of critical thinking, and, in fact, it's a true discipline with scholars, teachers, authors, and institutes. Developing critical thinking skills takes some dedication over time, requires work on practice exercises, and needs regular feedback from others. For this reason, it's not possible to truly teach critical thinking within the scope of this book. For those interested in critical thinking strategies, I've listed some Web-based and print resources beginning on page 258 in Appendix B.

However, what I will do here is briefly outline some key aspects of critical thinking and then provide some examples of how certain aspects are of particular relevance to research on the Web. This is intended to raise your awareness of the questions you should ask of yourself and of the creators of the sources you locate on the Web.

Although the discussion here barely skims the surface of what critical thinking entails, it should help the uninitiated to better understand the concept. Critical thinkers consider the following when encountering arguments and claims:

- What is the actual conclusion of the argument?
- Is the conclusion supported by the argument?
- What are the reasons offered in support of the argument?
- Are the language and words used clear and unambiguous?
- What kind of evidence is provided in the argument?
- What information is important that may be missing?
- What are the qualifications and authority of the person making the argument?

- Perhaps most importantly, is the reasoning sound? You should consider factors such as, what are the hidden assumptions? Can they stand on their own merits? Are there logical fallacies in the argument: That is, is the argument illogical? Examples of logical fallacies include citing a conclusion that does not flow from the reasoning; and using tautologies (using the initial premise of the argument to "prove" the argument). Are values being presented as objective evidence? Are the experts who are cited truly credible authorities?

Browne offers examples of how critical thinking skills can come into play when evaluating claims. The first relates to the always troublesome area of "causation"—that is, when you are presented with a claim that x occurred and thus y occurred, then y was caused by x. In the popular press, we often hear such causation arguments in relation to a health-related study—for example, the headline "Grapefruits are good for your heart!" in a news story that reports those who ate five grapefruits per week had 20-percent fewer heart attacks (thereby implying that eating more grapefruits must be good for your heart).

You'll also come across these types of claims in popular social science research or surveys, for example as in the following headline:

"Research Shows: Getting Married
Can Make You More Mentally Healthy"

Apparently a study of married people by the Family Research Council of Arlington, Virginia, showed that married people had 30-percent fewer visits to a mental health therapist than singles. But does this really mean that marriage causes better mental health? Could it mean that married people are more reluctant to go to a therapist? Or maybe it has nothing to with marriage, *per se*—it may be because married people also have children and tighter budgets and don't want to spend the money on therapists. Or maybe the entire study was done poorly, and married people actually do go to therapists as often, but the study involved a nonrepresentative sample of all married people. Perhaps mostly older couples or newlyweds, who generally go to therapists less often than middle-aged people, were involved.

You can see where I'm going with this. Critical thinkers don't accept that just because two phenomena are associated one is necessarily the cause of the other.

In the business arena, you might see research reports and company press releases with causal claims like:

- Growth in wireless Internet technologies boosts region's economy
- New software portal in workplace is improving company productivity
- Company's revenues are down in the wake of CEO scandal

In each case, you need to look for specific and credible evidence that the first factor is actually causing the second. Critical thinking means spending some time thinking about the claim, considering alternative reasons for the same conclusion, and then deciding whether the causation has actually been demonstrated by the argument presented.

Browne offers a simple exercise to practice critical thinking. When confronted with some claim, Browne says we should pose the following question to ourselves: "Is there any missing information that, were I to have it, I would be able to better make a decision about the conclusion."

For instance, say you find a Web page that states the following:

"GPS in Automobiles Forecasted to Soar."

"A study released by Steer-U-Right Research reported today that, between 2003–2007, half of all new automobiles will be equipped with a global positioning system (GPS) computer mapping system. The survey was based on a poll of 500 auto dealers who discussed increasing interest and an ongoing increase in GPS sales."

Hmmm, okay, well that's interesting. But what information is *not* here that, were I to have it, I would feel more confident about the claim that GPS sales are about to take off? I'd feel more confident if I had answers to these questions:

- How many automobiles were purchased this year, last year, and the year before that were equipped with GPS systems?
- What is the current additional price of adding a GPS system today? What was it last year and the year before? What is the expected price next year, and what is that figure based on?
- Which kinds of automobiles are being purchased with GPS? How are those automobiles categorized in the industry?
- Are there user-satisfaction surveys of those who've paid extra for a GPS?
- Which are the leading manufacturers of after-market GPS? What have their sales trends been? Are investment houses putting money into these firms? Why or why not?
- What is preventing more people from buying them now installed? Is it price or something else? If it is price, at what price do drivers seem to want them installed? If it isn't price, what is it?
- Are there less expensive alternatives that are being offered to car buyers who can't afford a full GPS? If so, who makes them and what do they cost?

One caveat in all of this: Critical thinking is of course a virtue, and it's hard to be too critical of being a critical thinker! Keep in mind that just because another person's argument fails to meet the standards of a critical thinker, it doesn't necessarily mean that his or her point is invalid. It could mean that the person doesn't have the skills to clearly articulate arguments. Or it could mean that he or she hasn't had the time or opportunity to marshal evidence. Or it could mean the person is operating from a more emotional, rather than rational, perspective.

This does not mean that they are wrong. But it does mean that you're unlikely to be convinced by that person's argument, based on what you are hearing. Instead, you'll need to think even bigger and consider such factors as whether this is a person who normally has shown keen insights and good judgment. Or is he or she in a position to see and understand certain things, and, if so, can you still pay attention to his claim? You should then use your own methods of asking good questions to tease out exactly why that person is thinking that way. Then decide for yourself whether their views are convincing or whether this is someone you should trust, even when the evidence is not there or is not well presented.

The Art of Asking the Right Questions

Critical thinking should be applied to all kinds of information and claims, in all types of media and sources. The Web has some special and unique attributes, and using it to do research calls for a certain set of critical thinking questions. I've listed these here, grouped into key topic areas for business searchers.

Before going to the Web for business research, ask yourself:

- Why am I choosing the Web to perform this research?
- Do my reasons make sense?
- For example, if it's because the Web is fast, why is that good?
- If it's because it's free, why is free information best? How much would I pay for good information?
- Is a search engine the best tool to find what I'm looking for on the Web? (See Chapter 2 for a description of the various information-finding tools.)
- Where else might I find the same type of information?
- Would a library or a fee-based database contain the data? If so, how would they compare in timeliness and comprehensiveness to what am I likely to find on the Web?

When you find a source of interest on the Web, ask yourself:

- Who put this information on the Web? Why?
- If it's free, why did the creator make it that way?
- Who gains from having this information on the Web?

When evaluating the authority of the publisher/creator of the information, ask yourself:

- What are the qualifications of this person or organization?
- Why should I trust them/it?

- Why are these opinions being offered here?

If a search engine doesn't return the information you're looking for, ask yourself:

- Did I use all the appropriate keywords and phrases?
- Did I follow the search engine's instructions?
- Could the search engine have failed to index the site that includes the information?
- Could the information be online, but as part of the "Invisible Web" that's inaccessible to search engines?
- Could it mean that the information isn't on the Web? If so, might it be available from other sources (the library, a journal database, a book or directory, an association, expert, etc.)?
- Could it be that what I'm looking for isn't the kind of information that's easily found on the Web? If so, am I better off trying a different type of resource altogether?
- Could it mean that the information simply doesn't exist?

When you find statistical data, ask yourself:

- What/who/where is the original source/creator of the data?
- Is this the most recent version/series of the data?
- Do I have the larger context from which this data was derived?
- Where can I find the methodologies and assumptions used to create these statistics?

On an online news site, ask yourself:

- What makes this a legitimate news-gathering and -reporting site?
- What is a legitimate news-gathering and -reporting site?
- Can I distinguish editorial from advertising on this site?

Note: Some of the checklists listed in Appendix A also provide a type of critical thinking for evaluating Web sites.

A few more thoughts on the importance of questioning. Browne explains that making the decision to ask a question means that we are "doing something or reflecting further, rather than just absorbing a declarative statement." We use questioning to work through the value and meaning of the new information being presented to us, and are deciding how it should be converted it into real, usable knowledge.

Although I'm a firm believer in the old "there's no such thing as a stupid question" adage, it's also true that some questions will be more helpful to you than others. Each question has an embedded assumption, and a certain question will have the power and capacity to call forth a specific answer. The best questions then will compel the most meaningful, useful, and insightful answers, and will have the following characteristics:

- They come from some position of knowledge and understanding. This allows the questioner to ask deeper, more probing questions.
- They will help shed light on the big picture and the matter under consideration.
- They probe the specific expertise or experience of the person being queried.
- They will surface hidden assumptions for a fresh look and analysis.
- They are open, honest, direct, confident, courageous, and polite.
- They don't take accepted orthodoxies for granted.
- They emphasize "why" over how, who, what, or when.
- They encourage communication as a way to create understanding.

The Use of Intuition

Just because you've learned how to be a critical thinker and to look at data skeptically doesn't mean that you don't also need to rely on your intuition—to listen to what your gut tells you when you find an unknown site. In fact, the more you become knowledgeable about a topic and the more you've learned to be a critical thinker, the more likely it is that your intuition will kick in. I don't pretend to have a definition for a force as mysterious as intuition. I do know that it is partially a function of embedded knowledge that you've absorbed from countless inputs and experiences that you have not consciously articulated to yourself.

The first steps in leveraging your intuition to better help you evaluate sites are, one, to recognize and acknowledge its existence, and, two, to recognize when it's trying to send you a message. Unless you're someone who already relies on intuition, meditates regularly, works with dreams, or is involved in some kind of spiritual training to tap into this kind of force, simply recognizing intuition can be tricky. Sad to say, many of us have been taught (perhaps by critical parents, teachers, or other negative forces) to distrust our feelings, thinking that someone else knows better.

If you're not used to listening to messages from your intuition, you need to first learn not to talk back or counter those messages as you hear them distantly in the background. They are soft but they can tug on you and make you feel a bit distracted and uncomfortable. Often your intuition will try to communicate some type of warning when you're about to make a decision based on what you think you're supposed or expected to do. Your gut tells you something isn't right. Start paying attention to those messages, as they generally represent a voice from a well with deeper knowledge and insight than you're used to encountering on the day-to-day surface.

Once you're aware of and learn to trust that voice, you'll see it appear more often, perhaps in even more mundane circumstances—such as when surfing the Web! You'll encounter, say, a company's Web site, which makes an odd-sounding claim about its product. But you realize that it just doesn't look right. It could be an unsettled feeling about some matter that's unresolved. When you feel that little tug, pay attention to it! It's your intuition trying to get your attention.

In fact, the phrase "just doesn't look right" is one that's fairly well-known among information professionals. It was used way back in the pre-Web days of the 1980s to alert librarians and researchers about the need to question information in print or on the fee-based databases that simply didn't "look right." Information guru Reva Basch has written about this "JDLR factor." She says she picked up the terminology some years ago from Don Ray, an investigative reporter in southern California, who used it in a presentation to a group of private investigators.

Basch explains that cultivating this JDLR antenna is more than just having a hunch. It comes from knowing the whole range of variables that go into how information is presented.

What do you do when you come across something that doesn't look or sound right? *The Modern Researcher*'s Barzun and Graff explain that when this occurs you have several options: accept the information, because it's coming from a trusted source; dismiss it because it doesn't square with what you already think; ignore it; or, as the authors advise, "suspend judgment until more information comes out" (p. 98). If your intuition gives you a caution warning, then take some of the practical strategies outlined earlier in this book (particularly regarding verification, as outlined in Chapter 4) to confirm your information.

Can you actually learn how to develop your intuition? I believe you can. First, as noted, understand what it is and be open to listening and trusting your own instincts. Acquire as much knowledge as possible in whatever areas you want to understand more deeply. Finally, use some relaxation or meditation techniques to help you quiet the distracting noises of everyday life—this will help make it easier for your intuition to reach your normal conscious state.

Whom to Trust

Ultimately, who or what you believe on the Web—or anywhere else—comes down to a matter of trust. And there is rarely, if ever, 100-percent certainty or confidence in the conclusions that you ultimately draw from the results of your research. As Barzun and Graff put it, "the historian arrives at truth through probability" (*The Modern Researcher*, p. 112).

In our daily business lives, we learn what sources—whether published or individuals—to rely on. These sources state something, and without going through an elaborate series of questioning or confirming, we put our trust in them. These sources have earned our trust, as they have proven to be reliable and trustworthy over time. We're usually not afraid to make decisions based on their advice. These types of sources are rare, and invaluable.

On the Web, of course, developing this kind of trust is a lot harder, for several reasons. First, you often encounter new sources or experts for the very first time, and you have no history or background to make a good assessment. There are also fewer cues for judging the value of a person's opinions and knowledge on the Web. In an office setting, we get to know colleagues and trusted advisors, how they behave in certain circumstances, a bit about their personal lives, visual cues, and so on. All this helpful input is missing on the Web. Instead, we have only the comments themselves, and perhaps an accompanying Web site.

You can use the various techniques and strategies I've already outlined to apply to unknown sources, but you still may not develop a deep trust in the source, only some level of confidence. So how do you come to trust a source on the Web? In the same way that you do in daily life: over time or through a referral from another trusted source. Specifically, this trust may occur as follows:

- You spend time on a discussion group and eventually find that a certain person regularly posts the most on-target, helpful, and insightful comments and suggestions to the rest of the group. Perhaps this person often has answers to your questions, and you come to expect that he or she is going to be of help. This person can become a trusted Web source.

- You visit a particular Web site on a regular basis and find that it's always easy to find what you need and that the information quality is consistently high. You come to rely on the site for a particular type of research, so it becomes a trusted site.

- You rely on a particular print newspaper, journal, or other traditional resource, and you learn that this source has launched a companion Web site. You should feel fairly confident that this source will be equally trustworthy.

So the key, when doing any type of research on the Web, is to build up a small but valued set of trusted sources. Then you can turn to them when you need help, and be fairly certain you'll receive quality information; this will help you avoid going through a questioning/ checklist type of procedure when you find information via a search engine or some other information hunt on the Net.

In the words of one well-known truth seeker, Bob Dylan, "If you want somebody you can trust, trust yourself" ("Empire Burlesque"). Remember that your own feelings about a source are your best guide.

Determining Truth

So far our discussion on evaluating the quality of what you find on the Web has focused on finding the best information. But what if you encounter deliberately created lies and misinformation on the Web? How can you avoid this?

Since this book is devoted to business-related research, I'll limit the discussion to business data that's most likely to be deceptive. From my experience, you mainly need to be careful in regard to:

- Investment-related sites, including stock manipulation
- Disgruntled employees, ex-employees, or others with a grudge spreading false information about a company
- Business-related urban legends and myths

Chapter 5 covered two other areas of business deception: one, companies that artificially inflate their earnings to make their financial health look better than it really is to encourage investment, and, two, overly rosy company and industry projections by research analysts.

The topic of investment research is beyond the scope of this book, but a full treatment of the hazards of searching for investment and stock data on the Web was comprehensively covered in Chapter 3 of Anne Mintz's book on avoiding misinformation on the Net, *Web of Deception: Misinformation on the Internet* (CyberAge Books, 2002).

Earlier, I covered the spreading of false information about a company, specifically the Emulex fake press release caper. But someone can spread bad data about a company a lot easier than going through the trouble of creating and disseminating a press release. All you need to do is to make a false statement about the company on one of the Web discussion groups.

For this reason, you should be extra cautious in respect to negative remarks about a company that appear in a discussion group. You'll want to consider the poster's possible motivations for making such comments, confirm the data with other sources, and assess the overall substance of the forum in which the remark was made. You might also try to contact the person who made the remark to get additional details, as well as a sense of his or her credibility and potential biases.

On the best and most active discussion groups there's often a kind of self-correcting mechanism when someone posts obviously false data, whether deliberately or not. Often what happens is that very quickly—normally within hours—one or more readers will challenge the information, and sometimes present alternative evidence or views. When someone posts something provocative, such as negative information about a company, you should watch for responses from others on the group.

If you're worried about misinformation being spread about your firm, there are online monitoring services that will track thousands of Web groups for mentions of the company name (or any other keyword you provide) and send you an excerpt of any such discussion.

There is a flip side to this problem, though. Some companies have had their representatives join certain Web discussion groups, not just to monitor what's being said about their company and their products, but to steer the conversation, counter others' points, and introduce topics that present them in a positive light. While this may not fall into the category of deliberate deception (it does in cases of misrepresentation), it certainly qualifies as information manipulation—an ethical gray area.

We have come to expect a certain amount of puffery in a press release or company brochure, but this type of attempt to put one's firm in the most positive light can be particularly insidious because we have no grounds for suspecting bias. There may well be an assumption on the part of the group that its membership only comprises people with a certain set of interests, while in fact someone may be simply using the forum to serve an interest that may be counter to its mission. This is clearly a deceptive practice and one that is likely to increase as the numbers of discussion group members grow.

How can you protect yourself from this kind of manipulation? There is no easy answer. First, if you wonder about someone, pay attention to your intuition. If it's important enough to you, take the next step and ask the person where he or she works. Are you satisfied with the answer? Try running the name of that organization through Google and see what comes up. Search the person's name through the Google Group function to see where else he or she has posted. (Of course it's always possible that the person is using an alias in the group, and so you won't be able to turn up any other information or postings.) If there are a couple of members in the discussion group that you trust, you could always e-mail them privately to ask if they know anything about the person. If you're still doubtful, then you're probably best off not heeding what that person says on the group.

This isn't to say that a company spokesperson cannot in some cases play a legitimate role in a discussion group. For example, on the BUSLIB group, when there's a discussion of a company's product or service, a representative of that company may join in. The key here is that the company representative doesn't pretend to be anyone else, so the rest of the group can judge his or her statements in context.

Business-Related Urban Legends and Myths

Remember hearing the story of a woman who visited a fast food restaurant and found that her french fries included a breaded mouse? Most of us have heard such stories—and this is but one example of a pre-Internet urban legend, a tale that spreads among the population but may have no basis in fact.

Well, the Web has proven to be the ideal urban legend propagation and dissemination vehicle. Many are hoaxes passed by e-mail, and typically involve things like nonexistent viruses, investment scams, and petitions to save National Public Radio. But are there other urban legends specifically related to business? Yes, there are.

Generally, these take the form of some outrageous story about what a company did or didn't do. Sometimes these "incredible but true" tales concern a certain company's product, or some egregious way that it dealt with its customers.

The following are just a few examples of *false* urban legends that relate to business. These have all been gathered from one of the leading collectors of false folk tales, The Urban Legends Reference Pages:

- Neiman-Marcus charged a customer $250 for its cookie recipe
- Starbucks Thailand turns away Asian customers
- Snapple is owned by the Ku Klux Klan
- The CEO of Procter & Gamble donates a portion of the company's profits to the Church of Satan
- Dr. Pepper is made with prune juice

There are many more, but in the interest of not propagating bad data I think this is enough to get the point across.

How can you protect yourself from falling prey to these fictitious stories? That's easy: If you read something outlandish in an e-mail or on an unknown Web site, simply disregard it. If you need to confirm it, don't do a Web search—that's likely to find more references, just as possibly false. Instead, check the Urban Legends Reference Pages, post a query to a reliable and relevant message board, or search a more reliable set of sources (such as a newspaper archive) to dig up some background on your own.

Seeking Larger Truths on the Internet

There is a growing tendency for everyone, business researchers included, to turn to the Web whenever they need an answer of any kind. The Web has, in fact, become a giant question-answering machine. We turn to it when we want to find answers to virtually any type of question, from the most mundane (what's the address of xyz company?) to more weighty issues (is now the right time for our company to go public?).

This has some interesting implications. On the positive side, it's now possible to quickly find answers to difficult or obscure questions that would have been almost impossible to find before the Web. Need to find out how Brazilian workers view the concept of telecommuting? Search for an international workers' organization. Wondering if anyone knows about the history of the vacuum cleaner? You'll find it by doing a search on Google, or, better yet, go to the Hoover Co. home page or one of several amateur sites devoted to the history of that appliance. Are U-Haul customers satisfied with the service they receive? You can find the answer on the Web.

But there's also a subtle downside to the surfeit of answers that are available on the Web. I believe that all of this information increases the danger that we fall prey to what is called self-confirmation bias—that is, only paying attention to the data that confirms what we already believe.

Here's why. The sheer number of articles, reports, anecdotes, and opinion pieces on the Web makes it easier than ever to find information that "confirms" your prior beliefs, theories, or suspicions. Do you suspect that e-books are an exploding market? Well, simply run a search on the Web with those keywords and you'll find some who concur with the belief that e-books are in fact an exploding market. But try entering "exploding market" for many other industries, or whichever other word combinations describe your research. You're almost always bound to find some people who are considering this as well, or who are positing a relationship between the two concepts. On the Web, the old adage about seeking and finding can now be updated to "seek and ye shall *surely* find."

When we find these relevant, matching sites on the Web, human nature tempts us to then view them as offering support for our pre-existing line of thinking.

Of course, the hazards of self-confirmation bias in research preceded the Web. Then, you could also skip over and ignore data that conflicted with your views. But doing research on the Web exacerbates this pitfall, for a couple of reasons. First, a keyword-search method on a search engine for finding information inherently limits what you'll view to those pages that include your concepts. So if you read only the information on those sites, you won't even find related discussions that may present conflicting evidence. In this case, it's not even necessary to ignore sources since you don't even need to encounter them at all. Secondly, the sheer amount of topic information that exists increases the probability that you'll find pages that match your keywords.

And just because you find sites where others say something that supports your hypothesis, as Ella Fitzgerald sang, "it ain't necessarily so."

On the other side of the coin, it can still prove to be a worthwhile lead if you do find reports or people who have had experiences that confirm your belief. It means that you may be on to something, so it's certainly worthy of further investigation. But it doesn't constitute any kind of ultimate proof or evidence.

So, when you're doing business research, remember that your choice of keywords is naturally going to limit what you retrieve. Try to broaden your searches to find related, associated pages that discuss issues on the edges of what you are researching. Don't assume that what you find on the Web represents comprehensive analysis of the subject you're researching. Remember to use resources that are not on the Web, such as scholarly and trade journal databases, governmental and association reports and white papers, and your own circle of knowledgeable colleagues.

The other hazard in turning to the Web to answer all your questions or problems is simply that while it can be a superb source for uncovering data, facts, opinions, and useful information, it's not the right source for discovering answers to big questions, finding answers to larger truths, and substituting for building your own knowledge. Questions like, "Should I move into such and such a career?" "Would a new venture in the exotic travel industry pay off?" and "Should I expand my business and open offices in other countries?" won't be "answered" with a few keyword searches.

In cases like this, you're not looking for facts or information but deeper insights. Such insights are not going to emerge from assembling facts and opinions off the Internet. Instead, they can come from deeper, more intangible wellsprings of knowledge: self-understanding, years of real-world experience, emotional intelligence, advice from trusted friends and colleagues, and the development of personal qualities like

Figure 8.1   *The Internet is only a source of data, facts, opinions, and information—not true knowledge and wisdom—though this site promises enlightenment!*

courage, self-discipline, and will. You can't get these from a Web search (despite the promises of Enlightenment.com—see Figure 8.1).

Neil Postman has been a longtime critic of the view that information itself is an answer to problems. He says, "If there are people starving in the world—and they are—it is not caused by insufficient information ... something else is missing." The Web does have a tendency to make us think that information is The Answer. In fact, though it can be used to find a good answer, that's not enough by itself.

So use the Web wisely, and don't count on it for wisdom.

CHAPTER 9

Prescreened Business Sites

As mentioned earlier, one of the best ways to make sure that the Web sites you use are of consistent high quality is to build your own list of trusted sources. It can take time to build up such a list, so I'll give you a head start with a listing of business research sites on the free Web that have been prescreened for quality. These sites are derived from two main sources.

The first list comprises selections that I made for the 2001–2003 period in my monthly Best Business Web Sites Eletter, which identifies and describes recommended business research Web sites. The second is a list of recommendations from several of FIND/SVP's "practice area" leaders, each of which focus on a particular industry or field (such as Consumer Products, Financial & Business, etc.). Several group leaders have provided me with the names and descriptions of some of their most trusted sites.

These lists are certainly not inclusive, by any means, but each source has been selected for its quality and value. All of them are available at no charge on the open Web.

Best of the Business Sites

Following are sites that I have personally checked and recommended to readers of the Best Business Web Sites Eletter. I've broken them down into the following categories:
- Advertising and Marketing
- Analyst Research

- Business Rankings
- Business Strategy/Knowledge Management
- Business Technology Web Journals
- Company Information
- Competitive Intelligence
- Corporate Finance
- Corporations—History and Management
- Country Information
- Economic Data
- Government Sources
- Industry Information
- International Business Research
- Market Research and Product Information
- Mergers and Acquisitions
- News Sources
- Patents and Trademarks
- Search Engines
- Statistical Information
- Venture Capital and Funding
- Weblogs
- Link Sites/Reference/Miscellaneous

Advertising and Marketing

Branding Resource List

http://makeashorterlink.com/?N2C312F34

A collection of resources and recommended readings on naming and branding strategies. Resources identified include books, articles and papers, Web sites, and case studies.

Analyst Research

Institutional Investor Online: Analyst Database

http://www.iimagazine.com (home page)

The Analyst Database section of Institutional Investor Online is a directory of sell-side equity research analysts, which includes all of Institutional Investor's ranked analysts since 1998, worldwide.

Business Rankings

Forbes Lists

http://www.forbes.com/lists

This site offers free access to several valuable business related lists created by Forbes.

List of Lists

http://www.specialissues.com/lol

The List of Lists is a database of ranked listings of companies, people and resources that are available for free on the Internet. The rankings are grouped into about 25 categories derived from the two-digit 1997 U.S. NAICS codes.

Ranking.com

http://ranking.com

Ranking.com provides a variety of statistical data on the 900,000 most visited sites on the Web.

Business Strategy/Knowledge Management

The American Productivity and Quality Center (APQC)

http://apqc.org

This site specializes in helping companies identify best practices, discover effective methods of improvement, adapt to changing environments, and be more competitive. Specialty areas include: benchmarking, knowledge management, process improvement, and quality programs.

BNET

http://www.bnet.com

BNET offers a wide range of documents to help businesses solve problems. It has a special focus in providing white papers, but also offers free case studies, Webcasts, audio conferences, book summaries, and other business related tools to increase effectiveness.

INSEAD Knowledge

http://knowledge.insead.edu/welcome.cfm

INSEAD provides abstracts and the full text to working papers and case studies on academically oriented business research topics. Specific areas covered include: change and innovation, competing, corporate development, entrepreneurship, finance and banking, globalization, green thinking, knowledge management, and marketing. INSEAD also provides interviews with professors and summaries of new business books.

Organizational Change: An Annotated Bibliography
    http://www.archives.gov/research_room/alic/staff_resources/
organizational_change_bibliography/bibliography_index.html
    This site is a compilation of selected publications and resources on organizational change. Specific topics include: balanced scorecard, benchmarking continuous improvement, leadership, learning organizations, organizational culture, outsourcing, performance measurement, and process management, as well as other aspects of organizational change.

Business Technology Web Journals

Business 2.0
    http://www.business2.com
    "A monthly magazine about business, technology, and innovation."

Darwinmag.com
    http://www.darwinmag.com
    The theme of this digital journal is "business evolving in the Information Age." Topics range from technology forecasts, to hot new products, strategic advice for high-tech firms, and the social implications of new technologies.

First Monday
    http://www.firstmonday.dk
    This peer-reviewed scholarly journal examines the social impact and implications of the Internet. According to the site, "First Monday publishes original articles about the Internet and the Global Information Infrastructure."

Journal of the Hyperlinked Organization (JOHO)
    http://www.hyperorg.com

According to the site, this journal "considers the subtle, pervasive and sometimes surprising effect of the Web (especially in the form of intranets) on how businesses work."

ReadMe

http://journalism.nyu.edu/pubzone/ReadMe

This site focuses on digital culture, technology news, e-business, and net art.

Company Information

Central Contractor Registration

http://www.ccr.gov

The CCR is the key database of vendors that are doing business with the U.S. federal government. The site permits visitors to search and obtain data supplied by the over 300,000 vendors that have registered with the CCS. A special section of this site also permits visitors to search a database of small business by clicking on the link called "Dynamic Small Business Search."

CorporateInformation.com

http://www.corporateinformation.com

This database provides a variety of useful company information, including company profiles, research reports, rankings, as well as country and state profiles.

Private Companies and Becoming an Expert

http://www.businessjournalism.org/content/3222.cfm

This page provides highlights from a presentation that identified, described, and provided links to sources that offer information on privately held firms.

The Wall Street Transcript Online: CEO Interviews

http://www.twst.com/ceos.htm

This site publishes the full text of transcripts of interviews with company CEOs and corporate leaders in a Q&A format.

WetFeet

http://www.wetfeet.com/research/companies.asp

This site offers over 1,600 snapshots of companies.

Directory of Corporate Archives in the United States and Canada, 5th ed.

http://www.hunterinformation.com/corporat.htm

This site provides a listing, and contact information for companies that maintain their own historical records, or use consulting firms to maintain their archive collection.

Company House

http://www.companies-house.gov.uk/info/

Company House offers details on all limited and public limited British firms, including active and dissolved firms.

zapdata

http://www.zapdata.com

This site provides free company profiles on 12 million businesses, reports on thousands of industries, and names of marketing prospects that match the criteria entered by the user (limited to 25).

American Customer Satisfaction Index (ACSI)

http://www.theacsi.org

The American Customer Satisfaction Index is a national economic indicator of customer satisfaction with the quality of goods and services available to household consumers in the United States.

The 2003 Global 500

http://www.fortune.com/fortune/global500

This site allows users to view industry data on Fortune magazine's Global 500 list. The listing can be viewed by company, CEO, industry, top performers, or by European and Asian firms. Data provided on the firms include address, Web site, CEO, number of employees. Also provided are revenue, profits, assets, and stockholders equity.

Industry Week 1000

http://www.industryweek.com/iwinprint/IW1000

This site provides data on the world's 1,000 largest publicly held manufacturing companies, based on revenue. The list provides the company name, a link to a short company profile, and its ranking for the current and previous year.

Ketupa.net

http://www.ketupa.net

Ketupa.net provides detailed profiles of 125 worldwide media companies. Among the types of media firms covered are newspapers and magazine publishers, recording companies, film and video production companies, broadcasters, and academic/technical publishers. Each entry also includes a company history as well.

MSN Money Ownership Profile

http://moneycentral.msn.com/investor/invsub/ownership/ownership.asp

This section of the MSN Money site offers a neat summary page of ownership of U.S. public companies. Enter a company ticker or name and the site will instantly present a chart that displays aggregate ownership data as well as the names and holdings of the largest institutional, mutual fund, and 5%+ individual owners.

The Scorecard Project

http://www.scorecard.org

The Scorecard Project provides detailed information on environmental hazards around the United States, down to a zip code level. The site describes the types of pollution and chemicals released and their hazards, provides interactive maps of the facilities that emit the specific pollutions, and provides contact and other information on the specific polluting facilities. The Scorecard Project covers manufacturing facilities that report their emissions under the U.S. "EPA's Toxics Release Inventory," and the 650 chemicals reported under this project.

Yahoo! Finance Company Profiles

http://finance.yahoo.com (enter ticker symbol; then click on "profile" in the selection box returned)

This section of Yahoo! Finance provides a wide range of descriptive and financial data on public companies, including: company description; recent events; officers names and salaries; summary of financial condition; ownership and insider stock purchase data; links to fee-based research reports, employee data, and more.

Zacks Free Research Center

http://www1.zacks.com/free.html

This site provides summaries and formatted tables with profiles, income statements, balance sheets, and additional data on U.S. public companies.

BusinessWire

http://home.businesswire.com

BusinessWire provides a searchable database of the last seven days of press releases from hundreds of companies, as well as short company profiles for some firms in its database.

Financial Ratios and Quality Indicators

http://www.onlinewbc.gov/docs/finance/fs_ratio1.html

This site identifies and explains the key business Ratios (e.g., current ratio, quick ratio, debt to equity, net profit margin).

Investor Canada

http://www.investorcanada.com/index.php

This site offers in-depth interviews of prominent CEOs, and other company executives of interest to business researchers.

ISI Emerging Markets

http://www.securities.com

This site delivers news, and company and financial data on emerging markets from about 30 countries in Europe, Latin America, and Asia.

Search-Sec.com

http://www.search-sec.com

This site provides access to SEC documents filed by U.S. public companies. Users can search by ticker symbol, and limit searches by company name, zip code, phone number, state, countries, SIC code, or form types.

WorldAtOnce.com

http://www.worldatonce.com

WorldAtOnce.com provides basic directory information on about 40 million firms around the globe. Users can search by region as well as by SIC code and yellow page headings to locate data on the firms in this database.

Competitive Intelligence

National Center for Charitable Statistics

http://www.nccs.urban.org/990

NCCS is a national repository of information on nonprofits in the United States.

The Virtual Chase

http://www.virtualchase.com/coinfo/index.htm

This site assists persons in the legal profession to perform research on the Web.

Eliyon Networking

http://networking5.eliyon.com/Networking

This site allows you to search for the names, titles, and years or employment for over 16 million past employees of large and small companies. A search is done by entering the name of a company.

Corporate Finance

IBM Guide to Financials

http://www.ibm.com/investor/financialguide

IBM's guide provides basic information on how to read the financial statements in a company's annual report. In a step by step manner, the guide provides beginners with definitions and instructions on how to understand annual reports, key financial reports (earnings, cash flow, etc.) the basics on analysis, and using the data for investment purposes. There is also a further resources section and a glossary.

CFO.com

http://cfo.com

This site serves as a complete reference and resource tool for senior finance executives.

Corporations—History and Management

The Corporate Library

http://www.thecorporatelibrary.com

The site, according to its creators, "is intended to serve as a central repository for research, study, and critical thinking about the nature of the modern global corporation."

Ad*Access and The Emergence of Advertising in America
http://scriptorium.lib.duke.edu/adaccess
http://scriptorium.lib.duke.edu/eaa

Ad* Access provides a searchable database of images and accompanying information for over 7,000 advertisements printed in U.S. and Canadian newspapers between 1911 and 1955 and covers five major areas: radio, television, transportation, beauty/hygiene, and World War II; The Emergence of Advertising in America covers over 9,000 images and information covering 1850-1920 in the areas of ephemera, broadsides, cookbooks, J. Walter Thomson house ads, tobacco ads, Kodak ads, and several other categories.

Country Information

Country Insights
http://globaledge.msu.edu/ibrd/countryindex.asp

Country Insights provides a description, statistics, resources, history, geographical information, and more on the countries of the world. This site also allows for statistical comparisons between selected countries.

BBC Country Profiles
http://news.bbc.co.uk/2/hi/country_profiles/default.stm

This site provides summary and detailed information for countries around the world. Data includes a general profile, key facts and statistics, leaders, media, an historical events timeline, broadcasts of historical events, and related links.

ExecutivePlanet.com
http://www.executiveplanet.com

This site provides "business culture guides" that contain information and advice on the appropriate etiquette and cultural do's and dont's when doing business in 40 countries around the world (including the U.S.). Topics covered include: making appointments, proper forms of addressing others, greetings, conversation, gift giving, and entertaining. There are accompanying discussion boards where site visitors can ask questions and make comments on this site's cultural advice.

NationMaster

http://www.nationmaster.com

This site takes publicly available statistical data on the world's countries, on everything from crime to education, the economy, demographics and more, and allows users to choose a country and/or a set of statistics to graph a comparison between designated countries. Sources include the CIA World Factbook, and various United Nations' publications.

Perry-Castañeda Library Map Collection

http://www.lib.utexas.edu/maps/index.html

This site provides links to a wide range of online maps including: world maps, continent maps, country maps, U.S. maps, county maps, city maps, historical maps, and current interest maps. Maps are in JPEG or GIF format.

Country Commercial Guides

http://www.state.gov/e/eb/rls/rpts/ccg

This site provides detailed business guides on countries around the globe.

United Nations Millennium Country Profiles

http://unstats.un.org/unsd/mi/mi.asp

The United Nations has created 48 social and economic indicators for countries around the globe. Among the statistics provided on this site: AIDS cases, access to essential drugs, CO_2 emissions, children immunizations, debt service, energy usage, Internet users, literacy rates, PC usage, poverty, telephone usage, and more.

Economic Data

Economagic

http://www.economagic.com

This site provides access to a huge number of key economic time series data, with a special emphasis on forecasting data.

The Beige Book

http://www.federalreserve.gov/FOMC/BeigeBook/2004

The Beige Book is a report from the U.S. Federal Reserve providing an up-to-date commentary of economic conditions and a commentary on economic trends for 12 selected regions around the country. The book is updated eight times per year and an archive of earlier reports is available back to 1996.

The Dismal Scientist

http://www.economy.com/dismal

This site provides daily coverage of macro-economic data worldwide, such as employment, GDP, monetary policy, commentary and analysis, forecasts, regional outlooks, economic tools and calculators, rankings, Federal Reserve news and analysis, and more.

Government Sources

FirstGov

http://www.firstgov.gov

FirstGov provides a one-stop access to over 30 million pages of information from the U.S. government.

Government Public Records

http://www.brbpub.com/pubrecsites.asp

This page contains links to over 300 state, county, and city offices that have made their public records available at no charge on the Web.

Energy Information Administration: Country Analysis Briefs

http://www.eia.doe.gov/emeu/cabs/contents.html

This site offers succinct, but detailed overviews on the role of energy for over 120 countries and regions. Each report begins with a country background, including an overview of its economy and environment, and then provides details on the use and importance of oil, natural gas, coal, electricity, nuclear power, synthetic fuels, and renewables.

Envirofacts

http://www.epa.gov/enviro

Envirofacts is a searchable database that provides in-depth data on institutions, regions, and other entities that have a connection to a known environmental hazard. Detailed maps are provided as well.

IMF Country Reports
http://www.imf.org/external/pubind.htm (Select "IMF Country Reports" under Series)

This site offers a searchable and browsable collection of economic reports published by the IMF on various topics for countries around the world. Sample recent reports: Republic of Mozambique: Statistical Appendix, Tunisia: Report on the Observance of Standards and Codes, and Forecasting Inflation in Indonesia.

The National Library for the Environment: CRS Reports
http://www.cnie.org/NLE/CRS

This site provides free access to over 1,200 Congressional Research Service (CRS) Reports on issues related to the environment, energy, water, science, and technology.

Industry Information

International Trade Data System:Industry Profiles
http://www.itds.treas.gov/commodityprof.html

This site assists businesses in locating industry data from the over 100 federal agencies involved in international trade and import/export activity.

International Trade Administration (ITA): Trade Development: Industry Analysts
http://www.ita.doc.gov/td/td_home/tdhome.html#top (then click on "Industry Analysts")

This site provides a directory of analysts and experts in the trade development office of the ITA.

Industry Data Finder
http://www.rh.edu/library/industry/industry.htm

This site identifies sources and provides links to over 30 key industries, ranging from aerospace and defense to toys and textiles.

Integra Information

http://www.integrainfo.com

If you click on "free stuff" you can get up to five free snapshot reports for over 900 industries, which includes growth rates, net profits, and margins.

Industry Resources Reports

http://www.valuationresources.com/IndustryReport.htm

Industry Resources Reports provides industry reports for about 220 industries, organized by SIC code. Click on an industry, and you'll find lists and links to a wide range of resources covering that industry, including publications, association reports, surveys, and more.

SmartBrief

http://www.smartbrief.com

SmartBrief is an industry news alert service sent directly to your e-mail. Subscribers obtain an HTML formatted message with headlines and abstracts of recent articles in specified journals and newspapers that relate to the particular industry selected.

Yahoo! Industry Center

http://biz.yahoo.com/ic

This site offers a wide range of industry information such as recent news, statistics, and profiles of industry leaders for about 100 different industries.

Strategic Advantage

http://www.strategy4u.com

One section of the site, devoted to business strategy, allows visitors to input their industry's SIC code and instantly obtain benchmark comparison data. There are also a variety of other tools whereby companies can comparethemselves in their strategic capabilities.

International Business Research

Trade Data Online

http://www.strategis.gc.ca/tdo

This site lets users generate customized reports on Canadian and U.S. trade with over 200 countries.

Documents Online

http://docsonline.wto.org

Documents Online provides access to the official documentation of the World Trade Organization (WTO), including the legal texts of the WTO agreements. The database includes over 100,000 documents, available in English, French, and Spanish.

World Competitiveness Yearbook 2003

http://www01.imd.ch/wcy/ranking

The World Competitiveness Yearbook studies the competitiveness of 59 world economies, and its companion Web site provides the overall ranking of the economies from least to most competitive. The ranking list is broken down into two categories: economies with a population greater than 20 million, and those with fewer than 20 million. The ranking is performed on a yearly basis.

Market Research and Product Information

Household Products Database

http://hpd.nlm.nih.gov/products.htm

This site provides a searchable database with health, safety, and manufacturer information on over 4,000 household products. You can browse by category or by brand name. Industries covered are: automotive, landscape, personal care, home maintenance, general household, and hobby/craft. Data provided for each product record includes: manufacturer name and contact information, health effects, handling/disposal, and chemical ingredients (unless a trade secret or proprietary formula). The record also allows the searcher to locate products with similar usage and locate other products by the same manufacturer.

Strategis: Create Your Own Market Research Report

http://strategis.ic.gc.ca/sc_x/engdoc/researching_markets.html?guides=e_res

On this section of Canada's national trade site, users can conduct a free search of the U.S. Department of Commerce's National Trade

Data Bank's market research reports. Searches can be restricted by country, world region, and specific industry.

International Market Research Center
http://www.fita.org/trade_info.html

The International Market Research Center offers a collection of resources, databases, guides, and links for conducting international trade. It includes business directories, statistical databases, trade show calendars, governmental resources, and more.

TradeStats Express
http://ese.export.gov/ITA2003_STATES/ITA_MapInfo_portal_page.htm

This database allows users to create and view color-coded graphical representations of import/export and trade balance data. Users can choose a specific product code, and then view charts and tables that display trade between the U.S. and user-specified countries for the product. Users can also select a state or region of the U.S. to the world, country, or region of the world and view its export data the same way.

InfoTech Trends
http://www.infotechtrends.com/freedemo.htm

This site extracts key market research data on the IT industry from about 100 key trade journals. The above URL allows visitors to try some free sample searches.

Marketing Virtual Library: KnowThis.com
http://knowthis.com

This site is a collection of the best and most substantive links on all major areas of marketing. Key topic areas include: advertising and promotion, careers and jobs, CRM, Internet marketing, market research, international marketing, selling and sales management, and more. Also provides basic definitions of terms, cross references, and specialty areas.

Mergers and Acquisitions

TheDeal.com
http://thedeal.com

This site provides both articles and various tools and data for those who need to track merger and acquisition activity.

M&A Activity Page

http://www.corporateaffiliations.com/dca/Executable/cn_mergers.asp

This page on the CorporateAffiliations.com site lists the largest firms (over $20 million in revenue) that have either merged, changed their name, or have gone out of business over a designated period of time.

News Sources

MagPortal.com

http://www.magportal.com

MagPortal.com allows you to conduct keyword searches on the Web versions of about 450 well-known magazines and Web-only publications.

Technology Review: Business Technology Review: Blog

http://www.technologyreview.com/topics/bus.asp (Business)
http://www.technologyreview.com/blog/index.asp (Blog)

Technology Review is a leading print publication that reports on new innovations and technologies that have a robust presence on the Web. The top URL links to business-oriented technology articles on the Web, and the bottom URL is a link to Technology Review's Weblog.

World News Connection (WNC)

http://wnc.fedworld.gov

World News Connection provides the full text of translated news from thousands of media sources around the world.

FindArticles.com

http://www.findarticles.com

An archive of hundreds of thousands of articles from 300 leading journals from The Gale Group.

JournalismNet

http://www.journalismnet.com/business

JournalismNet is a site designed to help journalists locate information on the Web.

ABYZ News Links

http://www.abyznewslinks.com

ABYZ News Links is a gateway to over 20,000 English-language media sources from all over the globe. The list includes newspapers, magazines, broadcasters, and Internet-only sites.

NewsNow

http://www.newsnow.co.uk

This news aggregator scans over 12,000 online news sources, sorts them into subject categories, and displays the latest headlines with links to the full stories.

Rutgers University Libraries: News Sources

http://www.libraries.rutgers.edu/rul/rr_gateway/research_guides/busi/busenews.shtml

This site identifies and provides links to various business news sources on the Web. Categories include: U.S.: General Business and Finance, E-Commerce and Internet Marketing; International Business News: Asia and Australasia, Middle East, Africa, Europe and CIS, and The Americas; and Industry-Specific News.

C-SPAN Archives

http://www.c-span.org

This site provides access to live C-SPAN broadcasts, as well as a searchable archive of the last 15 days of audio and video events. Also includes National Press Club luncheon speakers, which often feature speeches of well-known CEOs.

ClickZ

http://www.clickz.com/news

ClickZ provides timely news stories on topics related to interactive advertising. This includes e-mail marketing, pay-for-placement search, portals, Internet company activities, and wireless. Also covered are related consumer issues, such as demographic trends, Internet survey usage results, and so on.

News Directory.Com

http://www.newsdirectory.com

This site provides links to general and business newspapers from around the globe broken down by region of world and country.

Reuters.com

http://www.reuters.com

Reuters.com provides breaking business news, covering both the U.S. and the world. Topics reported on include company news and reports, consensus forecasts, economic indicators, fund stories, governmental filings, hot stocks, IPOs, mergers, and new issues.

Patents and Trademarks

Patent Alert

http://www.patentalert.com

Patent Alert helps you keep current with new patents filed in your field of interest by alerting you with an e-mail when a patent is awarded.

Search Engines

CyberJournalist SuperSearch

http://www.cyberjournalist.net/supersearch

CyberJournalist's SuperSearch provides visitors with the option to search a wide range of Web-based search engines from a single page. Included are general search engines, major news sites, specialty news sites, reference sources, company directories, legal searches, government sites, expert databases, people searching, and more.

SMEALSearch

http://smealsearch.psu.edu

SMEALSearch is a special purpose business-oriented search engine that allows users to search documents and citations of academically oriented business articles and data collections.

Statistical Information

Statistics.com

http://www.statistics.com

This site is a one-stop source for everything related to statistics.

Statistical Abstract of the United States

  http://www.census.gov/statab/www

  The Statistical Abstract is the official source of national statistics for the United States.

WebStat: Statistics on the Web

  http://webstat.stat.fi/etusivu_en.html

  This site is a searchable database of 3,200 statistical sources on the Web, classified by subject field and by country.

Statistical Resources on the Web

  http://www.lib.umich.edu/govdocs/stats.html

  Statistical Resources on the Web provides a list of filtered Web sites for a wide range of statistical topics.

Eurostat

  http://europa.eu.int/comm/eurostat

  This site provides a timely source for the latest statistical information on the European Union (EU).

PollingReport.com

  http://www.pollingreport.com

  This site aggregates current polling data from a wide range of opinion poll surveys conducted by polling organizations on current interest topics, such as political matters in the news, social issues, and business and economic subjects.

BizStats

  http://www.bizstats.com

  This site provides a wide range of substantive statistical data and summaries on various business topics with special attention to small business statistics. Categories include national business statistics such as employee productivity, and safest/riskiest businesses to begin, as well as statistical compilations for specific areas like construction, retail, and service industries.

Venture Capital and Funding

VentureWire

  http://www.venturewire.com

A Web site with an accompanying free e-mail alert that reports on the latest news on private firms and venture capital activity.

Weblogs

Analyst Blogs—Jupiter & Gartner

Jupiter: http://weblogs.jupiterresearch.com

http://sox.weblog.gartner.com/weblog/weblogIndex.php?pre=sox

These sites provide a forum where industry analysts can discuss news, trends, and developments in their fields, and offer up their analysis.

Michelle's Research Sources Online

http://michellelaycock.blogspot.com

This blog identifies and describes useful research services and sources on the Web, and includes related commentary on the information industry and on technology issues.

PaidContent.org

http://paidcontent.org

This site provides news, opinions, and comments on the digital content business, including online services, wireless, multimedia, digital devices, and other fee-based digital content products and services.

ResourceShelf

http://www.resourceshelf.com

Gary Price's Weblog provides news, commentary and links about the most important, useful, and substantive new research related sites on the Web. You can obtain his reports either by going to his site or signing up for Gary's free e-mail alert.

SiteLines

http://www.workingfaster.com/sitelines

SiteLines is a news blog that reports on developments and trends in Web searching.

The Weblog Guide

http://www.guardian.co.uk/weblog/special/0,10627,744914,00.html

The Weblog Guide offers a selection of "best" Weblogs in categories like news, technology, politics, and niche blogs. This page also includes information on how to start a blog, and has links to a wide range of news and media sites around the globe.

Link Sites/Reference/Miscellaneous

CEOExpress.com

http://www.ceoexpress.com/default.asp

CEOExpress.com offers links to hundreds of qualified, substantive business-oriented sites including news sites, company research sites, and search engines, and includes links to sources for doing research on topics like international business, banking, statistics, law, small business, bankruptcy, business reference tools, and more.

Google Zeitgeist

http://www.google.com/press/zeitgeist.html

This site provides listings, compilations, and charts identifying words and phrases Google users have searched on most frequently during the past month.

ClickZ

http://www.clickz.com/stats

ClickZ provides all in one place, a variety of sought-after statistical data, briefings, and research findings related to Internet use.

The Glossarist (Business glossaries)

http://www.glossarist.com/glossaries/business

Here you'll find a listing, brief description, and links to a wide range of business glossaries. These business glossaries are categorized into subtopics: advertising, communications, construction, e-commerce, freight and logistics, international trade, management, manufacturing, packaging, primary industry, occupational safety, printing, and real estate.

Iraq War and Business

http://www.lib.washington.edu/business/guides/iraq.html

This site has collected a variety of print, online, and Web resources that provide information on the impact of the 2003 Iraq War on business and the economy.

The Motley Fool: Web Resources List

http://www.fool.com/community/resource

This portion of the popular Fool.com investment and finance site provides a selection of the editors' favorite investment resources on the Web. Categories include: company research, economics and banking, stock selection criteria, international investing, and more.

Zimmerman's Research Guide

http://www.lexisone.com/zimmermanguide/index.html

Dictionaries and Glossaries

This site is an alphabetical encyclopedia providing descriptions, advice, and sources on over 1,000 different subject areas of interest to persons doing legal research.

Scandal Inc.

http://money.cnn.com/news/specials/corruption

The editors of CNN and Money have created a resource that provides a wide range of news, profiles, background information, and links about the various corporate scandals in the news.

CyberTimes Navigator

http://www.nytimes.com/library/tech/reference/cynavi.html

This site provides a set of links, created by The New York Times news team for use by its own journalists, as well as for the public. Sections include: Internet searching, reference, directories, publications, and more.

Financial Times: Special Reports

http://news.ft.com/business/specials

This site describes and provides links to various free special business reports created by The Financial Times. Topics are wide ranging, and include, for example: management and strategy, recent corporate scandals, profiles of companies in the news, industry surveys, and reports on business developments around the globe.

Librarians' Index to the Internet (Business Listings)

http://lii.org/search/file/business

This site provides links to selected business sites on the Web, organized into over 60 subcategories, ranging from accounting and advertising to women in business and zip codes.

National Institute for Research Advancement
http://www.nira.go.jp/linke/tt-link/index.html
This site describes and provides links to think tanks around the world.

OANDA: The Currency Site
http://www.oanda.com
This site offers a variety of useful currency tools, including background on 164 global currencies, currency rates, automatic currency conversions, forecasts, historical currency rates, and more.

Smarter Surfing: Better Use of Your Web Time
http://www.sree.net/stories/web.html
This site offers selections and descriptions of useful research and online search tools on the Internet. It covers reference sites, search engines, search tip sites, people finders, sites for journalists, and more.

Top Internet Sites for Business Research
http://www.washingtonresearchers.com/public/InternetGuide/InternetGuide.html
This site provides a selective list of annotated links to Web sites valuable to those conducting competitive intelligence. Categories listed include: search engines, corporate information, federal government sites, state government sites, international information by country/region, industry sites, and more.

A Sampling of FIND/SVP's Trusted Sites (By Industry/Practice Area)

FIND/SVP's team of expert researchers are broken down into "practice areas" that cover a specific industry or business practice. On the following pages are a selection of some of FIND/SVP's most trusted free sites, which are used by the members of these practice group areas.

(To learn more about FIND/SVP and its research capabilities, visit the Web site at www.findsvp.com.)

Some of these sites contain hundreds or even thousands of pages of useful information. As I mentioned earlier, it's often better to search a trusted site rather than the full Web to obtain quality information, and some sites do not have effective search engines. However, you can get around this limitation by using Google and instructing it to search for your keywords, but only within a particular site. For example, if you want to search the first site listed below, Advertising Age, on the topic of bottled water, you could link to Google and enter the following:

"bottled water" site:www.adage.com

Your results will include pages from the Advertising Age site that contain that phrase.

Advertising

Advertising Age
   http://www.adage.com
   News articles updated daily, account wins and losses, and a great deal of valuable statistical data.

Promo
   http://promomagazine.com
   Articles, special reports on promotion trends and spending, the annual agency report, the latest promotion news, and more.

Biotechnology

Biotechnology Industry Organization
   http://www.bio.org
   Excellent source of statistical data.

Banking

American Bankers Association
   http://www.aba.com
   Latest news, economic indicators, industry developments, and much more.

Consumer Bankers Association

http://www.cbanet.org

Information and research on retail banking issues. The association conducts several annual surveys and benchmarking studies to monitor the impact consumer issues have on retail banks. Also contains an auto finance survey of value to the automotive industry.

America's Community Bankers

http://www.acbankers.org

Industry issues, trends, online publications.

U.S. Regulatory Agencies

The Federal Reserve

http://www.federalreserve.gov

Official site of the U.S. Federal Reserve. Press releases, speeches, monetary policy, and more.

Federal Deposit Insurance Corporation

http://www.fdic.gov

Extensive resources from the FDIC, broken into the categories of deposit insurance, bank data, regulations and examination, consumers and communities, news, events, and more.

The Office of the Comptroller of the Currency (OCC)

http://www.occ.treas.gov

The OCC charters, regulates, and supervises national banks to ensure a safe, sound, and competitive banking system that supports the citizens, communities, and economy of the United States. The site provides news, publications, and information on new corporate applications.

The Office of Thrift Supervision

http://www.ots.treas.gov

The OTS is the primary regulator of all federally chartered and many state-chartered thrift institutions, which include savings banks and savings and loan associations. The site provides research, consumer information, industry news, and a searchable database of corporations.

Automotive Finance

National Automobile Dealers Association

http://www.nada.org

A resource for retail automotive news, consumer auto information, and dealer member services.

Automotive Digest

http://www.automotivedigest.com

Provides industry news and events, focusing on aftermarket, dealers, energy, fleets and rental of fleets, funding, global news, manufacturers, marketing, remarketing, and vehicle safety.

USAutoNews.com

http://www.usautonews.com

An automotive business portal focusing on news about and from the automotive industry.

National Automotive Finance Association

http://www.nafassociation.com

The National Automotive Finance Association is a trade association serving the non-prime auto lending industry. On the site are industry surveys, newsletters, conference reports, and more.

Credit Cards

RAM Research Group

http://www.ramresearch.com

A privately owned firm specializing in the collection of information regarding the global payment card and payment systems business. The site offers news on both U.S. and global developments.

Thomson Media (formerly Faulkner & Grey)

http://www.thomsonmedia.com/credit.html

Newsletters, Web sites, conferences, resources on credit cards.

CardWeb

http://www.cardweb.com

CardWeb.com, Inc. publishes information pertaining to all types of payment cards, including credit cards, debit cards, smart cards, prepaid cards, ATM cards, loyalty cards, and phone cards. Its site includes news, newsletters, surveys, featured cards, commentaries, and much more.

Mortgages

Mortgage Magazine
   http://www.mortgagemag.com
   Tools and news on loans, brokers, financing, and more.

National Association of Realtors
   http://www.realtor.org/rocms.nsf
   The official site of the National Association. Provides information on relocating, mortgage rates, housing prices, etc.

Mortgage Bankers Association
   http://www.mbaa.org
   The Mortgage Bankers Association of America is the preeminent association representing the real estate finance industry. The site provides industry news and tools. Covers federal and state developments.

Insurance

Insurance Information Institute
   http://www.iii.org
   Clearinghouse for information on the insurance industry. Covers facts and statistics, industry reports, and overviews; provides contacts and more.

National Association of Insurance Commissioners
   http://www.naic.org
   The National Association of Insurance Commissioners (NAIC) is the organization of insurance regulators from the 50 states, the District of Columbia, and the four U.S. territories. The site provides information on regulators, a calendar, financial reporting, a library, and more.

Annuity.com
   http://www.annuity.com
   Calculators, advice, and descriptions of the various types of annuities.

Consumer HealthCare

American Heart Association
   http://www.americanheart.org
   Advice on a variety of conditions including diabetes and stroke.

American Cancer Society
   http://www.cancer.org
   Cancer related statistics and more.

American Medical Association
   http://www.ama-assn.org
   Articles and statistics on doctors as well as medical students. Includes fee-based access to articles from JAMA and a doctor finder that includes mini biographies on doctors and their specialties.

Centers for Disease Control and Prevention
   http://www.cdc.gov
   Travelers' health requirements and profiles a lengthy list of disease conditions.

Healthfinder
   http://www.healthfinder.com
   Government health information site with details on virtually all diseases.

National Guideline Clearinghouse
   http://www.guideline.gov
   A public resource for evidence-based clinical practice guidelines.

National Women's Health Information Center
   http://www.4women.gov
   A gateway to federal information sources, and other sources regarding Women's health issues.

PharmaLive
   http://www.medadnews.com
   Pharmaceutical news and information.

World Health Organization
   http://www.who.int/en

International coverage not covered by the U.S. Centers for Disease Control (CDC).

Human Resources

Diversity Inc.

http://www.diversityinc.com

Offers a wide range of information on diversity.

Salary.com

http://www.salary.com

Salary data searchable by occupation and geographic area.

HR Guide

http://www.hr-guide.com

Detailed information on a variety of HR topics, including sample employee handbooks.

U.S. Bureau of Labor Statistics

http://www.bls.gov/oco

This governmental clearinghouse of labor data links to the Occupational Outlook Handbook of the Bureau of Labor Statistics and is a great resource for benchmarking the outlook for jobs, job descriptions, skills required, number of persons working in a particular field, etc.

Legal

Hieros Gamos

http://www.hg.org

A legal research portal that includes a diverse array of international legal sources.

LLRX.com

http://www.llrx.com

A great collection of sources and information useful to research legal issues.

Nolo

http://www.nolo.com

Easy to understand explanations of common legal concerns.

The Virtual Chase.com
http://www.virtualchase.com
Guides for business research and current updates on legal/business research sources and news.

Life Sciences and Medicine

Biospace
http://www.biospace.com
A specialized provider of Web-based products and information services to the life sciences. Offers breaking news, company information, investment reports, a buyers guide, career information, and more.

British Medical Journal
http://bmj.com
Free online access, including the archives. Covers weekly medical news in addition to clinical information.

Center for Devices and Radiological Health
http://www.fda.gov/cdrh
FDA clearinghouse on medical devices and diagnostics, including FDA approval dates.

Center for Drug Evaluation and Research
http://www.fda.gov/cder
FDA Clearinghouse on prescription and OTC drugs.

Drug Store News
http://www.drugstorenews.com
Current news in retail and prescription drug market.

Medlical Devicelink
http://www.devicelink.com
Coverage of medical devices plus the online Medical Device and Diagnostics Industry magazine.

New Hope Natural Media Online
http://www.nutritionbusiness.com
Marketing information and trends on the nutrition and supplement market.

PubMed

http://www.ncbi.nlm.nih.gov/entrez/query.fcgi

Access to over 12 million MEDLINE citations back to the mid-1960s and additional life science journals. PubMed includes links to many sites providing full-text articles and other related resources.

Marketing/Public Relations

1to1

http://www.1to1.com

This site from the Pepper & Rogers Group offers coverage of one-to-one marketing, customer relationship marketing/management, and other related topics. The Web site is a comprehensive resource of articles, papers, research, and other valuable tools.

Direct

http://www.directmag.com

A Primedia Publication, this site is targeted to senior direct marketing executives. Coverage topics include direct marketing, postal issues, creative lists, customer relationship management, direct response TV, and alternative media and database marketing.

DM News

http://www.dmnews.com

A Mill Hollow Corporation, DM News covers BtoB, catalogs, database, legal issues, lists and databases, and other topics. The Web site contains yellow pages of companies by category and a direct mail list directory. It also offers a daily e-mail that contains campaign information, industry data, and other valuable resources.

Direct Marketing Association

http://www.the-dma.org

This association offers excellent information, resources, research and current information on direct mail, telemarketing, lists, catalogs, interactive marketing, business-to-business, and international marketing issues. It also publishes Statistical Factbook, an extensive source of data and statistics on direct marketing.

HolmesReport.com

http://www.holmesreport.com

This site has PR firm search capabilities and an excellent "knowledge archive" of case studies, searchable by topic.

ODwyer's PR Daily

http://www.odwyerpr.com

You can find rankings for PR firms by specialty areas or geographically in one spot. Also, one of the only sources for searching for clients of PR firms.

Sales & Marketing Management

http://www.salesandmarketing.com/salesandmarketing/index.jsp

A VNU business publication that provides resources and information for sales and marketing executives. The publication features "The Best of Sales & Marketing," "Salary Survey," "Best Sales Forces," and "The Cost per Sales Call."

Selig Center for Economic Growth

http://www.selig.uga.edu

The Selig Center calculates data, for white, black, Asian, Native American, and Hispanic consumers.

Media & Entertainment

Arbitron (radio ratings)

http://www.arbitron.com

The radio ratings source releases dozens of valuable research findings on radio listening trends in its "Newsroom" section. Especially worthwhile are the series of annually published "Radio Today" reports that provide a good overview of commercial radio trends.

Motion Picture Association of America

http://www.mpaa.org

The "U.S. Economic Reviews" section provides two of the annually updated "Economic Review" and "Attendance Study," which are two of the industry's most useful reports that illustrate overall box-office revenue trends and cinema patron demographics.

Newspaper Association of America
http://www.naa.org
The "Circulation and Readership" section provides a vast collection of statistics and surveys illustrating newspaper readership trends.

Recording Industry Association of America
http://www.riaa.org
This site provides authoritative data on recorded music sales, including compact discs, cassettes, and other formats and an annual consumer survey illustrating demographic and genre trends.

Television Bureau of Advertising
http://www.tvb.org
The "Research Central" section provides details on monthly and weekly TV viewing trends, depictions of the top television markets, TV advertising revenues, and comparisons of TV's impact among other media formats.

Retail

About.com: Retail Industry
http://www.retailindustry.about.com
About.Com's expert links for news and resources on retailing is an excellent source.

International Council of Shopping Centers
http://www.icsc.org/rsrch/research.shtml
Statistical and analytical information about the shopping center industry.

Retail Chain Store Sales Index
http://www.btmny.com/reports/research/comment/Chain_Store_ Sales.htm
Detailed statistics from the Bank of Tokyo (don't let the rather zany Web site fool you—there is good data here).

Semiconductors

Semiconductor Industry Association
http://www.semichips.org

Semiconductor statistics, including book-to-bill ratios and the industry forecast.

Multi-Industry

FIND/SVP also recommends the various consultancies industry practice sites, which contain useful content for nonclients.

Accenture Industries
http://www.accenture.com/xd/xd.asp?it=enweb&xd=industries\ industries_home.xml

Capgemini
http://us.cgey.com/ind_serv/industry

Computer Sciences Corporation
http://www.csc.com/industries

Deloitte Consulting:
http://www.dcloitte.com

McKinsey & Co: Services:
http://www.mckinsey.com/practices

PriceWaterhouseCoopers Industries:
http://www.pwcglobal.com/gx/eng/about/ind/index.html

Web Site Evaluation Checklists

There are scores of sites that provide checklists for assessing Web site reliability. Below is one I developed, first published in *The Information Advisor*, followed by a list of several other evaluation checklists that I highly recommend.

Internet Information Credibility Indicators: One Checklist

I've provided here my own synthesized version of the various Internet quality checklists. I began using it a few years ago after reading through a number of checklists and adding my own particular evaluation methods. It can serve as a kind of quick sum-up of some of the more egregious and common problems related to information quality on the Web.

When you come across a site on the Internet, you can use the following indicators to make an assessment of the credibility of the information. This is a highly imperfect science, of course, but sites that meet a greater number of credibility indicators will more likely be reliable sources.

1. How was the site identified? Indicators of credibility:

__ The site was recommended or referred by a trusted source (this source could be print, online, or by word of mouth)

2. What is the organization behind the site? Indicators of credibility:

__ The site was created by, or is part of, a known institution of some kind

__ That organization provides full contact information, and can be contacted by mail or telephone, or visited in person

__ The organization identifies itself as an educational (.edu), or a government (.gov) site

3. Who is the author? Indicators of credibility:

__ The author was referred by another trusted source

__ The author's work has been quoted by others in the field

__ The author's site is often linked to on the Web. This technique for assessing credibility is the Internet equivalent to one of the standard methods for evaluating authors in the academic world, called citation analysis. With this method, scholars assess others' work by noting the number of times their published' articles have been cited in others' published work. (One way to check how often a Web site is linked to is to look up the site via the Google search engine's "who links to this page" advanced search function)

4. How does the author demonstrate his/her breadth of knowledge on the topic? Indicators of credibility:

__ Author cites theory and background, where relevant

__ Author quotes and/or paraphrases others' work and writings on the topic

__ Author demonstrates knowledge of others' work in the field

__ Author builds on others' work by adding new insights and by raising new questions

5. How does the author present his/her work? Indicators of credibility:

__ Author describes his/her methods of research, how conclusions were reached

__ Author provides or offers links to supporting evidence

__ Author identifies any limitations of his/her research

6. In what manner does the author present his/her material? Indicators of credibility:

__ Author's writing is clear

__ Author's writing is logical

__ Author's writing is organized

__ Author's writing shows evidence of thoughtfulness and analysis

__ Author's writing shows a caring, even a passion, for the topic

7. Is there evidence of any bias? Indicators of credibility:

__ The organization and/or author behind the site has no overtly stated political/ideological or other predetermined overriding agenda that would automatically detract from the credibility of the data presented

__ If there is an overriding political/ideological agenda, it is not hidden in any way to disguise its purpose, either by a misleading name or by other means

__ If there is an overriding political/ideological agenda, any research methods utilized (e.g., any polls or surveys performed or sources utilized) can stand scrutiny on their own

8. How current is the material? Indicators of date and currency:

__ The Web page displays a date

__ The date is clear as to its meaning (e.g., date of original source material, date Web site created, date most recently updated)

__ That date is timely for the purposes of your research

9. (Optional) For those sites where there is an existing equivalent source in some other medium (print, CD-ROM, online database):

__ The data presented on the Web page is as complete as the other media

__ The site describes any differences in coverage if the data is not as complete

10. Active Evaluation Strategies in addition to utilizing those credibility indicators listed here, another important way to evaluate the credibility of information found on the Net is by taking active evaluation strategies. I recommend the following:

• Perform a keyword search on the author's name (use quotation marks) to find out what, if anything, the author has had published on the Internet. Do a search on Google Groups to find any messages the author may have posted on Internet newsgroups.

- Contact the author and ask follow-up questions. This is useful for both making a better evaluation of the person's knowledge and having the opportunity to ask your questions.
- Confirm the author's information with at least one other source.

Other Recommended Evaluation Checklists

Evaluating Web Pages: Techniques to Apply and Questions to Ask from the library at the University of California, Berkeley.

www.lib.berkeley.edu/TeachingLib/Guides/Internet/Evaluate.html

The Virtual Chase: Evaluating the Quality of Information Found on the Internet by Genie Tyburski of the law firm Ballard Spahr Andrews & Ingersoll LLP

www.virtualchase.com/quality

Evaluating Internet Research Sources, created by Robert Harris, retired Professor of English at Southern California College, Costa Mesa, California

www.virtualsalt.com

Evaluating Information Found on the Internet and Practical Steps in Evaluating Internet Resources, Elizabeth E. Kirk, Electronic and Distance Education Librarian, Milton S. Eisenhower Library, Johns Hopkins University, Baltimore, Maryland

www.library.jhu.edu/elp/useit/evaluate

Evaluating Web Resources, Jan Alexander and Marsha Ann Tate, Wolfgram Memorial Library, Widener University, Chester, Pennsylvania

www2.widener.edu/Wolfgram-Memorial-Library/
webevaluation/webeval.htm

Evaluating Quality on the Net, Hope N. Tillman, Director of Libraries, Babson College, Babson Park, Massachusetts

www.hopetillman.com/findqual.html

How to Critically Analyze Information Sources

Jack Corse, W.A.C. Bennett Library, Simon Fraser University Burnaby, British Columbia

www.lib.sfu.ca/researchhelp/subjectguides/general/libguide5.htm
#How%20to%20Critically%20Analyze%20Information

Referenced Sites and Sources

http://books.infotoday.com/skepticalbiz

Listed here is a compilation, broken down by chapter, and listed in the order cited, of each Web site described or highlighted in this book. These sites are also listed and hotlinked in the companion Web site to this book, where they are updated on a semi-annual basis.

Chapter 1: The Business Researcher's Challenge

Google, www.google.com

NPR Segment on Internet Accuracy, www.npr.org/features/feature.php?wfId=1072660

Chapter 2: What to Do Before Using a Search Engine

Library of Congress American Memory, memory.loc.gov/ammem/amhom.html

Library of Congress Vatican Exhibit, www.ibiblio.org/expo/vatican.exhibit/exhibit/Main_Hall.html

Hoover's, www.hoovers.com

ResourceShelf, www.resourceshelf.com

EDGAR, www.sec.gov/edgar.shtml

U.S. Census Bureau, www.census.gov

Newslink, www.newslink.org

Public Records Online, www.netronline.com/public_records.htm

MarketResearch.com, www.marketresearch.com

MindBranch, www.mindbranch.com

Embassy.org, www.embassy.org

FirstGov, www.firstgov.gov

FedStats, www.fedstats.gov

ITA Trade Development: Industries and Analysts, web.ita.doc.gov/td/shared/tdindus.nsf/$$Searches?Openform

Thomas, thomas.loc.gov

Yahoo! Finance, finance.yahoo.com

New York Times, www.nytimes.com

TrackEngine, www.trackengine.com

WatchThatPage, www.watchthatpage.com

INFOMINE, infomine.ucr.edu

Social Science Information Gateway, www.sosig.ac.uk

SearchSystems, www.searchsystems.net

Librarians' Index to the Internet, www.lii.org

Profusion, www.profusion. com

BUBL LINK, bubl.ac.uk/link

Business.com, www.business.com

Alacra, www.alacra.com

Yahoo! business sites:

> dir.yahoo.com/Business_and_Economy/Business_to_Busines s/Marketing_and_Advertising/Market_Research

> dir.yahoo.com/Business_and_Economy/Trade/Statistics

dir.yahoo.com/Business_and_Economy/Business_to_ Business/Information

DMOZ—Open Directory Project, www.dmoz.org

To locate Internet discussion groups:

To sign up with BUSLIB, www.willamette.edu/~gklein/bus-lib.htm

To sign up with SLAB-F, www.slabf.org/slabf-l.html

To sign up with IRE-L, www.ire.org/membership/subscribe/ ire-l.html

To sign up with STUMPERS-L, domin.dom.edu/depts/gslis/ stumpers

Sample Weblogs:

Jim Romenesko, www.poynter.org/medianews

ResourceShelf, www.resourceshelf.com

The Shifted Librarian, www.theshiftedlibrarian.com

Librarian.net, www.librarian.net

Lisnews, www.lisnews.com

PaidContent.org, elearningpost.com

Peter Scott's Library Blog, blog.xrefer.com

Jeff Jarvis' Buzz Machine, www.buzzmachine.com

Marylaine Block's Neat New Stuff, marylaine.com/neatnew. html

Gwen Harris Internet News, www.websearchguide.ca/netblog

Gurteen Knowledge Log, www.gurteen.com

Guardian Blog, www.guardian.co.uk/weblog

Jupiter Research Analysts, weblogs.jupiterresearch.com

About.com, www.about.com

RSS Readers:

Amphetadesk, www.disobey.com/amphetadesk

NewsIsFree, www.newsisfree.com

NewzCrawler, www.newzcrawler.com

NewsMonster, www.newsmonster.org

NewsGator, www.newsgator.com

Radio Userland, radio.userland.com

Chapter 3: Precision Business Searching

Google, www.google.com

AlltheWeb, www.alltheweb.com

AltaVista, www.altavista.com

Yahoo! Search, search.yahoo.com

Teoma, www.teoma.com

Gigablast, www.gigablast.com

Vivisimo, www.vivisimo.com

IxQuick, www.ixquick.com

Query Server, www.queryserver.com

Search Engine Showdown, www.searchengineshowdown.com

Chapter 4: What to Do With Questionable Sites

Columbia University professor Sreenath Sreenivasan covers hoaxes on the Internet at the Poynter Institute site, www.poynter.org/content/content_view.asp?id=2957

Wall Street Journal Online, www.wsj.com

PubMed, www.ncbi.nlm.nih.gov/PubMed

COPAFS, members.aol.com/copafs

American Demographics Magazine, www.demographics.com

To Run a WHOIS search:

Verisign NetSol Revised: Network Solutions, www.netsol.com/ cgi-bin/whois/whois

Better-Whois, www.betterwhois.com

Register.com, www.register.com

SamSpade, www.sampade.org

To find Internet mailing list discussion groups:

Topix, www.topix.net

CataList, www.lsoft.com/lists/listref.html

Capital Research Center, www.capitalresearch.org

Center for Science in the Public Internet, www.cspinet.org/ integrity/corp_funding.html

Guidstar, www.guidestar.org

Common Cause, www.commoncause.org

OSHA Stats and Data, www.osha.gov/oshstats

Office of Thrift Supervision, www.ots.treas.gov/pagehtml. cfm?catNumber=25

FEC Transaction Query System, herndon1.sdrdc.com/fecimg/ query.html

Search Systems Net Public Records Locator, www.search systems.net

BRB Publications, www.brbpub.com/pubrecsites.asp

IRE Resource Center, www.ire.org/resourcecenter

IRE Tip Sheet, www.ire.org/resourcecenter/initial-search-tipsheets.html

Virtual Gumshoe: Investigative Resources Available on the Web, virtualgumshoe.com

LLRX, www.llrx.com/columns/roundup19.htm#New%20Jersey

Impropaganda Review: PR Watch: How to Research Front, Groups prwatch.org/improp/research_faq.html

Other interesting sites from the Center for Media and Democracy's PR Watch:

Spinning the Web, www.prwatch.org/prwissues/2002Q1/web.html

Impropaganda Review, ActivistCash.com; www.prwatch.org/improp/ddam.html

FedStats, www.fedstats.gov

AlltheWeb NewsSearch, www.alltheweb.com (click on "news")

Wayback Machine, www.archive.org

Chapter 5: Company and Industry Sources

EDGAR, www.sec.gov/edgar.shtml

The Corporate Library, www.thecorporatelibrary.com

Standard and Poor's Core Earnings, www2.standardandpoors.com/spf/pdf/media/CoreEarningsBrochure_NewJan2004.pdf

BestCalls.com, www.bestcalls.com

Thomson ccbn, www.ccbn.com

Other sources for corporate Webcasts:

Investor Broadcast Network, www.vcall.com

Street Events, www.fulldisclosure.com/highlight.asp?client=cb

EDGAR Spin-Offs:

FreeEDGAR, www.freeedgar.com

EDGAR Online, www.edgar-online.com

EDGAR Online Pro, www.edgarpro.com

EdgarScan, edgarscan.pwcglobal.com/servlets/edgarscan

10K Wizard, www.10kwizard.com

Search-sec.com, www.search-sec.com

LIVEDGAR, www.gsionline.com

MindBranch, www.mindbranch.com

MarketResearch.com, www.marketresearch.com

Reuters Research on-Demand, about.reuters.com/productinfo/researchondemand/material/RROD_BrochureUS.pdf

Thomson Research, http://research. thomsonib.com/www. investext.com

Research and Markets, www.researchandmarkets.com

Dialog (MarketFull), www.dialogweb.com

Profound (ResearchLine), www.profound.com

LexisNexis, www.lexisnexis.com

TechRepublic, www.techrepublic.com

Google Groups, groups.google.com

Yahoo! Groups, groups.yahoo.com

TileNet, www.tile.net

Catalist, www.lsoft.com/catalist

Information Week, www.informationweek.com

Institutional Investor, www.institutionalinvestor.com

Investars, www.investars.com

BitPipe, www.bitpipe.com

TechRepublic, www.techrepublic.com

ITPapers, www.itpapers.com

BNET, www.bnet.com

Hoover's, www.hoovers.com

Free company directory sites:

D&B Small Business Services, sbs.dnb.com/Default.
asp?bhcd2=1033393489

Zapdata, www.zapdata.com

Kompass, www.kompass.com/kinl/index.html

Yahoo! Finance, finance.yahoo.com

Thomas Register, www.thomasregister.com

Corporate Information, www.corporateinformation.com

World Chamber of Commerce Directory, www.chamberof
commerce.com

NIRA's World Directory of Think Tanks, http://www.nira.go.
jp/ice/nwdtt/#1

Chapter 6: Statistics, Polls, and Surveys

Government Printing Office: GPO Access, http://www.gpo
access.gov/index.html

U.S. Bureau of the Census, www.census.gov

U.S. Department of Commerce, www.commerce.gov

U.S. Bureau of Economic Analysis, www.bea.gov

U.S. International Trade Administration, www.ita.doc.gov

U.S. Department of Transportation, www.dot.gov

U.S. Environmental Protection Agency, www.epa.gov

FedStats, www.fedstats.gov

Statistical Programs of the United States Government, www.
whitehouse.gov/omb/inforeg/statpolicy.html

Statistics Canada definitions of Data Quality, www.statcan.ca/
english/concepts/inform.htm

Statistics Canada's Quality 2002 Assurance Framework, www.stat can.ca/english/freepub/12-586-XIE/12-586-XIE02001.pdf

OMB Watch, www.ombwatch.org

Union of Concerned Scientists, "Scientific Integrity and PolicyMaking," www.ucsusa.org/global_environment/ rsi/page.cfm?pageID=1322

United Nations National and International Data Sources and Links, unstats.un.org/unsd/methods/inter-natlinks/sd_natstat.htm

Statistics Finland: WebStat, webstat.stat.fi/etusivu_en.html

Principal Statistical Agencies, http://www.fedstats.gov/agencies:

The following are all federal agencies with statistical programs, which are described and linked via the above URL: Bureau of Economic Analysis; Bureau of Justice Statistics; Energy Information Administration; Economic Research Service; Environmental Protection Agency; Internal Revenue Service, Statistics of Income Division; National Agricultural Statistics Service; National Center for Education Statistics; National Center of Health Statistics; National Science Foundation's Science Resource Statistics; The Social Security Administration's Office of Research, Evaluation, and Statistics; Office of Management and Budget.

Statistical Abstract of the U.S., http://www.census.gov/prod/ www/statistical-abstract-03.html

Bureau of the Census: Economic Census, http://www. census.gov/econ/census02/WSSS

Bureau of the Census: American Factfinder, http://factfinder. census.gov/home/saff/main.html?_lang=en

United Nations: Links to Official Statistical Agencies, http://www.unece.org/stats/links.htm

United Nations: Millennium Country Profiles, http://unstats. un.org/unsd/mi/mi.asp

Global Statistical Finder: Finland's WebStat, webstat.stat.fi/etusivu_en.html

OECD, www.oecd.org

Pew Internet & American Life Project, www.pewinternet.org

Pew Research Center for the People and the Press, www.people-press.org

Comscore, www.comscore.com

ACSI Index, www.theasci.org/industry_scores/htm

PollingReport, www.pollingreport.com

ClickZ, www.clickz.com

Statistics.com, www.statistics.com

NationMaster, www.nationmaster.com

Fortune Lists, www.fortune.com/fortune/alllists

Forbes Lists, www.forbes.com/lists/

Best of the Business Web, www.bestbizweb.com

Zoomerang, www.zoomerang.com

SurveySite, www.surveysite.com

Additional source on survey creation and their proper use:

Bill Trochim's Center for Social Research Methods, trochim.human.cornell.edu

Chapter 7: News, Talk, and Blogs on the Net

CNNfn, www.cnnfn.com

New York Times, www.nytimes.com

AlltheWeb.com News, www.alltheweb.com

Google News, news.google.com

Yahoo! News, http://news.yahoo.com

American City Business Journals, www.bizjournals.com

FindArticles.com, www.findarticles.com

CBS MarketWatch Alerts, cbs.marketwatch.com/tools/alerts/createalert.asp?siteID=mktw

Google News Alerts, www.google.com/newsalerts

CNN Alerts, www.cnn.com/EMAIL/bnews.alerts

PaidContent, www.paidcontent.org

TechRepublic, www.techrepublic.com

DayPop, www.daypop.com

HighBeam, www.highbeam.com

TheStreet.com, www.thestreet.com

MSN Money, moneycentral.msn.com

National Public Radio, www.npr.org

C-SPAN, www.c-span.org

Fox News, www.foxnews.com

Nightly Business Report, www.nightlybusiness.org

CNBC/Dow Jones, www.cnbcdowjones.com

Topix.net, www.topix.net

Rocketinfo, www.rocketinfo.com

Newslink, newslink.org

ABYZ News Links, www.abyznewslinks.com

NewsDirectory.com, www.newsdirectory.com

SLA News Archive, www.ibiblio.org/slanews/internet/archives index.html

Factiva, www.factiva.com

BUSLIB-L: To sign up, www.willamette.edu/~gklein/buslib.htm

SlashDot, www.slashdot.org

AndrewSullivan.com, www.andrewsullivan.com

BloggerCon, blogs.law.harvard.edu/bloggerCon

WayPath, www.waypath.com

Tile.net, www.tile.net

CataList, www.lsoft.com/catalist.html

Epinions, www.epinions.com

WebFountain, www.factiva.com/webfountain

Biz360, www.biz360.com

Converseon, www.converseon.com

Technorati, www.technorati.com

New York Times: CyberTimes, www.nytimes.com/pages/
technology/index.html

Chapter 8: Knowledge, Intuition, and Trust

Recommended sources on critical thinking and media literacy:

Web sites

Learning about propaganda, www.propagandacritic.com

Listing of reviewed sites on the Web, directory.google.
com/Top/Science/Science_in_Society/Skeptical_Inquiry/
Critical_Thinking/?il=1

Print sources

Asking the Right Questions: A Guide to Critical Thinking
(Prentice Hall, 6th Ed. 2000) M. Neil Browne and Stuart M.
Keeley

Becoming a Critical Thinker: A User Friendly Manual
(Prentice Hall, 3rd Ed. 2000) Sherry Diestler

How to Watch TV News (Penguin USA, 1992) Neil Postman and Steve Powers

Urban Legends Reference Pages, www.snopes.com/snopes.asp

Hoaxbusters, hoaxbusters.ciac.org

Additional Recommended Resources

The following resources are also recommended for learning strategies and finding tips for evaluating business information quality on the Web.

Print sources – Books:

Finding Market Research on the Web (MarketResearch.com, 2003). By Robert Berkman. How to find and evaluate market research reports and conduct market research on the Web. Written by the author of this book and published in 2001; an updated version was published in 2003 by Sheri Lanza.

Find It Fast: How to Uncover Expert Information on Any Subject (HarperCollins, 5th ed, 2000). By Robert Berkman. *Find It Fast* is geared primarily to consumers, but contains an extensive discussion on how to evaluate the quality of Internet-based sources.

The Investigative Reporters Handbook (IRE, 4th ed, 2002). By Brant Houston, Len Bruzzese, and Steve Weinberg. How to investigate anyone or anything from top investigative reporters from a highly respected journalism association.

The Invisible Web (CyberAge Books, 2001). By Chris Sherman and Gary Price. Excellent guide for finding sources on the Net that search engines cannot retrieve. These are often high quality sites, such as databases and library catalogs, and may be of great worth to researchers.

The Modern Researcher (Wadsworth, 6th ed, 2003). By Jacques Barzun and Henry J. Graff. The bible for all types of serious researchers. *The Modern Researcher* is not at all focused on electronic sources or Internet research, but does provides the fundamentals of how any good researcher needs to approach his or her subject, and how to assess the veracity and trustworthiness of all kinds of information sources.

Web of Deception (CyberAge, 2002). Edited by Forbes' Chief Knowledge Officer Anne Mintz, this book provides a series of essays from expert searchers covering different perspectives on how to avoid encountering bad data and misinformation on the Web.

Print sources – Journals and newsletters:

The Information Advisor, Information Today, Medford, NJ; (609) 654-6266. Monthly newsletter. Founded and edited by the author of this book. Focuses on comparing and evaluating competing business information sources.

The CyberSkeptic's Guide to Internet Research, Information Today, Medford, NJ. (609) 654-6266. Monthly newsletter. Founded by Ruth Orenstein of BiblioData. *CyberSkeptic* reviews and analyzes information sources on the Web.

Web sources:

ConsumerWebWatch, www.consumerwebwatch.org

A spin-off of *Consumer Reports*, this site's mission is to help consumers evaluate Web sites and know who can be trusted online.

Fuld & Company Inc., www.fuld.com

Fuld & Company is a competitive intelligence firm founded and operated by well-known CI author and expert, Leonard Fuld. The site provides various tips and sources on conducting business research on the Web.

The Society of Competitive Intelligence Professionals (SCIP), www.scip.org

A large and well-known association of analysts, researchers, and others who work in the competitive intelligence industry.

Competia, www.competia.com

A competitive intelligence "community" with a magazine, library, conferences, resources, and tools for persons in the field of strategic planning, business research, knowledge management, and related fields.

Discussion groups:

BUSLIB-L, www.willamette.edu/~gklein/buslib.htm

A high quality mailing list discussion group for business librarians, who share research strategies, ideas, and new resources and pose their own difficult business research questions.

About the Author

Robert Berkman has been a writer, editor, teacher, and speaker in the information industry for more than 20 years. In addition to serving as an editor at McGraw-Hill Inc, Ziff-Davis, and What to Buy for Business, he is also the founder and editor of *The Information Advisor*, an international newsletter for business researchers, published by Information Today, Inc.

Berkman has written several books covering the field of effective research, business searching, and the online media. Among his published books are *Find It Fast: How to Uncover Expert Information on Any Subject* (5th ed. HarperCollins), *The Art of Being Well Informed*, co-authored with FIND/SVP President Andy Garvin (2nd ed. Avery Press, 1996), and *Rethinking the Corporate Information Center* (FIND/SVP, 1996). Berkman is on the faculty of the M.A., Media Studies program at New School University, and has an M.A. in Journalism from the University of Montana. He lives on Cape Cod in Massachusetts with his wife Mary.

INDEX

A

ABCNEWS.com, 164
ABI/INFORM, 31, 32, 102
"About Us," 74, 112, 122
About.com, 40–41, *42,* 240
ABYZ News Links, 168, 224
academic papers, 59
Accenture Industries, 241
access
  to archives, 23
  to government data, 149–152
  Internet, 16
  to librarians, 23
accounting practices, 118–119
accuracy, attention to, 10
Ad*Access and the Emergence of
    Advertising in America, 216
Adelphia, 119
Adobe PDF files, 50, *52,* 59, 64,
    120
advertising, 208, 231
Advertising Age, 231
advocacy groups, 85, 86
affiliations, research on, 79–82, 83,
    85
agendas, identification of, 84–90
Alacra, 37

alerts
  CBS MarketWatch, 164, 166
  CNN, 164
  e-mail, 27
  LII, 36
Allpar, 102
AllTheWeb, 46, 65, 66, *66,* 109
  links to news sites, 170
  News, 164
AltaVista, 46, 47–48, 49, 65
Amazon.com, 130–131, 179–180
American Bankers Association, 231
American Cancer Society, 235
American City Business Journals,
    164, 165
American Customer Satisfaction
    Index (ACSI), 212
American Demographics, 159
American FactFinder, 154
American Heart Association, 235
American Medical Association, 235
American Memory Collection, 23
American Productivity and Quality
    Center, The (APQC), 209
America's Community Bankers,
    232
Amphetadesk, 42
analysis, flaws, 156

Analyst Blogs—Jupiter& Gartner, 227

analyst research, 208

"AND" searches, 6, 51

AndrewSullivan.com, 171

anecdotes, 178

annual reports, 120

Annuity.com, 234

ANSI, 15

Arbitron, 239

archives
  government data, 148
  on the invisible Web, 28
  lack of, 11
  media, 23
  primary sources, 101
  The WayBack Machine, 109

ASCI Index, 155

Ask Jeeves, 67

Asking the Right Question: A Guide to Critical Thinking (Browne), 189

associations
  company information, 140
  Encyclopedia of Associations, 102, 140
  research on, 85
  studies, 28–29

assumptions, 128, 148–149, 196

asterisk (*), 51–52

audio programs, 28

Audit Committees, 119

authority, of sources, 156, 194–195

Automotive Digest, 233

automotive finance, 233

B

back issues, 23

ballot stuffing, 158

banking, 231–232

Bartlett's Familiar Quotations, 102

Barton, Chris, 74

Barzun, Jacques, 3, 10, 11–12, 84, 198

Basch, Reva, 8, 197

Bass, Michael, 73

BBC Country Profiles, 216

BBC online news, 43

Behar, Richard, 80

Beige Book, The, 218

Berinstein, Paula, 142, 155

Best Business Web Sites Eletter, 207–208

BestCalls, 121

biases
  Google rankings, 49–50
  hidden, 177
  identifying agendas, 84
  investment research, 132–133
  issues, 156
  in market research, 128
  of the researcher, 87–88
  self-confirmation, 6–7, 204
  self-selection, 157, 158, 160
  source credibility and, 107, 156
  wacky vs fringe thinkers, 181

biographies, 85

Biospace, 237

biotechnology, 231

Biotechnology Industry Organization, 231

biz360, 180

BizStats, 226

Block, Marylaine, *41*

bloggers. *see* Weblogs (blogs)

blogrolls, 174, *175,* 180

BNET, 209

Boards of Directors, 119

book reviews, 179–180

bookmarks, 23–24

books, 22

Boolean searches, 6, 66

bots, 12, 28

Branding Resource List, 208
BRB Publications, 90, 98, *99*
breaking news aggregators, 165
British Medical Journal, 237
brokerage research reports, 124
Browne, M. Neil, 189, 192
BUBL Link, 36–37, *38*
"Buddha" quote, 104–107
Bureau of Labor Statistics, U.S., 236
Bureau of the Census, U.S., *24*, 142, *144*, 154
Bush administration, 149–152
Business 2.0, 210
Business Filings Databases, 100
business rankings, 209
Business Statistics on the Web (Berinstein), 142
business strategy, 209–210
business technology Web journals, 210
Business Week, 186
Business Wire, 214
Business.com, 37, *38*
BUSLIB-L, 14, 39, 170, 202
Buzz Machine, *41*
Byrne, Peter, 105–106

C

C-SPAN, 167
C-SPAN Archives, 224
cache links, 62, 66
Calishain, Tara, 51
Canada, statistics, 145
Capgemini, 241
Capital Research Center (CRC) GreenWatch, 90, *91*
CardWeb, 233–234
cash flow, 119
CataList, 131
causation arguments, 191

CBS MarketWatch, 164, 166
CCBN, 121
censorship, 152
Center for Consumer Freedom, *86, 87*
Center for Devices and Radiological Health, 237
Center for Drug Evaluation and Research, 237
Center for Media & Democracy, 100
Center for Regulatory Effectiveness (CRE), *86,* 150
Center for Science in the Public Interest, 90, 92, *92*
Centers for Disease Control and Prevention, 235
Central Contractor Registration, 211
Centre for Digital Library Research, 36–37
CEOExpress, 228
CEOs, 122
CFO.com, 215
cgi-scripts, 28
Chambers of Commerce, 139
checklists, quality, 4–5
children's sites (.kid), 77
citations, primary sources, 75
claims, outlandish, 73
ClickZ, 155, 224, 228
CNBC/Dow Jones, 167
CNN Alerts, 164, 166
CNN.com, 164
CNNfn, 164, 167
Colón, Aly, 173
commentary, Weblog, *41*
commercial domains, 59, 77
Common Cause, 92, 94, *95*
company directories, 22, 136–139, 154

Company House, 212
company information
  from associations, 140
  business ranking, 209
  company-provided, *24,* 112–114, 122, 128
  credibility, 114–123
  exaggerations, 123
  financial results, 118–120
  home pages, *113*
  investment research, 132–134
  negative, 201
  red flags, 118
  sources, 111–140
  statistics, 141
  suspicious data, 118
  from think tanks, 140
  Web sites containing, 211–215
competitive intelligence, 215
competitor profiles, 124
CompuServe, 16
Computer Sciences Corporation, 241
Comscore, 155
conceptual information, 54, 204
conference reports, 28–29, 59
confidence ratings, 77–80
Congressional Research Service (CRS), 151, 219
Consumer Bankers Association, 232
consumer healthcare, 235–236
consumer surveys, 142
contact information
  for domains, 80
  reassuring signs, 74
  using, 109
  Web news and, 169
  on Web sites, 72
context, lack of, 156
controlled vocabulary, 31

Converseon, 180
COPFAS, 148
core earnings, 120
corporate finance sites, 215
Corporate Information, 137
Corporate Library, The, 119, 215–216
CorporateInformation.com, 211
corporation sites, 215–216
costs, 15–16
countries
  domain suffix for, 77
  information, 216–217
Country Commercial Guides, 217
Country Insights, 216
courses, 186
crawlers, 48
creativity, Weblog, *41*
credibility
  company information, 114–123
  evaluating, 70
  government data, 144–145
  jargon and, 108
  market research, 126–129, 127
  personal, 8–9
  press releases, 114–117
  reassuring signs, 74–75
  of sources, 3, 152–155
  Web site types and, 77–80
credit reports, 119
credt cards, 233–234
Cricket Web Forum, *176*
critical thinking skills, 189–194, 196–198
customer loyalty, 119
customer service, 127, 148
CyberAge Books, 142
CyberJournalist SuperSearch, 225
CyberTimes Navigator, 229

D

Darwinmag.com, 210
data definitions, 128, 156
data integrity, 3
Data Quality Act, 150
data sources, 127
dates, 74–75, 109
DayPop, 165, 172, 173, 174
D&B Small Business Services, 137
Deloitte Consulting, 241
Delphi, 16
demographics. *see also* U.S. Bureau
    of the Census
  consumer groups, 124–125
  Web sites, *24*
  Web surveys, 158
Department of Commerce, U.S.,
    142, 143
Department of Defense, 13
Department of Energy, 149
Department of the Treasury, U.S.,
    94
design
  astuteness in, 74
  emphasis on, 11
  outdated, 73
Dewey Decimal Classification, 37
Dialog, 15, 30, 125, 126
digital information industry, *41*
Direct, 238
Direct Marketing Association, 238
directories, 33–38
  company, 22, 136–139, 154
  newspapers, 169
  specialized, 22
  in URLs, 77
Directory of Corporate Archives in
    the United States and
    Canada, 212
discussion groups
  development of trust, 199
  disadvantages, 171
  leads from, 71
  monitoring, 201
  niche markets and, 178
  prescreened, 39
  research and, 170
  self-correcting mechanisms, 201
  wacky vs fringe thinkers,
      182–183
Dismal Scientist, The, 218
Diversity Inc., 236
DM News, 238
documents, primary, 23, 101
Documents Online, 221
domains
  query limiting by, 58
  search restrictions, 50
  server identification, 80
  suffixes, 59, 76, 77
  URLs, 76
Dornfest, Rael, 51
dot-coms, 59, 78
dot-edu sites, 4, 59, 76, 77, 79–80
dot-gov sites, 59, 79. *see also* gov-
    ernment, U.S.
Dow Jones market research, 125
Drug Store News, 237
Dylan, Bob, 200

E

e-mail
  address checking, 83
  alerts, 27
  knowledge building and, 188
  rumor spread via, 7
  survey by, 158
  Web site contact info, 72, 74
e-mail lookups, 84
Eastman Kodak, *96, 97*
Economagic, 217
Economic Censuses, 146, 154

economic data, 142, 217–218
Economist, The, 186
EContent, 56
EDGAR, *24, 26,* 111–112, 112, 121
editorial processes, 7
education sites (.edu), 4, 76, 77
elearningpost, *41*
eLibrary. *see* HighBeam
Eliyon Networking, 215
embassies, *24*
Embassy.org, *24, 26*
employee satisfaction, 119
employees, 122
Emulex, 116–117, *117,* 200
Encyclopedia of Associations, The, 102, 140
Energy Information Administration: Country Analysis Briefs, 218
Enlightenment.com, *206*
Enron, 114, 119
Entertainment industry, 239–240
EnviroFacts database, 149, 218–219
Epinions, 180
ERISA, 98
Eurostat, 226
evidence, 190, 193
Excel files, 50
ExecutivePlanet.com, 216–217
experts
    About.com and, 40–41
    analysis by, 125
    biography of, 177–178
    conceptual information and, 54–55
    credibility of, 107–108
    in-depth analysis, 179
    knowledge building and, 188–189
    locating, 14, 16
    names in queries, 56, 136
    Open Directory Project and, 37
    responses from, 108
    trust in, 199
extrapolation, false, 156

F

fact-checking, 7, 101, 102–107
Factiva.com, 169
Fair Disclosure Regulation, 112
Family Research Council, 191
Faulkner & Gray. *see* Thomson Media
FDIC Institution Directory, 94
Federal Deposit Insurance Corporation (FDIC), 232
Federal Election Commission, 94, *97*
Federal Reserve, The, 232
FedStats, *24,* 143–144, *145*
file types, 66–67
files, URL extensions, 77
Financial Accounting Standards Board (FSAB), 120
Financial Ratios and Quality Indicators, 214
Financial Times: Special Reports, 229
"Find" button, 63
FIND/SVP, *113,* 207, 230–241
FindArticles.com, 164, 165, 223
Finding Market Research on the Web (Berkman), 123–124
Finding Statistics Online (Berinstein), 142, 155
Finland Statistics, 152
First Monday, 210
FirstGov, *24,* 218
"Flash" format, 65
Forbes, 43, 186
Forbes Lists, 155, 209
forecasts, 128–129
Fortune, 43, 155, 186, 212

FOX News, 167
Front Groups, 100
FTP searches, 65–66
full word stemming, 51
Fulltext Sources Online, 170
funding, 90–94, 226–227

G

Gale Research, 140
General Motors, 182
Gigablast, 67
global positioning systems (GPS),
    192–193
Global Statistical Finder, 154
Glossarist, The (Business glos-
    saries), 228
Google
    alternatives, 65–68
    bloggers on, 173–174
    cache links, 62, *63*
    company information on, 2
    description, 37
    finding links, 83
    Groups link, 178
    indexed file types, 50
    knowledge building and, 188
    links to outdated pages, 147
    News, 164, 166
    news search tabs, 165
    page ranking, 147
    precision searching, 45–68
    Preferences page, 55
    ranking method, 60
    scan results, 60–63
    search box, 63
    search results, *46, 52, 53, 61*
    special features, 58–60
    value of links, 49
    Zeitgeist, 228
Google Hacks: 100 Industrial-
    Strength Tips & Tools
    (Calishain and Dornfest), 51

Gore, Albert, 13, 16
government data, 218–219
    access issues, 149–152
    censorship, 151–152
    on the invisible Web, 28–29
    links to outdated pages, 147, *147*
    "official" sites, 71
    PDF formats, 59
    preferred sources, 154
    statistics online, 142–154,
        143–144
    timeliness, 146–147
    Web sites, *24*
Government Printing Office (GPO),
    142, 150–151
Government Public Records, 218
government records, 88–89
government sites (.gov), 4, 76, 77
Graff, Henry J., 3, 9–10, 11–12, 84,
    198
grammatical errors, 72, 181
GrantMaker, 90, *91*
graphics, 11, 73
grassroots opinions, 40
GreenWatch, 90, *91*
Guardian Online Blog, *41*
GuideStar.org, 86, 92, *93*
guiding ideas, 87
Gurteen Knowledge Log, *41*

H

Harris, Gwen, *41*
Harvard Business School
        Publishing Corporation, *93*
headlines, 42
headquarters location, 122
healthcare, 235–236
Healthfinder, 235
Heffner, Steve, 128, 129, 130
Hieros Gamos, 236

HighBeam, 166
historical perspectives, 11
hoaxes, 3–4, 71, 116–117, 200,
    202–203
Holding Company Database, 94
HolmesReport.com, 239
Hoover's, *24, 25,* 136, *137,* 204
hot topics, 40
Household Products Database, 221
HR Guide, 236
HTML files, 50
http:, 76
human analysis, 9
human resources, 236
hype, 114, 122

I

IBM Guide to Financials, 215
images, 51
IMF Country Reports, 219
in-depth analysis, 179
in-house newsletters, 23
indexes, 31, 48
industry analysis, *24, 41,* 124–125
Industry Data Finder, 219
industry information, 141, 219–220
Industry Resources Reports, 220
industry sources, 111–140
Industry Week 1000, 212
INFOMINE, 30, 33, *34,* 56
Information Advisor, The, 12, 56
information gaps, 190, 192
information resources, *41*
Information Today, 56, 76
Information Week, 133
InfoTech Trends, 222
Ingebretsen, Mark, 71–72
INSEAD Knowledge, 209–210
Institutional Investor Online:
    Analyst Database, 208
insurance, 234

Insurance Information Institute, 234
Integra Information, 220
internal reports, 59
Internal Revenue Service, *93*
International business research,
    220–221
International Council of Shopping
    Centers, 240
International Market Research
    Center, 222
international statistics, 141,
    152–154, 154
International Trade Administration,
    U.S., 143
International Trade Administration
    (ITA): Trade Development
    Analysts, 219
International Trade Data Systems:
    Industry Profiles, 219
Internet
    access options, 16
    automated tools, 12
    benefits, 1–2
    changes in, 5–8
    conceptual information, 204
    editorial processes and, 7
    government statistics on,
        143–144
    government use of, 142–143
    hazards, 10–11
    history of, 12–17
    lack of archives, 11
    as verification tool, 71–72
Internet News, *41*
Internet Wire, 116
interviews, 70
intuition, use of, 196–198
inventories, 119
investigative reporters, 39, 69–73
Investigative Reporters & Editors
    Association (IRE), 100

investment research, 124, 132–134,
174–176, 200
Investor Canada, 214
Investor Relations, 112, *113,* 122
Invisible Web, 27–30, 195
Invisible Web, The (Price and
Sherman), 28
Iraq War and Business, 228
IRE Journal, 182
IRE-L, 39
ISI Emerging Markets, 214
ITA Trade Development: Industries
and Analysts, *24*
IxQuick, 46, 67–68, *68*

J
jargon, 64, 108
Jarvis, Jeff, *41*
JDLR (just doesn't look right) fac-
tor, 197 198
Journal of the Hyperlinked
Organization (JOHO),
210–211
journalism, *41,* 70–73
JournalismNet, 223–224
Jupiter Research Analysis, *41*

K
Kalorama, Inc., 128
Katz's Magazines for Libraries, 170
Kerstenbaum, David, 8
Ketupa.net, 213
keying errors, 3
keywords
bolded, 61
clarity, 55–56
hidden, 56
highlighting in results, 51
market research, *135,* 135–136
mind set of, 11–12

minus signs and, 60
search results and, 6, 48–49
selection of, 195
self-confirmation bias and, 204
Kmart, Whois search, 81–82
knowledge building, 185–189
knowledge gaps, 185–189, 190
knowledge management, *41,* 172,
209–210
KnowThis.com, 222
Kompass, 137

L
Ladner, Sharyn, 14
language selection, 55
laws, Web sites, *24*
learning, Weblog, *41*
LeFile, 120–121
legal, 236–237
legal documents, 23
legislature Web sites, *24*
Lexis/Nexis, 30, 125, 126
Librarian.net, *41*
librarians
access to, 23
BUSLIB-L, 15
company, 181
knowledge building and, 187
source evaluation by, 69–70
Librarians' Index to the Internet
(LII), 33, *35,* 36, 56, 188,
229–230
librarianship Weblog, *41*
libraries, 15, 22–23
Library Blog, *41*
library catalogs, 28
Library of Congress, 23
life sciences, 237–238
links
to blogs, 173–174
company Web sites, 112

links (*cont.*)
  evaluation, 82–84
  language use and, 109
  to news sites, 170
  search restrictions, 50
  Web pages, 49
Lisnews.com, *41*
List of Lists, 209
listservs, 83
LLRX.com, 100, 236

M

M&A Activity Page, 223
magazine sites, 80
Magazines, National Directory of,
    170
MagPortal.com, 223
mailing lists, 174
maps, 23, 217
margins of error, 161
market research
  aggregate reports, 125–126
  credibility issues, 126–129
  data, 123–131
  definition, 123
  elements, 124–125
  keywords, *135*
  Merrill Lynch fines, 129
  off-the-shelf, 126–128
  open Web sources, 134–136
  relevancy, 130–131
  reports, 123–131
  on the Web, 125–126
  Web sites, *24,* 221–222
marketing
  statistics, 141
  Web sites, 238–239
  websites, 208
Marketing Virtual Library:
    KnowThis.com, 222
MarketResearch.com, *24,* 126, 130,
    131

McGee's Musings, *172*
McKinsey & Co. Services, 241
McLuhan, Marshall, 9
Mead Data Central, 15
Meadnet system, 15
media
  archives, 23
  online services, 163–170
  politics, *41*
  Web sites, 239–240
Medical DeviceLink, 237
medicine, 237–238
Medline, 238
memos, 23
mergers and acquisitions, 222–223
Merrill Lynch, 129, 132
message boards, 175–176, *177*
messages, tracking posts, 83
methodologies
  explanation of, 75
  government data, 148
  market research, 127, 128
  surveys, 159–160
Michelle's Research Sources
    Online, 227
military sites (.mil), 76
MindBranch.com, *24,* 126
Minow, Nell, 119
Mintz, Anne, 118
minus signs, 51, 60
Modern Researcher, The (Barzun
    and Graff), 3, 9–10, 11–12,
    87, 100, 198
Morningstar, 133
Mortgage Bankers Association, 234
Mortgage Magazine, 234
mortgages, 234
Motion Picture Association of
    America, 239
Motley Fool, The: Web Resources
    List, 229

MS Word files, 50, 59
MSN Money, 167
MSN Money Ownership Profile, 213
myths, 202–203

N

Nader, Ralph, 182
National and International Data Sources and Links, 152
National Association of Insurance Commissioners, 234
National Association of Realtors, 234
National Automobile Dealers Association, 233
National Automotive Finance Administration, 233
National Center for Charitable Statistics, 215
National Directory of Magazines, 170
National Guideline Clearinghouse, 235
National Institute for Research Advancement, 230
National Library for the Environment, The: CRS Reports, 219
National Press Club, 224
National Public Radio (NPR), 167, *168*
National Science Foundation, 13
National Women's Health Information Center, 235
NationMaster, 155, 217
"NEAR" proximity operators, 65
Neat New Stuff, *41*
Netscape Open Directory Project (ODP), 37
network sites (.net), 76

New Hope Natural Media Online, 237
New York Times, 27, 43, 166, 181
news
  aggregators, 165, 169
  alert services, 166
  authority of, 195–196
  evaluation tips, 169
  industry sites, 167
  online services, 163–170
  RSS feeds, 167
  searchable databases, 165–166
  sources, 223–225
  types, 164–169
  Weblog, *41*
NewsDirectory.com, 168, 225
NewsGator, 42
NewsIsFree, 42
NewsLink, *24,* 168
NewsMonster, 42
NewsNow, 165, 224
Newspaper Association of America, 240
newspapers
  development of trust, 199
  directory listings, 169
  on the Invisible Web, 28–29
  Web sites, *24*
Newspapers.com, 168
NewzCrawler, 42, *43*
Nexis/Lexis, 15
Nightly Business Report, 167
990 filings, *93*
"no robots" command, 28
Nolo, 236
nonprofit organizations, 59, 85
normal ranges, 155
Notess, Greg, 46, 57, 68
NY Times Tracker, 27
nytimes.com, 164

O

OANDA: The Currency Site, 230
Occupational Safety and Health
    Administration (OSHA), 94,
    96
ODwyer's PR Daily, 239
OECD, data quality, 154
Office of Management and the
    Budget (OMB), 145, 150,
    151
Office of the Comptroller of the
    Currency, The (OCC), 232
Office of Thrift Supervision, The
    (OTS), 94, 232
OMB Watch, 149, *150*
1to1, 238
"OR" searches, 51
Organizational Change: An
    Annotated Bibliography, 210
organizations, backgrounds, 85

P

paid listings, 37
PaidContent.com, *41,* 164, 167, 227
Parrinder, Geoffrey, 105–107
passwords, 28
Patent Alert, 225
patents, 225
Peck, M. Scott, 10
peer review, 7
Perry-Castañeda Library Map
    Collection, 217
Pew Internet and American Life
    Project, 155, 158
Pew Research Center for the People
    and the Press, 155
PharmaLive, 235
phone books, online, 84
photographs, historical, 23
plus signs, 51

political candidates, 89, *95*
political contributions, *95*
PollingReport.com, 155, 226
polls, 142, 153, 157–161
pop-up advertisements, 62
popularity ranking, 49, 147
Postman, Neil, 189, 206
PowerPoint files, 50, *52, 59*
Poynter Institute, 173
PR Watch, 100
precision searching techniques, 52
press releases
    credibility, 114–117
    currency of, 73
    dating, 108
    information within, 116
    on the Invisible Web, 28–29
    puffery, 201
    sample, *115–116*
    value of, 200
Price, Gary, 28, *41,* 65, 227
PriceWaterhouseCoopers Industries,
    241
primary sources
    citations, 75
    documents, 23, 101
    market research, 128
print versions, 3
Private Companies and Becoming
    an Expert, 211
product statistics, 142
Profound (ResearchLine), 126
Profusion 33, *36*
Promo, 231
PROMT database, 32
proofreading, 7
propaganda techniques, 86
ProQuest, 30, 31, *31,* 166
proximity operators, 65
proximity scores, 49
public companies, *24*
public issues Weblog, *41*

public records
company filings, 111–112
government records, 88–90
Search Systems, 30
Web sites, *24,* 94–97
Public Records Locator, 98, *99*
Public Records Online, *24*
public relations, 238–239
publications, 186
PubMed, 238
puffery, 201

Q

quality
checklists, 4–5
evaluation of, 3
government data, 144–145
sources and, 152–155
survey instruments, 160
Quality 2002 Assurance Framework
(Statistics Canada), 145
QueryServer, 46, 67–68
questions, the art of, 194–196
quotation marks, 51
quotations, 102, 104–107

R

Radio Userland, 42
RAM Research Group, 233
randomization, surveys, 160
ranking algorithms, 49, 60
Ranking.com, 209
rates of change, 156
Ray, Don, 197
ReadMe, 211
reality, definition of, 8
recent activity, 72–73
Recording Industry Association of
America, 240
referrals, 80, 107, 174

registration, 28
Regulation FD, 120
regulatory agencies, 232
relevancy, market research,
130–131
relevancy ranking, 6, 49
reputation management, 180
Research and Markets, 126
research documents, 59
ResourceShelf, *24, 25,* 28, 29–30,
41, 227
resumes, 59, 85
Retail Chain Store Sales Index, 240
retail Web sites, 240
Reuters Research On-Demand, 126
Reuters.com, 225
reverse directories, 84
Road Less Traveled, The (Peck), 10
"Robin Good," 181
robots, 12, 28
Rocketinfo, 168
Romenesko, Jim, *40, 41*
Rosen, Jeffrey, 83
Ross, Patrick, 75, 83
RSS Feeds, 41–44, *43,* 167,
180–181
RSS Master, 181
RSS Reader, 168
rumors, spread of, 7
Rutgers University Library: News
Sources, 224

S

Salary.com, 236
Sales & Marketing Management,
239
sales statistics, 124
Salvemini, Gaetano, 88
Sayings of Buddha, The (Parrinder),
105
Scandal Inc., 229

Scorecard Project, The, 213
Scott, Peter, *41*
screening, 9, 23–24
screens, reload times, 55
search engines
    choice of, 194, 195
    context and, 10–11
    function, 48–49
    Google, 46–68
    keyword mind set of, 11–12
    news search tabs, 165
    trends, 6
    Web sites on, 225
search protocols, 51
Search-Sec.com, 214
Search Systems, 30, 98, *98, 99*
Searcher, 56, 58
secondary sources, 118, 128
Securities and Exchange
    Commission, 111–112, 118,
    120–121
selection bias, 6–7
self-confirmation bias, 6–7, 204
self-reports, issues, 156
self-selection biases, 157, 158, 160
Selig Center for Economic Growth,
    239
Semiconductgor Industry
    Association, 240–241
semiconductors, 240–241
server identification, 80
Shenk, David, 185
Sherman, Chris, 28, 57
Shifted Librarian, The, *41*
Singer, S. Fred, *92*
SiteLines, 227
SLABF-L, 39
SlashDot, 171
"Smart Cars," 102–104
SmartBrief, 220
Smarter Surfing: Better Use of Your
    Web Time, 230

SMEALSearch, 225
social/demographic statistics, 142
Social Science Information
    Gateway, 30
Soft Money Laundromat, 94, *95*
sources
    authority, 156, 194–195
    biases, 156
    choice of, 194
    confirmation of data, 177
    credibility of, 3
    data quality and, 152–155
    evaluation of, 137–138, 169
    identification of, 2
    market research, 128
    news, 223–225
    original, 101
    primary, 75
    print, 186, 187
    reliability of, 107–109
Spahr, Ed, 148
Specials Libraries Association, 39
speeches, 59
speed, hazards of, 11
spelling errors, 72
spiders, 48
Spielberg, Steven, *97*
sponsorship of surveys, 159
Sprintnet, 15
Standard and Poors (S&Ps), 120
Standard Periodical Directory, 169
starting points, 155
Statistical Abstract of the United
    States, 144, 154, 226
Statistical Programs of the United
    States Government, 145
Statistical Resources on the Web,
    226
statistics
    basic concepts, 155–156

data sources, 141–142
documentation on the Web, 148
international agencies, 152–154
market research, 127
methodology, 3
preferred sources, 154–155
selection of, 195
source quality, 152–155
U.S. government, 142–154
Web sites, *24,* 225–226
Statistics Canada, 145, *146*
Statistics.com, 155, 225
Steer-U-Right Research, 192
"stop" words, 51
Strategic Advantage, 220
strategies
  asking questions, 194–196
  choosing Web sources, 194
  pre-research steps, 186
  pre-search engine, 21–44
  preparation for searches, 53–55
  refining searches, 64–65
  search statements, 55–58
Strategis: Create Your Own Market
    Research Report, 221–222
Strathclyde, University of,
    Glasgow, 37
STUMPERS-L, 39
style, emphasis on, 11
Sullivan, Danny, 57
survey organizations, 153
surveys
  goals of, 159
  hazards, 158
  methodologies, 159–160
  quality issues, 157–161
  questionnaires, 160
  reporting of results, 161
  sample sizes, 160
  sponsors of, 159
SurveySite, 157

T

tautologies, 191
tax returns, nonprofits, 85
technical help, 148
Technology Review, 223
technology Weblog, *41*
Technorati, 181
TechRepublic, 131, 164, 167
Television Bureau of Advertising,
    240
Teoma, 46, 67
terminology
  search refinements, 64
  in surveys, 160
  undefined, 156
  wacky vs fringe thinkers, 181
text, chunking of, 11
textbooks, 186
TheDeal.com, 222–223
TheStreet.com, 167
think tanks, 140
Thomas Register, *24,* 137
Thompson Research, 126
Thomson Media, 233
tilde (), 60, 72
Tile.net, 131
timeliness
  company directories, 138, 139
  government data, 146–147
  indications of, 74–75
  market research, 127–128
Top Internet Sites for Business
    Research, 230
Topix.net, 167
TrackBack function, 180
TrackEngine, 27
Trade Data Online, 220–221
Trade Development Analysts, 219
trademarks, 225
TradeStats Express, 222
transfer protocols, 76

translation options, 55
trends, 40, 128–129
truncation, 51
trust, giving of, 198–200
truth, determination of, 200–202
2003 Global 500, The, 212
Tymnet, 15

U

Union of Concerned Scientists,
    151–152
United Nations
    data quality, 154
    Millennium Country Profiles,
        217
    National and International Data
        Sources and Links, 152
    Reports, 28–29
*Unwanted Gaze, The: The
    Destruction of Privacy in
    America* (Rosen), 83
updates, 60, 74–75
urban legends, 202–203
Urban Legends References Pages,
    203
URLs (Uniform Resource Locators)
    alerts to changes in, 27
    clues provided by, 62
    company Web sites, 112
    with dates, 61, *61*
    search restrictions, 50
    Technorati search on, 181
    timeliness of data, 147
    understanding, 76–77
usability, government data, 148
USAutoNews.com, 233
Usenet groups, 83, 170, 174

V

Value Line, 133

Vatican library, 23
venture capital, 226–227
VentureWire, 226–227
veracity, online sources, 2
verification, importance of,
    100–102
Virtual Chase, The, 215
Virtual Chase.com, The, 237
Virtual Gumshoe: Investigative
    Resources Available on the
    Web, 100
Vivisimo, 46, 57, 67–68

W

wacky thinkers, 181, 182–183
Wall Street Journal, 119
Wall Street Journal Online, 71
Wall Street Transcript Online, The:
    CEO Interviews, 211
WatchThatPage, 27
WayBack Machine, 109
Waypath, 174
Web Forums, 174–175
Web indexes, 33–38
Web journals, 210
*Web of Deception: Misinformation
    on the Internet* (Mintz), 118,
    200
Web sites
    activity level, 72–73
    agendas, 84–90
    "branded," 71
    dating of, 109
    development of trust, 199
    evaluation, 69–110
    evaluation checklists, 243–246
    evaluation of links to, 82–84
    new, 50
    pages in URLs, 77
    "personal," 72
    prescreened, 23–27, *24,* 207–241

reassuring signs, 74–75
red flags, 72–71
type of, 77–80
Webcasts, 112, 121
WebFountain, 180
Weblog Guide, The, 227–228
Weblogs (blogs), 171–173
  Gary Price's, 28
  prescreened, 39–41
  research and, 170
  trustworthy, 173–174
  Web sites, 227–228
webs of trust, 180
WebStat, 152, 226
Weinberg, Steve, 182
Wells, Matt, 67
WetFeet, 211
white papers, 59, 133–134
Whois searches, 80–82
word limits, 52
workshops, 59, 186
World Chamber of Commerce
  Directory, 139
World Competitiveness Yearbook
  2003, 221
World Directory of Think Tanks,
  140

World Health Organization,
  235–236
World News Connection (WNC),
  223
World Trade Organization (WTO),
  221
WorldAtOnce.com, 214–215
WorldCom, 119
Wright Investor's Service, 137

Y
Yahoo!
  Alerts, 166
  Finance, *24,* 37, 137, 213
  Industry Center, 220
  News, 164
  news search tabs, 165
  Overture division, 65
  Search, 66–67

Z
Zacks Free Research Center, 214
zapdata, 212
Zimmerman's Research Guide, 229
Zoomerang, 157

More Great Books from Information Today, Inc.

Choosing and Using a News Alert Service

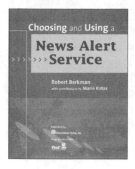

By Robert Berkman

There are dozens of competing firms that offer an e-mail based news alert service. But how to know which one is best? This comprehensive new guide explains how these tools work and then identifies, compares, and evaluates more than two dozen free, inexpensive, and fee-based alert services. It not only helps you pick the right one, but also advises how to get the most out of the news alert once you begin the service. A detailed appendix also compares specific news source coverage for the major news alert vendors.

2004/127 pp/softbound/ISBN 0-57387-224-5 • $79.95

The Extreme Searcher's Internet Handbook
A Guide for the Serious Searcher

By Randolph Hock

The Extreme Searcher's Internet Handbook is the essential guide for anyone who uses the Internet for research—librarians, teachers, students, writers, business professionals, and others who need to search the Web proficiently. Award-winning writer and Internet trainer Randolph "Ran" Hock covers strategies and tools (including search engines, directories, and portals) for all major areas of Internet content.

There's something here for every Internet searcher. Readers with little to moderate searching experience will appreciate the helpful, easy-to-follow advice, while experienced searchers will discover a wealth of new ideas, techniques, and resources. Anyone who teaches the Internet will find this book indispensable.

As a reader bonus, the author maintains "The Extreme Searcher's Web Page" featuring links, updates, news, and much more. It's the ideal starting place for any Web search.

2004/296 pp/softbound/ISBN 0-910965-68-4 • $24.95

Business Statistics on the Web
Find Them Fast—At Little or No Cost

By Paula Berinstein

Statistics are a critical component of business and marketing plans, press releases, surveys, economic analyses, presentations, proposals, and more—yet good statistics are notoriously hard to find. This practical book by statistics guru Paula Berinstein shows readers how to use the Internet to find statistics about companies, markets, and industries, how to organize and present statistics, and how to evaluate them for reliability. Organized by topic, both general and specific, and by country/region, this helpful reference features easy-to-use tips and techniques for finding and using statistics when the pressure is on. In addition, dozens of extended and short case studies demonstrate the ins and outs of searching for specific numbers and maneuvering around obstacles to find the data you need.

2003/336 pp/softbound/ISBN: 0-910965-65-X • $29.95

Super Searchers on Madison Avenue
Top Advertising and Marketing Professionals Share Their Online Research Strategies

By Grace Avellana Villamora
Edited by Reva Basch

Research professionals in the advertising and marketing game are a rare breed. Working in one of the business world's true pressure cookers, these super searchers find and analyze the information that fuels today's most successful product launches and advertising campaigns. Their market research expertise provides critical strategic support to new business teams, account managers and planners, copywriters, and sales promotion specialists at every major international ad agency. Here, Grace A. Villamora—director of knowledge management at Euro RSCG Tatham Partners—gets 13 research pros from such firms as TBWA/Chiat/Day, Leo Burnett, and Interpublic to share the tips, techniques, and resources that have made them the best in the business.

2003/244 pp/softbound/ISBN: 0-910965-63-3 • $24.95

International Business Information on the Web

Searcher Magazine's Guide to Sites and Strategies for Global Business Research

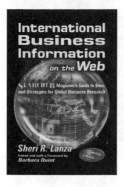

By Sheri R. Lanza
Edited by Barbara Quint

Here is the first ready-reference for effective worldwide business research, written by experienced international business researcher Sheri R. Lanza and edited by *Searcher* magazine's Barbara Quint. This book helps readers identify overseas buyers, find foreign suppliers, investigate potential partners and competitors, uncover international market research and industry analysis, and much more. As a reader bonus, a companion Web directory features links to more than 1,000 top sites for global business research.

2001/380 pp/softbound/ISBN 0-910965-46-3 • $29.95

The Web Library

Building a World Class Personal Library with Free Web Resources

By Nicholas G. Tomaiuolo
Edited by Barbara Quint

With this remarkable, eye-opening book and its companion Web site, Nicholas G. (Nick) Tomaiuolo shows how anyone can create a comprehensive personal library using no-cost Web resources. And when Nick say "library," he's not talking about a dictionary and thesaurus on your desktop: He means a vast, rich collection of data, documents, and images that—if you follow his instructions to the letter—can rival the holdings of many traditional libraries. If you were to calculate the expense of purchasing the hundreds of print and fee-based electronic publications that are available for free with "the Web Library" you'd quickly recognize the potential of this book to save you thousands, if not millions, of dollars. (Fortunately, Nick does the calculating for you!) This is an easy-to-use guide, with chapters organized into sections corresponding to departments in a physical library. *The Web Library* provides a wealth of URLs and examples of free material you can start using right away, but best of all it offers techniques for finding and collecting new content as the Web evolves. Start building your personal Web library today!

2003/440 pp/softbound/ISBN 0-910965-67-6 • $29.95

Web of Deception
Misinformation on the Internet

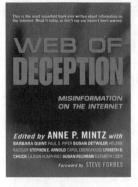

Edited by Anne P. Mintz
Foreword by Steve Forbes

"Experts here walk you through the risks and traps of the Web world and tell you how to avoid them or to fight back ... Anne Mintz and her collaborators have done us a geuine service"

—Steve Forbes, from the Foreword

Intentionally misleading or erroneous information on the Web can wreak havoc on your health, privacy, investments, business decisions, online purchases, legal affairs, and more. Until now, the breadth and significance of this growing problem for Internet users had yet to be fully explored. In *Web of Deception*, Anne P. Mintz (Director of Knowledge Management at Forbes, Inc.) brings together 10 information industry gurus to illuminate the issues and help you recognize and deal with the flood of deception and misinformation in a range of critical subject areas. A must-read for any Internet searcher who needs to evaluate online information sources and avoid Web traps.

2002/278 pp/softbound/ISBN 0-910965-60-9 • $24.95

Naked in Cyberspace, 2nd Edition
How to Find Personal Information Online

By Carole A. Lane
Foreword by Beth Givens

"Perfect for someone trying to trace a person with whom contact has been lost, or to build a profile of a potential business associate ... arguably the only essential manual for the work of today's private investigator."

—The Electronic Library

In this fully revised and updated second edition of her bestselling guide, author Carole A. Lane surveys the types of personal records that are available on the Internet and online services. Lane explains how researchers find and use personal data, identifies the most useful sources of information about people, and offers advice for readers with privacy concerns. You'll learn how to use online tools and databases to gain competitive intelligence, locate and investigate people, access public records, identify experts, find new customers, recruit employees, search for assets, uncover criminal records, conduct genealogical research, and much more. Supported by a Web page.

2002/586 pp/softbound/ISBN 0-910965-50-1 • $29.95

Smart Services
Competitive Information Strategies, Solutions and Success Stories for Service Businesses

By Deborah C. Sawyer

"Finally, a book that nails down what every service business needs to know about competition and competitive intelligence. Smart Services *offers competitive information strategies that firms can put to immediate use."*

—Andrew Garvin
CEO, FIND/SVP

Here is the first book to focus specifically on the competitive information needs of service-oriented firms. Author, entrepreneur, and business consultant Deborah C. Sawyer illuminates the many forms of competition in service businesses, identifies the most effective information resources for competitive intelligence (CI), and provides a practical framework for identifying and studying competitors in order to gain a competitive advantage. *Smart Services* is a roadmap for every service company owner, manager, or executive who expects to compete effectively in the Information Age.

2002/256 pp/softbound/ISBN 0-910965-56-0 • $29.95

Super Searchers on Competitive Intelligence
The Online and Offline Secrets of Top CI Researchers

By Margaret Metcalf Carr
Edited by Reva Basch

*"*Super Searchers on Competitive Intelligence *features the insights and experiences of some of the best in the business. The referenced sites alone are worth the price of the book"*

—Carolyn M. Vella, SCIP Meritorious Award Winner
and author, *Bottom Line Competitive Intelligence*

Here are leading CI researchers in their own words, revealing their secrets for monitoring competitive forces and keeping on top of the trends, opportunities, and threats within their industries. Researcher and CI pro Margaret Metcalf Carr asked experts from 15 CI-savvy organizations to share tips, techniques, and models that can be successfully applied to any business intelligence project. Includes dozens of examples of CI research in action and a range of strategies that can help any organization stay several steps ahead of the competition.

2003/336 pp/softbound/ISBN 0-910965-64-1 • $24.95

Building & Running
a Successful Research Business
A Guide for the Independent Information Professional

By Mary Ellen Bates
Edited by Reva Basch

This is *the* handbook every aspiring independent information professional needs to launch, manage, and build a research business. Organized into four sections, "Getting Started," "Running the Business," "Marketing," and "Researching," the book walks you through every step of the process. Author and long-time independent researcher Mary Ellen Bates covers everything from "is this right for you?" to closing the sale, managing clients, promoting your business, and tapping into powerful information sources.

2003/360 pp/softbound/ISBN 0-910965-62-5 • $29.95

Super Searchers on Mergers & Acquisitions
The Online Research Secrets of Top Corporate Researchers and M&A Pros

By Jan Davis Tudor • Edited by Reva Basch

The sixth title in the "Super Searchers" series is a unique resource for business owners, brokers, appraisers, entrepreneurs, and investors who use the Internet and online services to research Mergers & Acquisitions (M&A) opportunities. Leading business valuation researcher Jan Davis Tudor interviews 13 top M&A researchers, who share their secrets for finding, evaluating, and delivering critical deal-making data on companies and industries. As a reader bonus, "The Super Searchers Web Page" features links to the most important online information sources for M&A research.

2001/208 pp/softbound/ISBN 0-910965-48-X • $24.95